SPECIAL FEATURES OF THE BEST BOOK OF ITS KIND ANYWHERE AT ANY PRICE

—A logical sequence of presentation that enables you to read it straight through for a complete personal education in all phases of good grammar, from the basics to the fine points

—A superb index that lets you go instantly to any area where you have practical questions to answer

—Authoritative and sensitive combining of traditional rules with the latest developments in approved usage

—A clarity of style that makes it accessible to the novice, yet comprehensive information that makes it invaluable even at the highest level of education

D0449400

About the Author

JOHN B. OPDYCKE was born in Doylestown, Pa. Before his death in 1956, he lectured at New York University, Columbia University and Johns Hopkins.

He was a contributor to leading newspapers and magazines and is the author of such books as *Literature of Letters, Telling Types in Literature, Say What You Mean, Lexicon of Word Selection, Handbook of English Usage, Get It Right* and *Mark My Words*.

HARPER'S ENGLISH GRAMMAR

by John B. Opdycke, Ph.D.

WARNER BOOKS

A Warner Communications Company

To: *T.H.*

WARNER BOOKS EDITION

Copyright © 1941, 1965 by Harper & Row, Publishers, Incorporated
All rights reserved.

This Warner Books Edition is published by arrangement with
Harper & Row,
10 East 53rd Street,
New York, N.Y. 10022

Warner Books, Inc.,
666 Fifth Avenue,
New York, N.Y. 10103

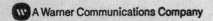 A Warner Communications Company

Printed in the United States of America

First Warner Books Printing: July, 1983

10 9 8 7 6 5 4 3 2 1

EDITOR'S FOREWORD

Readers familiar with the original edition of John B. Opdycke's *Harper's English Grammar* will find that this revised edition represents something of a departure from the original. Not only have some of the author's viewpoints been modified, many of the examples changed and the exercises eliminated entirely, but the chapter dealing with sentence analysis has been completely recast. This was done to incorporate into the new version some of the more recent developments in English grammar study, especially the work of the structural linguists.

The conventional classification of the parts of speech has been retained not just consciously, but deliberately. The editor's feeling is that, while systems of classification like that of Charles C. Fries are admirable as linguistic analysis, they are familiar to so few that there is little purpose in attempting to use them in a reference grammar of this type. Further, it has always seemed paradoxical that a number of these systems (not specifically Fries') frequently turn to using the standard denominations of the parts of speech anyway.

One change that has been made is a result of the attempt to introduce greater precision in the area of levels of usage. The basis for this has been the conventionally accepted designation of standard and substandard levels, with formal and informal functional varieties of the standard level. This system has replaced some of the rather imprecise designations found in the original.

A final observation: many comments by contemporary students of English appear to indicate disapproval of all reference grammars on the grounds that such books must necessarily be private and arbitrary in their standards. That is, as some are fond of saying, if a grammar purports to describe standards of correctness, these must be some individual's standards of correctness. This notion contains a certain bit of truth, but essentially it is ridiculous. A poll of all English teachers in the United States might very well show a surprising lack of agreement about the acceptance of contractions in formal writing or some comparable problem; there is no doubt, however, that areas of agreement about correctness

5

would be enormous. So, on a few points, this book may take what some call arbitrary positions, yet on most it details what even the most ardent critics of grammatical authoritarianism will have to concede are generally accepted usages in formal writing.

This revision, then, tries to steer a middle-of-the-road course between Varro and Zellig Harris without being vacillating. Hopefully it will prove palatable to all schools of grammatical taste, from traditionalism through structural linguistics to the most advanced experimentalism.

Stewart H. Benedict

CONTENTS

PART ONE

Introduction • The Parts of Speech

THE PARTS OF SPEECH

This term—**the parts of speech**—is a covering term for the eight general divisions into which the 750,000 words of the English language are classified according to their various functions, meanings, and uses in sentence structure. The word **speech** must not be taken to refer to oral expression only; it is used, rather, in the broader sense of language or discourse. Though its Anglo-Saxon original did mean the faculty of uttering articulate sounds (words) to express thought—the physical power of expression—the modern word **speech** is used to denote any and every form of thought expression that the evolution of language has brought with it—oral **and** written address, discourse, discussion, disquisition, dissertation, eloquence, harangue, oration, oratory, sermon, and so forth. Even sign language is sometimes loosely referred to as speech. Moreover, it is speech rather than writing that decides usage for the most part; it is speech that comes first in the individual's development of power in expression, just as it was speech that came first in the evolution of expressional power.

These eight classes of words are **noun, pronoun, adjective, verb, adverb, preposition, conjunction, interjection.** Noun is from the Latin **nomen** meaning name; and **pronoun** is from two Latin words—**pro** meaning for or in place of, and **nomen.** **Adjective** is from two Latin words—**ad** meaning to or pertaining to, and **jacio** meaning throw; thus, to throw to or to pertain to (noun and pronoun). **Verb** is from the Latin **verbum** meaning word. **Adverb** is from two Latin words—**ad** and **verbum;** thus, pertaining to word (verb, adjective, adverb). **Preposition** is from two Latin words—**pre** meaning before, and **pono** meaning place; thus, to place before (a preposition is usually placed before its object to indicate relationship between that object and an action or a being or a thing named before it). **Conjunction** is from two Latin words—**con** meaning together, and **jungo** meaning join; thus, to join or connect. **Interjection** is from two Latin words—**inter** meaning between, and **jacio** (as in **adjective**); thus, thrown between (any ejaculation or thrown-in word or expression).

In the following these eight parts of speech appear in the dress parade of a sentence:

(conjunction)	(interjection)	(pronoun)	(verb)
But	oh,	they	rush
(adverb)	(preposition)	(adjective)	(noun)
madly	toward	the	goal!

It will be noted that all these names of the parts of speech come from Latin. All of them were adapted to the terminology of grammar as early as the grammarian Marcus Terentius Varro (B.C. 116-27), and all were used in general senses as well as in specific grammatical senses. **Verbum,** thus, took on the limited technical meaning of **verb, nomen** of **noun, con jungo** of **conjunction,** and so on, while each was retained in general usage—**word, name, union,** respectively. Attachment of a specific meaning to a word in general usage is by no means an uncommon phenomenon in language. In English this characteristic adds a richness of fluidity and adaptation unequaled in any other tongue.

Latin was the language not only of ancient Rome, but, up to modern times, the language also of church and school and state in all of Western civilization. By virtue of its importance and general use, Latin became the most highly organized vehicle of expression. This means that, among other things, its grammar became highly systematized and articulated; and since English has drawn most heavily from Latin in its appropriation of words from foreign sources, it has likewise drawn much from Latin grammar, including even the names of its tools of expression or the parts of speech.

For a long time, indeed, it was thought that Latin would survive English as a world language, and that all of the early attempts to extend and broaden the use of English must fail. English authors, feeling that English was to be short-lived, wrote their works in Latin. Later, seeing the stubborn persistence of English, they gambled with fate by writing them in both Latin and English. The double task thus assumed would, they thought, be a guarantee of permanence. It is quite by the way, but nevertheless interesting to note, that survival has depended upon content rather than upon medium. The output of our literary forefathers lived or died primarily in accordance with the worth of its subject matter; the advertising value of the language in which it was expressed was imponderable. And in this resides an enduring principle.

In the days of Pompey one Dionysius Thrax, student of the Greek grammarian Aristarchus, wrote a grammar for Roman schoolboys. Its principles were derived chiefly from the old Greek grammar, and it served as model for both Latin and English grammar down to almost the time of Shakespeare. As a matter of fact, many of its principles are still used in English grammar, as, for instance, a pronoun agrees with its antecedent in person and number but its case depends upon the structure of the clause in which it stands (page 268).

When Ben Jonson (1573-1637) "made" his English grammar, he did so, he said, "to free the English language from the opinion of the rudeness and barbarism wherewith it is mistaken to be diseased." In other words, he wrote his grammar to influence writers of his day to use English rather than another medium, principally Latin; and to make this influence as powerful as possible among those who believed Latin to be an enduring vehicle and English but an ephemeral one, he held his English to the same rigid proprieties to which Latin was and is and must be held. If he were living today he might well take the view that, although the two are related in vocabulary, they are in fact distinctly different languages; thus very few rules of grammar in Latin are relevant to English.

Fortunately, however, as English has evolved, it has tended to become more and more simplified. Many of the old rules of Latin grammar as well as those even of Jonson's English grammar are modified in present-day usage. Just as Latin grammar, according to Thrax, had fewer inflections than its basic Greek—fewer changes and modifications in words as they were fitted together to express ideas nicely—so English grammar today has fewer such changes and modifications than Latin and the early English grammar.

Nouns in English today may be inflected for gender, number, case; pronouns for gender, number, person, case. Verbs may be inflected for voice, mood, tense, number, person. Conjunctions, prepositions, and interjections are not inflected at all. Adjectives and adverbs (most but not all) undergo a kind of inflection in degrees of comparison, but these are changes in a word itself to denote for the most part differences in quality or quantity rather than changes to adjust one word to another in grammatical relationship. Some authorities regard nouns, pronouns, and verbs as the only inflectable parts of speech, and thus classify the remaining parts as uninflectable. A list or table or paradigm (page 58) of inflections for nouns and pronouns is called **declension;** for verbs, **conjugation.**

The parts of speech are sometimes also grouped as **substantives** (nouns and other words or word groups used as nouns are used), **predicatives** or **modals** (verbs), **modifiers** (adjectives and adverbs), **connectives** (conjunctions and prepositions). Interjections, being detached or unrelated terms, are unclassifiable; they were once listed as **independents** and are now sometimes called **isolates.**

The following order of treatment of the parts of speech means little or nothing by way of their relative importance or their arrangement in expression. Noun, pronoun, adjective are usually grouped together for discussion only because they are to a degree interrelated—a pronoun is a substitute for a noun, and an adjective may modify a noun or a pronoun and nothing else. Verb and adverb naturally fall together inasmuch as most adverbs pertain to or modify verbs. Prepositions, being more numerous than conjunctions and having more complex ramifications by way of relationship and connection, are usually treated before conjunctions. Interjections, having least significance, require least exposition and are, as a rule, last to be considered.

The parts of speech may be used in any order, though words (nouns and pronouns as a rule) used as subjects usually precede words (verbs) used as predicates. Words used as modifiers (adjectives and adverbs as a rule) usually precede words modified. Prepositions and conjunctions usually fall between terms related or connected. Nouns and verbs are the most important parts of speech—the master parts—for practically all talk and all writing are concerned primarily with names and with actions and conditions. To meet expressional demands more nouns and verbs than other parts of speech have therefore been evolved in the language. Pronouns, adjectives, adverbs, prepositions, conjunctions, interjections may all freely function as nouns or verbs, and nouns and verbs may in turn function as adjectives and adverbs (usually with some slight changes in form). This facility in functioning—this transference or interchange of function—is made possible in English partly because of the fact that it is not a highly inflected language, and partly because of the fact that its diction is drawn from so many linguistic sources. Both advantage and disadvantage result from this fluidity in usage: It yields color and convenience beyond the power of most other tongues; it tempts to looseness or carelessness that may easily lead to substandard usage.

In **And is overused**, a conjunction functions as noun (subject). In **He ohs too much**, an interjection functions as verb (predicate). In **It out-herods Herod**, a proper noun functions as verb. In **They drove close upon**, both **close** and **upon** are adverbs, but in **Upon my word these are close quarters, upon** is a preposition and **close** is an adjective. In **I shall close the door, close** is a verb. In **I shall bring the meeting to a close, close** is a noun. Now, though **close** in the first two examples is a different word derivatively from **close** in the last two, and is pronounced differently, here are nevertheless four different parts of speech represented by exactly the same spelling. Note, further, the word **fell:** a verb in **I fell downstairs** and **I fell trees** and **She will fell the seam**, a noun in **I walked around the fell** and **The needle pierced the fell**, an adjective in **He made a fell attack.** Here is one word—one spelling and one pronunciation—having six different kinds of significance and serving as three different parts of speech. For purposes of English grammar, it does not at all matter that the word is Anglo-Saxon in one instance or old French in another or old Norse in still another. But it is important for the student of English grammar to observe that, spelling and pronunciation and derivation aside, the versatility of a word in "playing" first one part (of speech) and then another constitutes for him an unusual expressional opportunity as well as an unusual expressional danger.

Close and **fell**, that is to say, and numerous other words like them, require setting, demand relationship with other words in an expression, before they may be induced to reveal the part (of speech) they are going to portray. In the same way many words require others in relation before the complete cataloging of their grammatical functioning can be arrived at. **John**, for instance, is on sight a masculine singular proper noun; its case and person cannot be told until it is seen at work with associated words. The personal pronoun—the most highly inflected part of speech in English—is the only one that gives all or nearly all of its parsing secrets away on its very face. **He**, for instance, is masculine, singular, third, nominative, though what its nominative relationship is cannot be explained until other words accompany it. But **you** is "in the dark" as to number, gender, case, until it is built into a construction.

It has been suggested that versatility in the use of the parts of speech may be disadvantageous if legitimate liberty within rule is permitted to become license. If, for instance, a word is strained or wrenched too violently out of its natural functioning it becomes a questionable usage. To say to a person who is inclined to surround a problem with many conditions that he "ifs" too much, may be an impressive comment, used once at a highly provocative moment. But it is a liberty in language to be used discreetly and sparingly. To say **I buicked down town** and **If you allow yourself to become napoleonized you will eventually be waterlooed** is to carry transference of grammatical function too far (as writers of advertising copy may well note). **Buick** and **Napoleon** and **Waterloo** are preferably and intrinsically proper nouns, not verb and adjective and verb respectively. Abuse of their grammatical functioning as here illustrated constitutes impropriety.

Chapter One

NOUN

DEFINITION AND CLASSIFICATION

A noun is a name—a name of anything—animal, condition, material, object, person, place, quality. A **common noun** is one that denotes a general group or class or indefinite animal, condition, material, object, person, place, quality, as **dog, illness, silver, box, child, city, honesty.** A **proper noun** is one that particularizes or distinguishes or individualizes, and that is useless except to point out and mark off from the general, as **Denver, Horace, Rover, Magna Carta, Quaker.** A common noun is not capitalized except occasionally in figurative uses. A proper noun is always capitalized (**proper** is from a Latin word meaning **one's own**). A noun, or any word or group of words used like it, is sometimes called a **substantive**, that is, the substantial part of thought or that part of an expression that contains the substance.

Sometimes a proper noun is extended to denote a class or group having the characteristics of the individual that it originally specified. It thus becomes generalized in application. Used in figurative allusion—to bring a group under a particular name—such proper noun remains capitalized, as **The oratorical contest revealed potential Patrick Henrys** and **The ingenue imagines herself a Bernhardt.** But used in reference to a group or class in order to extend the individual name to mean quality or characteristic, such converted proper noun loses right to an initial capital letter and becomes really a common noun, as **buncombe** (from Buncombe County, North Carolina), **mocha** (from Mocha, Arabia), **vaudeville** (from Vaudeville, Normandy), **mackintosh** (from Charles Mackintosh), **ohm** (from G. S. Ohm), **wistaria** (from Caspar Wistar), and **china, sandwich, sherry, spruce,** and a host of others.

A **collective noun** is one that denotes a number of things constituting a unit-group or whole, as **audience, class, club, fleet, flock, regiment, team.** Note that these nouns indicate aggregate or mass or sum whereas such nouns as **girls, men, animals, benches** indicate individual and unrelated units. Collective nouns are usually common nouns, but they may be proper also especially when they stand for an individual group or whole, as **College of Cardinals, Conclave, Congress, Electoral College, Parliament.**

A **concrete noun** is the name of any material object having attributes that are capable of being conceived through the senses, as **ball, can, desk, shirt, stone, tin.**

An **abstract noun** is the name of an idea or quality or attribute or condition, as **Catholicism, fear, happiness, height, knowledge, perfection, strength.** Your idea of **stone,** for instance, is obtained through the exercise of the senses—you see it, you feel it, you may hear it. But you may abstract such qualities or attributes of stone as **hardness, roundness, heaviness,** and regard them as separate from any single object conceived through the senses or as general attributes of many objects. Note these abstract nouns in relation to adjectives: **distant, distance; good, goodness; great, greatness; honest, honesty; just, justice; noble, nobility; patient, patience; prudent, prudence; pure, purity; silent, silence; stupid, stupidity; temperate, temperance; true, truth; useful, usefulness; wide, width; wise, wisdom.** Note these in relation to verbs: **advise, advice; behave, behavior; believe, belief; choose, choice; conceal, concealment; deceive, deceit; employ, employment; learn, learning; move, motion; please, pleasure; protect, protection; reveal, revelation; seize, seizure; serve, service; subtract, subtraction; weigh, weight.** Note these in relation to other nouns: **bond, bondage; captain, captaincy; child, childhood; friend, friendship; hero, heroism; kin, kinship; leak, leakage; mayor, mayoralty; martyr, martyrdom; prude, prudery; rascal, rascality; thief, theft.** Abstract nouns, especially those of Anglo-Saxon origin, are frequently formed from adjectives by suffixing **ness** or **t** or **th** or **ty.** Those formed from verbs and other nouns frequently suffix **age, ment, ship, t,** or **ty.** But this is a broad generalization. There is no hard and fast rule.

It is important as well as interesting to observe that a noun may be concrete in one use and abstract in another. In **She wore a precious jewel, jewel** is concrete. In **His speech was a jewel of oratory, jewel** is abstract.

A **diminutive noun** is a derivative indicating something small, young, or loved, and (occasionally) something belittled. It is formed usually by means of suffix; animal**cule**, bagate**lle**, maid**en**, cyg**net** (young swan), kitchen**ette**, bird**ie**, aster**isk**, negr**ito**, lamb**kin**, speck**le**, book**let**, weak**ling**, hill**ock**, sched**ule**, dear**y(ie)**. Sometimes an internal change takes place also, as in gosling. (It is not to be assumed, however, that **etiquette** means little Etta; **hamlet**, little ham; or **worldling**, little world!) Note that young cougars are either **kittens** or **cubs**; young antelope, **kids**; young moose and reindeer, **fawns** (sometimes **calves**).

An **agent noun** is one that indicates a being or a thing that acts for or in place of another, one that acts by authority, one that does. The suffixes **er, ist, or** usually denote nouns of agent, as **adviser, pianist, donor.** The opposite or **recipient noun** indicates one who receives something, one to whom an act is done or upon whom a privilege is conferred. It is frequently suffixed **ee**, as **grantee, mortgagee, payee,** antonyms of **grantor, mortgagor** (also spelt **mortgager**), **payer** respectively. Do not confuse the diminutive ending **ie** with the **ee** ending.

GENDER

Gender is that difference or distinction made among nouns and pronouns (no other part of speech has gender) that indicates whether they signify male sex, female sex, either sex, or neither sex. Nouns signifying male sex are called **masculine**, as **boy, Julius, landlord, horse;** those signifying female sex are called **feminine**, as **girl, Julia, landlady, mare;** those signifying either sex are called **common** or **indeterminate** in gender, as **assistant, buyer, citizen, driver, friend, helper, lawyer, listener, monarch, relative, worker;** those signifying absence of sex, or sexlessness, are called **neuter**, as **chair, desk, fear, fund, share, trip, wagon, zeal.** It is important to remember that the terms **masculine, feminine, indeterminate, neuter** belong to the idea of gender, not to the idea of sex.

There are three different ways of indicating gender for nouns. Sometimes an entirely different word is used to differentiate masculine from feminine, as

Masculine	Feminine	Masculine	Feminine
bachelor	spinster	brother	sister
boar	sow	buck	doe
boy	girl	bull	cow

Masculine	Feminine	Masculine	Feminine
cock	hen	man	woman
colt	filly	master	mistress
drake	duck	monk	nun
earl	countess	nephew	niece
father	mother	rajah	ranee
gander	goose	ram	ewe
groom	bride	sir	madam
horse	mare	sire	dam
husband	wife	son	daughter
king	queen	uncle	aunt
lord	lady	widower	widow

This is a short list only, used as illustration. There are many other pairs of "gender words" in the language. There are certain others that cannot be paired. The masculines **boor, clown, satyr, squire,** for instance, have no feminine partners; and the feminines **amazon, brunette, dame, dowager, milliner, shrew, virago,** have no masculine. Note, too, that it is wrong to call **wife** the feminine of **husband, boy** the masculine of **girl, daughter** the feminine of **son,** and so on, inasmuch as there is nothing in any of the above words to denote sex or gender. Each word in a pair denotes a different being, and this difference, in turn, happens to denote difference in sex or gender. In colloquial usage, some of the words above listed denote common gender; that is, we speak of **duck** and **goose** and **horse** in general conversation without thinking of gender at all, regarding them merely as creatures or animals. In England, the wife of an earl is a countess, but on the continent **count** is the corresponding masculine form of **countess.** The suffix **ster** once signified feminine, as **seamster, songster, spinster.** Later it came to mean the opposite, namely, masculine, as well as one skilled in a particular kind of work, as **drugster** and **teamster;** and **stress** was substituted to signify feminine, as **seamstress** and **songstress.** Today it may have a belittling or derogatory connotation, as **gamester, rimester, trickster.**

Gender is sometimes indicated by a foreign or once-foreign suffix—**ess, ina (a), ine, trix**—which may or may not involve some change in root form. In words that undergo no such internal change, the tendency is to make the masculine form serve as both masculine and feminine. As language evolves it

tends toward simplification; this means that special gender
(and other endings) tend to disappear. Unfortunately **aviatrix**
is generally used as the feminine form of **aviator**, but this is a
newspaper affectation. We have long ceased to say **editress** for
woman editor, **doctress** for woman doctor, and **mediatrix** for
woman mediator. Note the following more commonly used
suffixed gender forms:

Masculine	Feminine	Masculine	Feminine
abbot	abbess	hunter	huntress
actor	actress	Joseph	Josephine
administrator	administratrix	lion	lioness
adventurer	adventuress	marquis	marchioness
baron	baroness	margrave	margravine
benefactor	benefactress	master	mistress
czar	czarina	murderer	murderess
don	dona or	prophet	prophetess
	donna	prosecutor	prosecutrix
duke	duchess	protector	protectress
emperor	empress	shepherd	shepherdess
enchanter	enchantress	signor	signora
executor	executrix	sorcerer	sorceress
god	goddess	sultan	sultana
governor	governess	testator	testatrix
hero	heroine	tiger	tigress
host	hostess		

In the time of Shakespeare the **ess** forms were much more
extended than they now are. Such feminines as **butleress,
championess, vassaless, wagoness, warrioress** were commonly
used. And up to half a century ago **deaconess, poetess, lec-
turess, songstress** were. But now, happily, we say **chairman** for
a woman who presides at a meeting, and **postmaster** for a
woman in charge of a post office, in preference to **chairwoman**
and **postmistress**. The **trix** ending is now rarely met except in
legal phraseology (with the exception of the affected **aviatrix**
above referred to). Do not make the mistake of thinking all
ess, ine, trix endings indicate feminine, as, for instance, in ad-
**dress, mattress, success, doctrine, marine, quarantine, cicatrix,
matrix.** Most of the words in the above list are of French,
Greek, or Latin origin (**hunter** and **shepherd** are from Anglo-
Saxon). The French **Monsieur** is not used in English, but its

plural **Messieurs** is used in abbreviated form—**Messrs.** The English equivalent of **Monsieur**—in French abbreviated **M.** in the singular and **MM. (Messieurs)** in the plural—is **Mr.** The feminine singular **Mrs.** or **Miss** is used in English, but the French **Mesdames** is frequently made the English plural, though **Ladies** is increasingly used and is recommended. The two masculines **bridegroom** and **widower** are formed from the feminines.

In the third place, gender is sometimes indicated by pre-fixing or compounding, as **bull-calf, cow-calf; cock-sparrow, hen-sparrow; he-goat, she-goat; he-wolf, she-wolf; landlord, landlady; maidservant, manservant.** But these gender distinc-tions are tending also to disappear; the biblical **manchild** and **womanchild** have long since disappeared. The more common usage, when such distinction is considered necessary, is now the prefixing of **male** and **female,** as **male giraffe** and **female giraffe, male elephant** and **female elephant,** and so on.

As pointed out on pages 15-16 gender belongs to the individ-ual and independent noun itself and is not influenced by other words in sentence association. For instance, in **Every citizen lost his vote, citizen** remains indeterminate in gender as a part of speech, the pronoun **his** being regarded also as common or indeterminate. This is a much easier expression than **Every citizen lost his and her vote.** The neuter **its** is frequently used to refer to **child,** as in **The child has lost its rattle;** but, again, **child** as a part of speech remains common or indeterminate. Contrarily, gender is given to inanimate objects when they are personified. As a rule, names of things that convey the idea of force and power and destructiveness are made mascu-line, those that convey the idea of delicacy and fertility and graciousness are usually made feminine. Thus, we say **War has unleashed his hounds** and **Earth has brought forth her fruit.** But a ship is usually spoken of as **she,** and the pronoun **her** is colloquially applied to practically anything, as **Let her go, Turn her** (car, door, furniture, etc.) **a little to the right, Lightning has taken her** (barn, house, tree, etc.) **top off,** and so on.

Gender in English is sometimes called natural or rational gender, that is, it follows sex. **Man** indicates a person of the male sex, and the word **man** is, therefore, masculine. But in many other languages gender denotes not a natural distinction but a purely and arbitrarily grammatical one. Many objects without sex are regarded as masculine or feminine in these languages. The French word **gaffeau,** small boat, is masculine; the German word **Beleidigung,** insult, is feminine; the Latin word **res,** thing, is feminine. Anglo-Saxon and early English likewise had this so-called grammatical gender, that is, arbitrary gender; the nature of the object itself had nothing to do with deciding its gender. This is one of the difficulties in the study of a foreign language, especially in view of the fact that adjectives and pronouns modifying nouns may have to be given gender endings in agreement with the nouns.

PERSON

Person, as a grammatical term, indicates that relation of words by which is indicated the one speaking, the one spoken to, the one spoken about. In **I (Bill) work hard and long,** the noun **Bill** (like the pronoun **I**) indicates the speaker and is, therefore, said to be in the first person. In **Bill, bring me that book, Bill** is spoken to and is, therefore, said to be in the second person. In **Bill did that for me, Bill** is spoken about and is, therefore, said to be in the third person. Person applies to nouns, pronouns, and verbs only.

Note that it is impossible to use an English noun in the first person without accompanying it with a personal pronoun in order to key the person. Omit it in **I (Bill) work hard and long** and **Bill** becomes second person. When Polly says, "Polly wants a cracker," she is placing herself modestly in third person rather than making her name first person. First-person proper nouns appear as a rule only in legal phraseology, as **I, James Sunden, will and bequeath,** and in biblical phraseology, as **I, Thomas, do exhort you.** But it must be observed that the use of commas instead of parentheses to set off the proper noun may make for ambiguity: **James Sunden and Thomas** may be regarded as of second person. In such expressions as **we girls** and **us boys** and **we the people,** in which the first-person noun is placed in close emphatic apposition with its preceding pronoun, neither commas nor parentheses are necessary to set it off.

Most usage involves the **third person,** which is, as a rule, clear and sufficient without pronominal assistance. But for emphasis you may say **He, John J. Johnson, is the man we want.** The repetition of the personal pronoun after a noun, as

in **Tom he went** is now regarded as an impropriety, though it
was once allowable and was, of course, a common construction in the old ballads. Remember that person designates a
relationship, not an independent or isolated quality of a noun.
A noun standing alone has no person. A personal pronoun
has (page 16) as have also a few forms of the verb. In the old
verb forms third person was denoted by eth—**doth** (formerly
doeth), **hath** (formerly **haveth**), **loveth, maketh;** the second
person by st or est—**dost** (formerly **doest**), **hast** (formerly
havest), **lovest, loved'st, fearest, feard'st** (page 156).

A noun in the second person does not, as a rule, require a
personal pronoun for clarification, but in some instances it is
necessary. In **Tom, speak** and **Robert, be careful,** it is perfectly clear that Tom is being addressed in the one case, and
Robert in the other. But in **To you, women, have been assigned important tasks** the pronoun cannot well be omitted
without having **women** taken as of third person. Like the informal first-person usage above pointed out, the informal
second-person usage is arrived at by merely omitting the commas—**To you women have been assigned important tasks.**
This is a colloquial or conversational form, and is fixed in
English idiom.

Grammatical person is of signal importance in the formation
of two figures of speech, apostrophe and personification. The
former means the addressing of the absent or the dead or an
abstract idea or an imaginary object as if present and able to
understand and respond, as **Tremble, thou earth, at the
presence of the Lord.** The latter means the representation of
inanimate objects or abstract ideas as having personal attributes, as **The heavens declare the glory of God, and the
firmament showeth his handiwork.** Apostrophe employs the
second person; personification, the third. Some authorities call
apostrophe the second-person form of personification.

NUMBER

Number is that property of nouns and pronouns by which
is indicated one or more than one. Verbs, likewise, have the
property of number derivatively through agreement. But the
other five parts of speech are not inflected for number. A
form indicating one is said to be of **singular number;** indicating more than one, of **plural number.** In Greek, there are

three numbers—singular meaning one, dual meaning two, plural meaning more than two. Old English also had the dual number, but it has been dropped, and modern English happily has but two numbers—singular and plural. Anything up to and including one is singular; anything over and above one is plural; hence, 1½ or 1¼ or 1¾ is plural.[1]

The regular plural of nouns is formed by adding **s** to the singular whenever it unites readily with the sound of **s** without forming an extra syllable, as **boy, boys; book, books; foe, foes; answer, answers; time, times; picnic, picnics.**

But when **s** does not readily and easily so unite, that is, when a singular ends with **s, x (ks), z, ch** (soft), **sh**, then **es** is added to the singular to form a pluralizing syllable, as **adz, adzes; alias, aliases; arch, arches; box, boxes; branch, branches; bush, bushes; church, churches; fox, foxes; gas, gases; lass, lasses; marsh, marshes; match, matches; speech, speeches; surplus, surpluses; tax, taxes; topaz, topazes; waltz, waltzes; wish, wishes.** Of course, singular nouns with final **e** (see above) end with **es** when the pluralizing **s** is added, and this may or may not be pronounced as a separate syllable; thus, **due** and **dues, toe** and **toes,** but **face** and **faces, abuse** and **abuses, expense** and **expenses, science** and **sciences.**

Note in the above illustrations the sound of pluralizing **s** and **es.** In nouns ending with the sound, **f, k, p, t,** or voiceless **th,** the **s** is usually pronounced soft—**reefs, books, wraps, fats, breadths.** There is much custom and some authority, however, for the hard **s** (**z**) sound after **th** endings, as **baths** and **laths** and **paths.** In nouns ending with a vowel sound or with the sound **b, d, g** (hard), **l, m, n, ng, th** (voiced), or **v,** the **s** is pronounced hard, that is, like **z.** In other words, the added **s** and the end of the word must both be pronounced as sonant or as surd, or they may automatically form two syllables. Pronounce **bags** with soft **s** and you get **backs;** so you must pronounce the plural of **bag, bagz,** the plural of **pod, podz,** the plural of **fall, fallz,** the plural of **plan, planz.** Misunderstanding in pronunciation does not always result by not doing so, but this is only because there is no homonym of the soft

[1] This represents weight of authority, though it is sometimes ruled that anything less than two should be regarded as singular.

pronunciation. Note these plurals, in order of the endings listed above: **cubs (cubz), beds (bedz), bugs (bugz), ells (ellz), plums (plumz), duns (dunz), rings (ringz), lathes (lathz), leaves (leavz).** The soft s pronunciation yields, in order, **cups, bets, bucks, else, plumps, dunce, rinks, laths, leafs (liefs).** The s is sounded z in the es pluralization after the **j, s, x, z, ch** (soft), and **sh** endings, as **trench** and **trenches (trenchez).** Note that when final **ch** is hard, **s** alone is added and no extra syllable is necessary—**monarch** and **monarchs, epoch** and **epochs.** It should be observed here (as will be noted later) that the foregoing plural formations, as well as those explained just below, apply to the third person singular present indicative verbs; thus, **hate** and **hates** and **he hates, clash** and **clashes** and **he clashes, thief** and **thieves** and **he thieves, fancy** and **fancies** and **he fancies, echo** and **echoes** and **he echoes.** But note **loaf** and **loaves** and **he loafs.**

Nouns ending with **f** or **fe** preceded by a long vowel or by **l,** and descended from pure English source, change the **f** and **fe** to **ves** to form the plural, as **calf, calves; elf, elves; half, halves; knife, knives; leaf, leaves; life, lives; loaf, loaves; self, selves; sheaf, sheaves; shelf, shelves; thief, thieves; wife, wives; wolf, wolves.** But the long **oo** in **hoof** and **roof** does not superinduce the change, their plurals being **hoofs, roofs. Beef, scarf, turf, wharf** are pluralized in both ways—**beefs** and **beeves** (the former especially in western America in reference to fattened oxen ready to kill), **dwarfs** and **dwarves, scarfs** and **scarves, turfs** and **turves, wharfs** (preferably in England) and **wharves. Staff** is pluralized **staffs** when it means personnel; **staves,** when it means rods and sticks (**stave** is really the singular). **Tipstaffs,** however, is preferable to **tipstaves.** The following take **s** regularly (many of them from foreign source): **bailiffs, beliefs, bluffs, briefs, carafes, chefs, chiefs, clefs, cliffs, cuffs, fiefs, giraffes, griefs, gulfs, handkerchiefs, kerfs, mischiefs, plaintiffs, proofs, puffs, reefs, safes, serfs, skiffs, reliefs, strifes, waifs, whiffs.**

There are no dependable rules for the pluralizing of nouns ending with **o.** Some, especially those that have been long used in English and that have a consonant immediately before final **o,** add **es;** some, especially those that come from Italian and that have a vowel immediately before final **o,** add **s.** Some are spelled either way. The following lists may be helpful, but the dictionary must be your final guide:

es plurals (o following consonant)

archipelago	archipelagoes	lingo	lingoes
bilbo	bilboes	manifesto	manifestoes
bravado	bravadoes	mosquito	mosquitoes
cargo	cargoes	mulatto	mulattoes
dado	dadoes	Negro	Negroes
echo	echoes	no	noes
go	goes	potato	potatoes
grotto	grottoes	tomato	tomatoes
hero	heroes	tornado	tornadoes
innuendo	innuendoes	torpedo	torpedoes
jingo	jingoes	veto	vetoes

s plurals (o following vowel)

bamboo	bamboos	portfolio	portfolios
cameo	cameos	radio	radios
embryo	embryos	ratio	ratios
Florio	Florios	rodeo	rodeos
folio	folios	Romeo	Romeos
hoodoo	hoodoos	studio	studios
oratorio	oratorios	voodoo	voodoos

s or es plurals

buffalo	buffalos	buffaloes
calico	calicos	calicoes
desperado	desperados	desperadoes
domino	dominos	dominoes
flamingo	flamingos	flamingoes
fresco	frescos	frescoes
halo	halos	haloes
hobo	hobos	hoboes
mango	mangos	mangoes
memento	mementos	mementoes
portico	porticos	porticoes
volcano	volcanos	volcanoes
zero	zeros	zeroes

But note these exceptions to the first list above; that is, the following nouns ending with **o** preceded by a consonant are generally spelled with **s** only:

albinos	cellos	major-domos	scherzos
altos	chromos	octavos	silos
autos	decimos	pianos	siroccos
banjos	dynamos	piccolos	solos
bassos	Eskimos	Platos	sombreros
boleros	Filipinos	provisos	sopranos
broncos	hidalgos	quartos	stilettos
burros	inamoratos	ranchos	tobaccos
cantos	juntos	ridottos	torsos
casinos	kimonos	rondos	tyros
Catos	lassos	salvos	violoncellos

Nouns ending with y preceded by a consonant change y to i and add es to form the plural; ending with y preceded by a vowel, add s; thus,

ally	allies	alley	alleys
berry	berries	attorney	attorneys
body	bodies	boy	boys
city	cities	chimney	chimneys
comedy	comedies	donkey	donkeys
daisy	daisies	journey	journeys
fancy	fancies	galley	galleys
folly	follies	key	keys
lady	ladies	kidney	kidneys
lily	lilies	medley	medleys
mercy	mercies	money	moneys
quantity	quantities	monkey	monkeys
sky	skies	trolley	trolleys
story	stories	turkey	turkeys
sty	sties	valley	valleys
tragedy	tragedies	volley	volleys
whisky	whiskies	whiskey	whiskeys

The old plural **monies** is now little used, but some authorities prefer it to **moneys** to indicate sums of money. Note **colloquies, obloquies, soliloquies,** plurals respectively of **colloquy, obloquy, soliloquy. Obsequies** occurs, as a rule, only in the plural. The **qu** is the consonant combination **kw** in pronunciation, and the **y** is, therefore, changed to **i** and **es** is added. The noun **fly,** with its several meanings, is preferably pluralized regularly—**flies.** But usage varies and the dictionary should be consulted.

There are few **en** plurals. **Oxen** is one. **Brethren** is another old plural (page 33). **Chicken,** though frequently used in provincial parts as a plural, is singular, the **en** indicating diminutive; it is from the Anglo-Saxon **cycen** which is in turn diminutive of **coc** or **cock. Children** is really a double plural, the **r** being remnant of one **(childer)** and the **en** of another. **Kine,** old plural of **cow,** is now archaic. **Swine** is both singular and plural meaning hog or hogs, not necessarily sow or sows alone. In addition to these special forms, the following remain as the most irregular plurals in everyday English usage: **dormouse, dormice; foot, feet; goose, geese; louse, lice; man, men; mouse, mice; tooth, teeth; woman, women.**

Foreign nouns coming into English tend to adopt regular **s** or **es** pluralization the longer they remain in English usage. On first adoption, however, they retain their own foreign plural forms, and foreign technical and scientific terms may retain these plurals permanently. The simple English plurals are recommended for all foreign nouns that are even in occasional use. But care should be taken not to add **s** or **es** to forms that are already plural in other tongues, as, for instance, **memorandas** for **memoranda** (plural of **memorandum), phenomenas** for **phenomena** (plural of **phenomenon), termini** for **termini** (plural of **terminus), theseses** for **theses** (plural of **thesis), chassises** for **chassis (chassis** being both singular and plural), and **cherubims** for **cherubim,** and **seraphims** for **seraphim** (see page 33). Note that foreign nouns ending with **us** in the singular usually have **i** in the plural; those with **um** have **a;** those with **on** also have **a;** those with **a** have **ae;** those with **x** or **ex** have **ces** or **ices;** those with **eau** add **x;** those with **is** have **es** or **ides.** In the lists below, the English plural is not given in case the foreign noun has not yet adopted it; that is, in case the foreign plural is as yet used as an English plural.

Foreign singular	Foreign plural	English plural
addendum	addenda	addendums
administratrix	administratrices	administratrixes
alga	algae	
alumna (f)	alumnae	
alumnus (m)	alumni[1]	

[1] For the sake of convenience this form—**alumni**—is being more and more generally used as both masculine and feminine plural.

Foreign singular	*Foreign plural*	*English plural*
amanuensis	amanuenses	
analysis	analyses	
antithesis	antitheses	
antrum	antra	antrums
apex	apices	apexes
aphis	aphides	
apotheosis	apotheoses	
appendix	appendices	appendixes
arboretum	arboreta	arboretums
arcanum	arcana	arcanums
arena	arenae	arenas
auditorium	auditoria	auditoriums
automaton	automata	automatons
axis	axes	
bacterium	bacteria	
bandit	banditti	bandits
basis	bases	
beau	beaux	beaus
bureau	bureaux	bureaus
calyx	calyces	calyxes
candelabrum	candelabra	candelabrums
chapeau	chapeaux	chapeaus
chateau	chateaux	chateaus
cheval	chevaux	
chrysalis	chrysalides	chrysalises
classis	classes	
cortex	cortices	cortexes
crisis	crises	
criterion	criteria	criterions
cumulus	cumuli	
curriculum	curricula	curriculums
datum	data	
decennium	decennia	decenniums
desideratum	desiderata	desideratums
dictum	dicta	dictums
dilettante	dilettanti	dilettantes
dogma	dogmata	dogmas
drachma	drachmae	drachmas
effluvium	effluvia	effluviums
ellipsis	ellipses	
emporium	emporia	emporiums
erratum	errata	
executrix	executrices	executrixes

Foreign singular	Foreign plural	English plural
focus	foci	focuses
formula	formulae	formulas
fungus	fungi	funguses
genus	genera	genuses
gladiolus	gladioli	gladioluses
glottis	glottides	glottises
gymnasium	gymnasia	gymnasiums
hiatus	hiatus	hiatuses
hippopotamus	hippopotami	hippopotamuses
honorarium	honoraria	honorariums
humerus	humeri	
hypothesis	hypotheses	
iris	irides	irises
lacuna	lacunae	lacunas
larva	larvae	larvas
madame	mesdames	madams
magus	magi	
matrix	matrices	matrixes
maximum	maxima	maximums
medium	media	mediums
memorandum	memoranda	memorandums
miasma	miasmata	miasmas
minimum	minima	minimums
minutia	minutiae	
momentum	momenta	momentums
monsieur	messieurs	misters
nebula	nebulae	nebulas
nucleus	nuclei	nucleuses
oasis	oases	
octopus	octopi **or** octopides	octopuses
parenthesis	parentheses	
paries	parietes	
phenomenon	phenomena	
polypus	polypi	
propaganda		propagandas[1]
radius	radii	radiuses
radix	radices	radixes
referendum	referenda	referendums
sarcophagus	sarcophagi	sarcophaguses
seraglio	seragli	seraglios
sinus	sinus	sinuses

[1] Rare.

Foreign singular	Foreign plural	English plural
spectrum	spectra	spectrums
sphinx	sphinges	sphinxes
stadium	stadia	stadiums
stimulus	stimuli	
stratum	strata	stratums
syllabus	syllabi	syllabuses
symposium	symposia	symposiums
synopsis	synopses	
synthesis	syntheses	
tableau	tableaux	tableaus
tempo	tempi	tempos
terminus	termini	terminuses
thesis	theses	
thrombus	thrombi	thrombuses
triumvir	triumviri	triumvirs
trousseau	trousseaux	trousseaus
vertebra	vertebrae	vertebras
vertex	vertices	vertexes
vibrio	vibrioni	
virtuoso	virtuosi	virtuosos
vortex	vortices	vortexes

Do not use foreign plurals simply for the sake of showing off your vocabulary. Foreign words that occur in the average conversational vocabulary may follow regular English pluralization. In a few cases somewhat different meanings may be conveyed by different plural forms (page 33).

Hyphened compounds usually take pluralization on the principal part—the part that is described or explained by the other part or parts of the compound—as **arm-chairs, foot-stools, mouse-traps, ox-carts, wagon-loads. Major-generals** follows suit for here a general is indicated and **major** is a modifier. But the plural of **attorney-general** may be **attorneys-general** or **attorney-generals.** Webster now omits hyphen from both of these military terms.

A few hyphened compounds have both parts pluralized, as **knights-templars, lords-justices, menservants, womenservants** (the last two are increasingly written solid). Compound terms in which an adjective follows a noun are usually pluralized on the latter—**courts-martial, knights-errant**—but **court-martials** and **knight-errants** are allowable forms, as so too, of course, is **tête-à-têtes.**

The pluralization of hyphened compounds that denote legal relationships occurs on the part denoting the relationship, as **aunts-in-law, cousins-in-laws, brothers-in-law, daughters-in-law, fathers-in-law, mothers-in-law, sisters-in-law, sons-in-law, uncles-in-law.** And other similar compounds—those consisting of a noun and a descriptive or explanatory word or phrase—follow suit, as **hangers-on, lookers-on, maids-of-honor, men-of-war, stoppers-by.** But a compound noun composed of words not nouns is pluralized regularly, as **forget-me-nots, go-betweens, hand-me-downs, six-per-cents.**

Solid compounds are pluralized regularly, that is, at the end of the word, as **bookcases, bookshelves, horsemen, jury-women.** This applies to the so-called step solids—**stepaunts, stepbrothers, stepchildren, stepdaughters, stepfathers, stepmothers, stepsisters, stepsons, stepuncles.** It applies also to the ful solid compounds, as **armfuls, bucketfuls, handfuls, spoonfuls,** in which the emphasis is always upon the quantity measured rather than upon the agency of measurement. If you say **five spoons full** you mean five different spoons. If you say **five spoonfuls** you mean one spoon filled five times, the spoon being merely a unit of measure. The latter is the intended meaning in most usage. The plural of **Dutchman, Englishman, Frenchman, Norseman, Northman** is respectively **Dutchmen, Englishmen, Frenchmen, Norsemen, Northmen,** following **man** and **men.** But note that in **Brahman, Burman, dragoman, German, Mussulman, Norman, Ottoman, talisman,** the last syllable, though spelled **man,** is pluralized **mans** rather than **men.** If the first part of a hyphened form is in the possessive case, pluralization takes place on the last member of the compound, as **bird's-eye-views, cat's-paws.**

Certain nouns have two plurals of different meanings, as

bandit	bandits (individuals)	banditti (organized body)
brother	brothers (family)	brethren (group or society)
cannon	cannons (individual guns)	cannon (collective quantity)
cherub	cherubs (individuals)	cherubim (order of angels)

cloth	cloths (kinds of cloth)	clothes (wearing apparel)
die	dies (coining stamps)	dice (gaming cubes)
fish	fishes (individual)	fish (quantity or species)
game	games (sports)	game (prey in hunting)
genius	geniuses (talented persons)	genii (spirits)
heathen	heathens (individuals)	heathen (collective group)
index	indexes (in books)	indices (in mathematics)
memorandum	memorandums (separate lists)	memoranda (items listed)
pea	peas (distributive)	pease or peas (collective)
penny	pennies (coins)	pence (quantity or value)
seraph	seraphs (individuals)	seraphim (order of angels)
shot	shots (distributive)	shot (collective)
stamen	stamens (in seed growths)	stamina (fibers, energy)
stigma	stigmas (of pistil, kinds)	stigmata (spots, soilure, scars)

Some nouns are plural in form but singular in use and meaning; scientific terms ending with **ics** predominate in this group.

acoustics	linguistics	poetics
aeronautics	mathematics	polemics
aesthetics	measles	politics
athletics	mechanics	pyrotechnics
billiards	metaphysics	shingles
civics	mnemonics	statics
dynamics	molasses	statistics
economics	news	tactics
glanders	optics	whereabouts
hydrostatics	physics	woods

Some of these are frequently heard and seen as subjects of plural verbs, especially **politics** and **tactics**. But in most of these words the final **s** is not a sign of the plural at all, and most of them have no corresponding singular form. Drop the s from the **ics** endings and adjectives result as a rule.

Certain nouns that denote pairs are usually treated as plural, namely, **breeches, drawers, pincers, pliers, reins, scales, scissors, shears, spectacles** (for the eyes), **tongs, trousers, tweezers.**

The plural forms **alms, bellows, eaves, entrails, riches** are now generally regarded as words without singulars and are used preferably in plural constructions, though the first two may be construed as either singular or plural; the singular form **eave** is now almost archaic; **riches** is the French **richesse,** not **rich** plus **es,** and was once regarded as singular.

Amends, means, odds, pains, tidings, wages are sometimes construed as singular, sometimes as plural. Euphony (page 258) has something to do with their number; thus, **Many tidings are coming in** and **Good tidings is received, These odds are discouraging** and **This odds is too much, Great pains is taken** and **All possible pains are taken.** Used in reference to a single manner or method, **means** is singular; to more than one manner or method, plural; thus, **No other means is at hand** and **All possible means are to be resorted to.** Any plural noun, it naturally follows, is correctly construed as singular when it is used in a unit or collective sense, as **That fifty dollars you owe me is due.** Here, though **dollars** is normally plural, it has singular significance, and both its modifier **that** and its predicate **is** are accordingly singular (pages 93-94).

While the plurals listed just above are sometimes designated as false or disguised plurals, the following may be set down as plural nouns that are rarely or never used in the singular though singular forms, sometimes with different meaning, exist (those given in the preceding paragraph are not repeated):

annals	dregs	nuptials	spectacles
ashes	gallows	oats	suds
athletics	goods	obsequies	victuals
blues	lees	proceeds	vitals
clothes	links	remains	works

But usage varies in regard to these. **Athletics,** for instance, is regarded as singular when it refers to a system of training, as plural when it refers to many different kinds of sport. **Gallows** has a regular plural form—**gallowses**—but **gallows are** is much more commonly used than **gallows is.** Do not use **gallow** as the singular form or as a modifying form. Say **The condemned man walked up to the gallows platform unafraid.** In the same way speak of **scissors blades,** not scissor blades; **spectacles frame,** not spectacle frame; **trousers pockets,** not **trouser pockets.**

Note that the plural of a noun does not always mean merely more than one of its singular but may have an entirely different meaning; thus, **good,** moral force, and **goods,** merchandise; **draught,** air or drawing or demand, etc., and **draughts,** game of checkers; **domino,** mask, and **dominoes,** game; **spectacle,** display, and **spectacles** for eyes.

Figures, letters, signs, symbols, hieroglyphs, and other characters, are pluralized by the apostrophe and s—'s—**Dot your i's and cross your t's, There are two r's and two s's in embarrass, The *'s and &'s confuse me, We have three ¶'s to memorize, There are two 0's in 100.** In stock quotations, however, no apostrophe is used—**3s, 6s, 7s, 1945s, 4½s** being quite clear under general stock headings. In detached copy **3s** might mean three shillings, and **Write u's clearly** is different from **Write us clearly.** The plurals of names and words used without regard for meaning or context once followed this rule, as **and's** and **if's, There are too many but's in this sentence.** But this form of pluralization is now used decreasingly. **Capitalize your Georges and make your pros and cons clear** is correct.

Proper nouns are pluralized by means of s and es in accordance with rule, as **Ednas, Ethels, Jameses, Johns, Joneses, Leos** (page 27), **Maries, Shapiros, Stevenses, Virginias, Wyomings.** But **Carry, Harry, Mary** follow the anomalous dry and are pluralized, in defiance of the final-y rule, **Carrys, Harrys, Marys.** Titles used before names are usually pluralized rather than the names themselves, with one exception, namely **Mrs.** This exception is made to prevent pronunciation confusion with **Misses** before feminine names to mean unmarried (or single), and also to prevent the awkward **Missises.** Thus, the **Misses Ferguson** is somewhat better than the **Miss Fergusons,** the Misses Alice and Gertrude Ferguson than Miss Alice and Gertrude Fergusons, the Messrs. Smith than the Mr. Smiths; likewise say the Drs. Munson, Drs. Albert and Horace Munson, Professors Noe and Soe, Fathers Breen and McQuillan, Sisters Althea and Rosaria, Reverends Yea and Nay. Note, however, as suggested above, that the Mrs. Hansons is correct to indicate two married women surnamed Hanson. The article *the* before a title is a formal and professional usage, not a business one; it is usually capitalized in very formal notes. Titles that follow names are not pluralized. You do not say Henry James and Wilbur Holmes, A. M.'s, but Henry James, A. M., and Wilbur Holmes, A. M.

A great many nouns are spelled the same in both singular and plural, particularly the names of animals, diseases, grains, materials, measures, as barley, cod, cord, deer, gold, granite, gross, grouse, hundredweight, mackerel, perch, plover, quail, rheumatism, salmon, sheep, silver, trout, wheat. You may say that you saw three deer, caught ten bass, sold twenty hundredweight (hundredweights is also correct). But such nouns used as names of species are regularly pluralized, as the deers of Canada, the wheats of Hungary, the sheeps of Australia, the malarias of interior Africa.

Certain nouns that denote measure and quantity and weight may be used in the singular after a word signifying plural, such as brace, dozen, gross, head, load, pair, sail, score, ton, yoke. Thus, three brace of partridges, five dozen of eggs (page 92), three gross of pencils, twelve head of cattle, two load of hay, six pair of shoes, a fleet of fifty sail, four score of boxes, four ton of coal, three yoke of oxen are correct, but many authorities consider it better form to pluralize such nouns in keeping with their modifiers, as three dozens, six pairs, and so on. Certain common and proper nouns, such as chassis, corps, series, species, and Burmese, Chinese, Japanese, Portuguese, Siamese, are the same in form for both singular and plural.

Abstract nouns frequently become concrete through pluralization. In the pursuit of happiness, happiness is an abstract noun. In He was able to bring to her little daily happinesses, the pluralized form of the word becomes concrete, enabling the mind to picture actual objects and events. In the same

way, **hope** and **generosity** and **hardship,** and a host of other
abstract nouns, lose their general qualitative character when
they are pluralized and take on images of actualities. But
such abstract nouns as **courage** and **manhood** and **earnestness**
are always abstract and singular.

A collective noun is singular in form but its construction
may be either singular or plural. You may say **Majority rules**
and **The majority of those present were boys and girls, The
jury has entered** and **The jury disagree.** When such collective
nouns as **cabinet, class, committee, company, corporation,
crowd, generation, group, nation, number, people, public,
rest, remainder** denote solid unity, they take singular verbs;
when they denote division or split, plural verbs. When you
say **The number of students is smaller today,** you are thinking of an isolated and unified group. When you say **A number
of students are certain to fail,** you are thinking of scattered or
diversified students.

CASE

Case in grammar means the relationship of nouns and
pronouns to other words in a sentence. Nouns and pronouns
are the only parts of speech that are inflected for case. Any
being or thing named in a sentence as the subject of thought
is said to be in the **nominative case.** This case is called nominative in other languages also. Any being or thing named in
a sentence as the object of thought is said to be in the
objective case, whether it follows a verb or a preposition expressed or understood. This case is called **accusative** or **dative**
(see below) in other languages. Any being or thing indicated
in a sentence as possessing is said to be in the **possessive case.**
This case is called **genitive,** as a rule, in other languages. It is
sometimes called genitive in English when it is denoted by **of.**
When denoted by **'s** or **s'** or **'** it is called **inflected possessive.**
English nouns are not changed in any way for the nominative
and objective case relationships; they are changed for the inflected possessive and sometimes for the genitive (pages 44
and 46). It follows, therefore, that nominative case and objective case are discernible only through thought connection
and the order of words thus required, the nominative usually
(but not always) coming early in a sentence and before verb
forms, the objective usually (but not always) coming late and
after verb forms.

In **Good books build both mind and character**, **books** indicates the subject of thought and is, therefore, in the nominative case; **mind** and **character** indicate the objects of thought, the things acted upon, and are, therefore, in the objective case. You may reverse the order, and thus the cases, if you wish: **Both mind and character are built by good books**. Now, **mind** and **character** are in the nominative case, and **books** is in the objective.

A noun is in the nominative case when it is **subject** of a verb, as **The boy struggled**, in which **boy** is subject of **struggled**.

A noun is in the nominative case when it is used as **predicate nominative**, that is, when it follows the predicate but means the same thing as the subject or closely explains or describes it, as **Buffalo Bill was a great marksman**, in which **marksman** is the predicate nominative. Other names for this construction are **predicate noun, attribute complement, subjective complement**.

A noun is in the nominative case when it is used in **direct address**, as **Mary, do your work**, in which **Mary** represents a person directly addressed. This construction is sometimes called **vocative**, that is, the **called** case. If such noun is expressed with emotion, as **Police! save my child** and **Heart of my heart! the woman comes**, it is called by some authorities **nominative of exclamation**.

A noun is in the nominative case when it is unrelated to other words in a sentence and stands as the expression of an independent idea, as **The car having stalled, we got out and walked**, in which **car** is **nominative independent** or **nominative absolute**. The car having stalled is detached or "untied" from the rest of the sentence. As far as form is concerned it might just as well be called objective. But a fundamental rule of grammatical construction says that a noun or a pronoun not dependent upon or related to any other word in a sentence, is correctly regarded as of the nominative case.

The nominative absolute is, as a rule, the equivalent of an adverbial clause, as **I being a coward, the thief was allowed to get away**, that is, **Inasmuch as I am a coward, the thief** was allowed to get away; Jenkins being out of the office for a moment, the clerk telephoned his best girl, that is, While Jenkins was out of the office for a moment, the clerk telephoned his best girl. Note that this absolute construction is frequently expressed with understood noun or subject in general usage, as in The hymns are to be sung standing and Generally speaking, John is a good boy; that is, in the first, the congregation standing, and in the second, one or a person generally speaking. Don't confuse nominative absolute with dangling participle (page 144). Though it often has participial modification, the participle is not essential to an absolute construction; in The mountains rose like a celestial stairway, peak after peak, the phrase peak after peak is nominative absolute.

A noun is in the nominative case when it is attached to another nominative noun by way of appositive or emphatic or explanatory adjunct, as The teacher, a vigorous young man, was taken suddenly ill, in which man, in apposition with teacher, is an explanatory modifier of it, and is called nominative by apposition. Apposition derivatively means placed near. Its position must very often be depended upon to distinguish it from attribute complement. In Charles, the captain, has been taken ill, captain is appositive to Charles. In Charles, who has been taken ill, is the captain, captain is attribute to Charles, or predicate nominative.

A noun in apposition may be in objective case or in possessive case, in agreement with the noun that it explains. As a rule it agrees with that noun also in gender and number, but not always. In Ten girls, the whole class, failed, girls is feminine and plural, whereas class is intrinsically common and singular. Again, in Harold, the tennis-player, has won again and Mary, the tennis-player, has lost again, the noun in apposition—tennis-player—is masculine in the one and feminine in the other. This is one of the very few instances in which a feminine ending might help the beginner in English. Note, again, that a single noun may have more than one noun in apposition with it, as Harrison—captain, president, student, editor—has made an enviable record. Here Harrison is the singular subject and requires a singular predicate, the four appositives having no influence on number. The words as, of, or are sometimes used as introductory to the appositive (pages 206 and 210); thus, Adams, as our representative, did his best for us and **Nectarines, or peach-plums, of best quality come from South Africa.**

It is said above that the nominative noun usually comes early in a sentence and precedes the predicate. But it has been seen that this is not true when the nominative noun is attributive or appositive to an attribute, and it is not necessarily true of a nominative absolute or of a nominative by direct address. Note the position of the italicized nominative in each of the following: **Please give me that,** *Bill.* **Has** *Jenny* **done her work yet? There is a** *book* **on the table. Were** *I* **able I would help him. I cannot accept your explanation, neither can the other** *members* **of the team. Alone stands our** *hero!* **"This," said** *he,* **"is the end of all."** These various placements of the nominative show the facility of English in adjusting itself to interrogation and exclamation, and in lending itself to emphasis and variety.

A noun is in the objective case when it is the object of a predicate, of a participle, or of an infinitive, as **Jim saved his money,** in which **money** is the **direct object** of **saved;** and **Jim saving his money became rich** (object of participle), and **Jim determined to save his money** (object of infinitive).

A noun is in the objective case when it is used as **cognate object** of a predicate, that is, when it repeats the meaning of an otherwise intransitive verb or yields a meaning similar to that of the verb, as **He prayed a solemn prayer** and **They lived their routine lives,** in which **prayer** and **lives** repeat the idea contained in their respective verbs and are **direct cognate objects.** The repeated idea in the object should usually be intensified by a modifier; otherwise there is no purpose in repeating it (page 106).

A noun is in the objective case when it means the same thing as the direct object or explains or describes it, as **We made Horace leader,** in which **leader** defines the direct object **Horace.** This is not to be confused with a noun in apposition. Note that **leader** completes, that the sentence without it is absurd—**We made Horace.** The noun in apposition is not necessary for completion, but is added and gratuitous in a construction. In all such expressions—**They elected Roosevelt president, They named the boy Harrison, They chose Bill**

captain—the completing noun—**president, Harrison, captain** —is called **objective complement;** it is also called **factitive object, predicate objective, appositional object, resultant object, secondary object.** Such verbs as **appoint, call, choose, constitute, elect, find, make, name, ordain, think** are followed very often by objective complements denoting rank, office, position, name, and the like. Note that the objective complement follows the direct object.

A noun is in the objective case when it is in apposition with another noun in the objective case (see above), as **We took the old route, our childhood haunt,** in which **haunt** is in apposition with the direct object **route** and is, therefore, in the objective case.

A noun is in the objective case when it is used (with understood preposition before it) to denote distance, measure, space, time, manner, value, weight, and the like, as **They strolled a few *blocks*, She stayed a *month*, The wall is three *yards* high, It weighs ten *pounds*, She drove full *speed*,** in which the italicized words are the objects of prepositions understood, as **They strolled for a few blocks, She stayed for a month, The wall is high to the extent of three yards, It weighs to ten pounds, She drove at full speed.** This construction is called **adverbial adjunct** or **adverbial modifier** or **objective of weight or measure,** and so on. Do not confuse this construction with cognate object. This is an objective having strictly adverbial nature whereas the cognate is a noun repetition of the verb idea.

A noun is in the objective case when it is used as object of a preposition, the preposition showing from what word or words the idea starts and to what word or words it is directed, as **He is going to Boston, They arrived from the East, The boy is at the circus,** in which **Boston** and **East** and **circus** are in the objective case, objects respectively of **to, from, at.**

A noun is in the objective case when it is used as subject of the infinitive, as **They expected the girls to be interested,** in which **girls** is subject of the infinitive **to be interested.** Note that the sentence does not mean that they expected the girls. That is a completely different idea. The direct object of the verb **expected** is the infinitive phrase **the girls to be interested** as a unit; separation of one part of the phrase from another is impossible if the exact meaning of the sentence is to be retained.

A noun is in the objective case when it is used as **indirect object,** that is, an object indicating the person to or for or on behalf of whom something is done, as **Pass** *Mary* **the butter, Telegraph** *Blaine* **our terms, Tell the** *boy* **a story, Do** *Harry* **this favor,** in which italicized nouns are indirect objects with to or for understood before them. But the preposition may be expressed before an indirect object, as **Buy a car for the** *boy,* **Give my best wishes to your** *sister,* **Find a position for** *Mary.* When the preposition is understood before an indirect object, the indirect object always precedes the direct object; when the indirect object follows the direct object, the preposition must be expressed. The verbs after which the indirect object is to be expected are those denoting getting, giving, providing, telling, as **allow, ask, buy, deny, find, give, grant, hand, make, obtain, offer, pass, pay, procure, promise, provide, secure, send, telegraph, telephone, tell, write,** and a few others. After **ask,** it should be noted, the indirect object may be governed by the preposition **of,** as **We asked the principal no favors** or **We asked no favors of the principal.** Note also that **make,** meaning build or construct, takes an indirect object, as **Make John a new chair;** meaning appoint or constitute, it takes an objective complement, as **They made Mary queen.** The archaic forms **meseems** and **methinks** are really forms of the indirect object—**seems to me** and **thinks to me** (both mean **It seems to me**). The indirect object also occurs after certain adjectives and adverbs; thus, **like Carrie,** is really **like to Carrie; unlike Mary, unlike to Mary; near Alice, near to Alice; opposite Sally, opposite to Sally.** The indirect object is sometimes called **dative.**

A noun is in the objective case when it is used as **retained object,** that is, when an object of an active verb is "held over" as object of the same verb in the passive voice. In **I taught John a lesson, lesson** is the direct object and **John** the indirect object. In **John was given a lesson by me, lesson** is the retained object after the passive form of the verb. In the other passive reading—**A lesson was given John by me, lesson** is made subject and **John** is indirect object.

It is said above that the objective noun usually follows the predicate, and this is natural order. But for the sake of variety or emphasis it may be given other placement. In **A scarf he gave to me, scarf** is object of **gave,** yet stands before it. In **John I bought it for, John** is object of the preposition **for,** yet it is placed as far away from it as it can be. In **Two weeks we stayed in that one-horse town,** the adverbial adjunct **weeks** carries emphasis as a result of placement out of natural order, which, incidentally, is usually true in English.

The possessive case denotes possession, origin, source—indicates that to which something else belongs or with which it is connected. The possessive case of nouns is their only inflected case, the inflection consisting of **'s** or **s'** or of the apostrophe alone. The **of** possessive or genitive does not invariably make use of possessive inflection (page 48). Up to the latter part of the seventeenth century the possessive case was indicated by **es** or **is** or **ys** at the end of a noun, and this case ending made a separate syllable. The vowels in these endings were later supplanted by the apostrophe. The **'s** sign is not to be regarded as a shortened form of **his** or **its.**

The possessive singular of nouns is usually formed by the addition of **'s,** as **boy's prize, day's work, week's visit, Bill's pencil, Jane's dress, May's bonnet.** If, however, a singular noun ends with **s** or other hissing sound and consists of two or more syllables after the sign of the possessive is added, the apostrophe alone may be used in order to prevent awkward pronunciation and disagreeable sound, as **Dickens' novels** instead of **Dickens's novels, St. James' Square** instead of **St. James's Square, Achilles' wrath** instead of **Achilles's wrath, Jesus' name** instead of **Jesus's name, Knox' gelatin** instead of **Knox's gelatin, goodness' sake** instead of **goodness's sake, conscience' sake** instead of **conscience's sake, righteousness' sake** instead of **righteousness's sake, Demosthenes' speeches** instead of **Demosthenes's speeches.** There is an old rule to the effect that proper names ending with a hissing sound must form their possessive by the addition of **'s,** no matter how awkward or ineuphonious the pronunciation may be; thus, **Dickens' novels, St. James' Square, Thomas' book** are considered wrong under this rule. "As language evolves it tends to become simplified." There are many persons now who disregard this old rule, and there are many who insist upon the conservative possessive forms—**Dickens's novels** and **St. James's Square.** In England this proper-name rule is rigidly observed. In America it is not, advertising copy having done much to popularize the simpler form.

The possessive plural of nouns that end with s is formed by adding the apostrophe alone. When, however, the plural noun does not end with s, the possessive is formed by 's as it is in the singular noun; thus, **girls' shoes, doctors' offices, babies' bottles, women's activities, people's interests.**

Compound nouns take the sign of possession at the end, that is, the sign of possession is always placed nearest to the name of the thing possessed, as **mother-in-law's cake, major-general's uniform, mothers-in-law's cakes, major-generals' uniforms.**

Two or more names used in succession to denote joint possession take the sign of possession on the last only. Similarly, two or more successive words (usually proper names, as in a title) carry the sign of possession on the last; thus, **Canby and Opdycke's** *Good English,* **Funk and Wagnalls'** *Practical Standard Dictionary,* **Germany and Russia's Trade Treaty, The Guaranty Trust Company's buildings, The Standard Oil Company of New Jersey's employes** (see below). But if joint possession is not indicated, the sign of possession must be placed at the end of each name; thus, **Harry's and Tom's cars** means two cars, one owned by Harry and one owned by Tom; **Harry and Tom's car** means that Harry and Tom have one car between them. Nouns in apposition follow the above rule of possessive proximity, that is, the sign of possession is placed nearest the thing possessed, as in **Brainerd, the treasurer's, report has been made.** Both Brainerd and the noun in apposition with it—treasurer—are in the possessive case, but the sign of possession is placed on the appositive only. Note that the appositive is set off by commas just the same. If it were not, the appearance of such expression might cause confusion —Brainerd and any other word similarly placed might be taken as a vocative. All the possessive constructions treated in this paragraph are sometimes called **phrasal possessives.**

Note that a singular possessive may modify a plural noun, a plural possessive a singular noun, as **man's feet** and **men's room.** Note, too, that there are certain "frozen" or habitual possessives in which no apostrophe is necessary, as in such

titles as **Teachers College** and **Mechanics Bank,** rather than
Teachers' College and **Mechanics' Bank.**

The pronunciation of the possessive **s** is the same as that of
the plural-number **s** (page 25); that is, it is **z** in those uses in
which the plural **s** is **z,** and in those uses in which the plural
es makes an extra syllable the **'s** does the same; thus, **dogs,
dog's, dogs'** are pronounced **dogz,** and **daughters, daughter's,
daughters'** are pronounced **daughterz; minxes** and **minx's** are
pronounced **minxez,** and, like the above illustrations, are
heard to be exactly the same. The ear can distinguish such
forms as these only by the context or the complete expression.
But not only are nominative plurals and possessive singulars
and plurals in **s** thus confusing; sometimes even the context
or the complete expression fails to clarify them to the ear. If
you say **The fox's head was turned in wrath,** the singular **head**
makes **fox's** clear. But if you say **The fox's feet carried guilt of
blood,** the plural **feet** does not make the preceding possessive
clear; it may be either **fox's** as here, or **foxes'.** In writing, no
confusion exists, of course, for the eye sees the placement of
the apostrophe. In speaking, it is better to use the **of** possessive
in case there is likely to be misunderstanding, as **the feet of
the fox** or **of the foxes.**

As a rule, the possessive case of a noun as shown by **'s** is
the same as the possessive or genitive case formed by the
preposition **of,** as **Roosevelt's career** and **the career of Roosevelt.** The use of **of** instead of **'s** is always recommended (1)
when a phrasal possessive is long and awkward, as **The policies
of the Society for the Investigation of the Increase in Taxes,**
rather than **The Society for the Investigation of the Increase
in Taxes' policies;** and (2) when a series of possessives make
a bungled and confusing sequence, as **the brother of the
cousin of Joe's partner,** rather than **Joe's partner's cousin's
brother.** The latter is sometimes called the "tandem" possessive and should be avoided.

But note that the **of** possessive may lead to ambiguity, context alone being depended upon to clarify. Thus, if you say
the depredations of the enemy, you may mean the depredations suffered by the enemy or the depredations committed
by the enemy upon others. It is necessary to use the preposition **by** or **against** to make meaning clear, or to supply modifying phrases, as **depredations by the enemy** or **depredations**

against the enemy or **depredations of the enemy in** or **against foreign territory** or **depredations committed by the enemy.** Note, again, that the **'s** possessive is no clearer used before a noun that means both act and condition, as **the enemy's persecutions.** Such ambiguous construction is called **subjective possessive** when the possessive or genitive noun denotes subject; **objective possessive** when it denotes object; thus, if the enemy did the persecuting, the construction is subjective; if the enemy were persecuted, the construction is objective. Such expressions as **love of God, love of mother, Mary's picture, John's painting** *are invariably* ambiguous in both the **of** possessive and the inflected possessive. The last, for instance, may be a painting owned by John, one that he made, one of him, one that he is carrying, one that he has hanging temporarily in his room.

The possessive case of a noun or a pronoun (page 144) is usually required before a participle used as a noun, as **Mary's arriving was well timed** and **The woman's going was hurried.** In both of these examples it is the action—**arriving** and **going** —about which the predicate makes an assertion and on which the thought of the sentence is based. And in most such participial construction this is true; it would thus be wrong to say **Mary arriving was well timed** and **The woman going was hurried.** But note the difference between **On the employer's entering a silence fell upon the meeting** and **On the employer entering there fell a book from the top of the door.** In the former **entering** is correctly modified by the possessive **employer's,** for **entering** is the important word of the phrase. In the latter, **employer** is object of the preposition **on** and it is modified by **entering.** In the second example above, it is possible to convey the meaning that the woman herself was hurried, that is, a hurried woman was going—**The woman going was hurried.** The meaning would be that the woman had a confused and hurried manner as she went. But this would be an unusual understanding of such a sentence, to say the least.

The **'s** form of the possessive (that is, the inflected possessive) is or should be confined to names of living beings or personified objects, and to certain idiomatic expressions denoting time or space or measure. Thus, you say **the horse's bridle, the ship's deck** (because ship is so frequently personified), **stone's throw** and **week's wages** and **arm's length** and

a month's visit and a dollar's worth and an hour's work and
journey's end. You do not say the barn's mow, the celery's
price, the room's size, the lawn's grass, the can's top.

By **double possessive** is meant those idiomatic expressions in
which both the inflected possessive and the of possessive are
used, as a poem of Wordsworth's and a story of Poe's. In all
such expressions the plural of the first noun is understood
after the inflected possessive, as a poem of (among) Wordsworth's poems and a story of (among) Poe's stories. A poem
of Wordsworth, a story of Poe, that home run of Brown are, as
a matter of fact, correct, but they are not idiomatic. The substitution of by for of in such expressions makes the apostrophe
s unnecessary, as a poem by Wordsworth and a story by Poe.
In such of expressions as the tautological month of May and
year of 1776 and city of San Francisco, the two nouns are
logically in apposition—the month, May, and the year, 1776,
and the city, San Francisco. But the of is idiomatic, as well as
sometimes emphatic and oratorical. In family names it has
very largely become condensed, as Davidson for son of David.
And in certain geographical names it is never used; we say
Hudson River, not river of the Hudson; Sierra Nevada Mountains, not mountains of the Sierra Nevada.

The inflected possessive always precedes the noun that it
limits. The of possessive usually follows it. Like the nominative and the objective, the possessive may, however, be
wrenched out of its natural order for the sake of emphasis, as
Of John's oils I like this the best instead of I like this the best
of John's oils. The inflected possessive may stand alone with
a nominative or an objective understood after it, as John's
pleases me most and I like John's best.

A paradigm (page 58) is a graph or tabulation by which
is shown at a glance all the declension forms of nouns and
pronouns, the conjugation forms of verbs, the comparison
forms of adjectives and adverbs. The following are declension
paradigms for nouns:

	Singular	*Plural*
NOMINATIVE AND OBJECTIVE	dog	dogs
	conscience	consciences
	Duke of Windsor	Dukes of Windsor
	father-in-law	fathers-in-law
	foot	feet
	mouse	mice
	Pius	Piuses
	stepson	stepsons
	Teddy	Teddys
	tooth	teeth
	XII	XII's or XIIs
	z	z's or zs
POSSESSIVE	dog's	dogs'
	conscience' or conscience's	consciences'
	Duke of Windsor's	Dukes of Windsor's
	father-in-law's	fathers-in-law's
	foot's	feet's
	mouse's	mice's
	Pius' or Pius's	Piuses'
	stepson's	stepsons'
	Teddy's	Teddys'
	tooth's	teeth's
	XII's[1]	XIIs'[1]
	z's[1]	zs'[1]

[1] These can be formed but they would hardly be used.

Chapter Two

PRONOUN

DEFINITION AND CLASSIFICATION

A pronoun is a word used as a substitute for a noun or another pronoun; it is used in place of the one or the other (or both) to prevent awkward or monotonous repetition; it "officiates" as a noun also in certain instances where there can be no noun to take its place. In **Bill took Bill's sister the box that Bill's sister asked Bill to bring Bill's sister,** the repetition is both clumsy and ridiculous. Much more facile and convenient and pleasant **and economical,** as result of pronouns, is **Bill took his sister the box that she asked him to bring her.** In **It rains ceaselessly** and **What does Jacobs say** the pronoun serves as a noun that cannot be definitely substituted (see below).

There are expressions, to be sure, in which repetition of a noun is required, where the substitution of an agreeing pronoun will not do. In **Mary's mother says that she doesn't think she cares to go to the party,** the reference of the pronouns she is somewhat confused. The first **she** may refer to either **Mary's** or **mother;** the second obviously refers to **Mary's,** but it may under special circumstances refer also to **mother.** There is a good grammatical rule to the effect that a pronoun cannot take as an antecedent a noun in the possessive case. This makes it impossible, therefore, for either **she** to refer to **Mary's.** But since this rule is little respected by writers and authors—if, indeed, known—such a sentence as this must be reconstructed if it is to be made entirely clear to the average understanding. It must read **Mary's mother says that Mary doesn't think she cares to go to the party** or **Mary's mother says that she doesn't think Mary cares to go to the party** or **Mary's mother says, "I don't think Mary cares to go to the party"** or **Mary's mother says, "I don't think I care to go to the party"** (there are still other possibilities). Direct discourse, as in the last two, is always preferable for the clarification of such ambiguous use of pronouns.

Note that in **It rains** and **It snows** and **It is said,** the pronoun **It** does not take the place of any noun but stands, rather, independent of all noun reference or relationship. Try to substitute a noun for **It,** and you will find none that will quite do. The best possible substitutes are **The rain (rains)** and **The snow (snows)** and **The saying (is said),** and these are ridiculous repetitions. **It** in such usage is sometimes called an **expletive pronoun** (page 64).

The noun or other pronoun to which a pronoun refers is called its **antecedent** (from two Latin words meaning to go before). It does not always go before but it usually does. The pronoun **It** in the sentences just above has no antecedent. But in **John brought his mother the book that she sent him for,** **John** is the antecedent of **his** and **him, mother** is the antecedent of **she, book** is the antecedent of **that.** The antecedent of a pronoun is usually a noun, but it may be another pronoun, as **He who wanted you has left,** in which the pronoun **who** refers to **he.** But note that **he** has no antecedent, in the sentence at least. It is identified by the clause **who wanted you,** and its true antecedent is the name of the person referred to.

While, as stated above, a noun in the possessive case may not stand as an antecedent of a pronoun, a pronoun in the possessive case may—usually must—have an antecedent. The pronoun **I** is, as a rule, used without an antecedent; it would be extremely awkward for a person to repeat his own name after **I** every time he used this pronoun, as **I (Bob Harkness) want a ticket to Rochester** and **I (Horace Wainwright) would like a drink of water.** Yet, the name referred to by **I** is always implied or understood. And the awkward repetition is common to legal phraseology, as **I, James Stillson, do hereby will and bequeath.** This makes certain of no misunderstanding; it "tightens" the expression (page 23).

The second-person **you** follows **I** in this respect. Just as the real antecedent of **I** is the person speaking, the person himself, so the real antecedent of the person spoken to is the person addressed, and additional identification is superfluous. With the third-person pronouns the situation is different. While actual repetition of name is by no means always made, and should not be, identification has somewhere to be made clear by name (or by pointing!), inasmuch as the person spoken about is presumably not present as **you** and **I** are. In legal phraseology repetition is customary in all three persons.

Certain pronouns may stand for a group of words coming before or after them, and such group may be regarded as an antecedent. It will usually be a group that may easily be "translated" into a noun or a pronoun. In **To be or not to be —that is the question,** that stands for the compound phrase **to be or not to be.** In **Whatever he may do, it can make no difference to me,** it stands for the introductory clause **whatever he may do.** In both examples the group of words referred to may be called appositives; some grammarians use the term **antecedent appositive** for such pronominal reference. In **It is certain that he will come,** the clause **that he will come** they call **subsequent appositive.**

The pronouns **who** and **which** and **what,** used interrogatively, frequently have no antecedents. As will be pointed out later, they may refer to a word or to words in the answer to a question, but their antecedence may be indefinite or unrevealed, even after the answer is given. Antecedence may be general or indefinite again in such expressions as **Whoever sins must pay the penalty** and **We cannot tell what you mean.** If you understand **he** or **the man** before **whoever** in the first, and **thing** or some other general term after **what** in the second, you nevertheless still have indefinite antecedence for the pronouns.

Pronouns are inflected for gender, person, number, case, as nouns are. But many pronouns are more highly inflected than nouns. A pronoun must agree with its antecedent in gender, person, number, but its case depends upon the construction of the clause in which it stands. This rule cannot apply, of course, to pronouns without definite antecedence, such as those above mentioned. Pronouns are classified as **adjective, demonstrative, indefinite, interrogative, personal, relative.** There are a few subdivisions in addition; these are treated below under the proper headings.

ADJECTIVE

An **adjective pronoun** (sometimes called **pronominal adjective**) is one that may be used as an adjective, to modify a noun or another pronoun. Some authorities classify demonstrative pronouns and indefinite pronouns as adjective pronouns. All pronouns herein listed as demonstratives and indefinites may be used as adjectives and as pronouns, and may thus be called adjective pronouns. Some authorities rule that any adjectives that may be compared—**certain, few, little, much, many**—have more adjective than pronoun nature, and are, therefore, to be regarded as pronominal adjectives; that any such uncompared words as **all, any, each, every, both,** are more correctly called indefinite pronouns. This is probably hair-splitting, and may be disregarded provided you understand the definitions and their application.

If you say **Few men are ill, few** is a pure adjective modifying **men.** If you say **Few are ill, few** is made to substitute for a noun (and is thus a pronoun) and to limit meaning of an understood subject (and is thus an adjective); hence, it is an adjective pronoun. Since it does not specify definitely who are ill, it may likewise be called an indefinite pronoun. Even the possessive case forms of personal pronouns may be called adjective pronouns when they modify, as **my hat, her hand, its fur, his case, your sister, their fault,** but the possessive personals that do not directly modify—**mine, hers, ours, theirs, yours,** and sometimes **his** and **its**—are pure possessives, not adjective pronouns, as in **This book is mine and that is hers** and **This is yours not his** and **You have your hair and the horse has its.**

The forms **mine own, none other, thine honor** are now archaic in general usage but are still to be found, of course, in poetical and religious expression, but **mine** and **none** and **thine** were once commonly used before nouns beginning with vowel sounds or with silent **h.** The simple **my** and **no** and **thy** are now used in their place. The demonstratives **that, those, this, these,** and the interrogatives and relatives **which** and **what,** and the relative **that,** are often used adjectively. **Who** is never used as an adjective pronoun inasmuch as it has the regular possessive form **whose** which may stand alone as well as modify.

DEMONSTRATIVE

A **demonstrative pronoun** is one that designates or points out, one that functions chiefly in specifying something referred to. There are but two demonstratives—**this** and **that,** with their plurals **these** and **those. This** and **these** denote close at hand; **that** and **those,** farther away or remote. **This** and **these** may be used synonymously with **latter; that** and **those** with **former;** thus, **Music and literature are cultural subjects, this (the latter)** acquired rather than innate, that (the former) innate rather than acquired.

Demonstrative pronouns take not only nouns but also phrases, clauses, and sentences as antecedents; in **He has returned unexpectedly but what that means I cannot tell** and **You will probably make a go of it but this alone will not satisfy you,** the demonstrative in each instance takes the entire preceding clause as antecedent.

Be sure to use **this** and **that** to modify singular nouns; **these** and **those** to modify plural ones. Mistakes in such agreement are likely to be made before **kind, sort, style, type,** and a few similar nouns. **This kind** and **these kinds, that type** and **those types** are correct. Don't say **these kind** or **that types.**

The personal pronoun **them** is sometimes wrongly used for **these** or **those,** as **them books** and **them things.** Such expressions are substandard.

Although there is little authority for the usage of **this** and **that** as adverbs of degree, their use is increasing. Thus, while **this big** and **this much** and **that high** are quite acceptable in informal usage, **so big** and **so much** and **so high** are preferred in formal usage.

INDEFINITE

An **indefinite pronoun** is one that is general and indeterminate in its reference to objects and living beings. The most commonly used indefinites are **all, another, any, anybody, any one, anything*, aught*, both, certain*, divers*, each, either, else*, every, everybody, every one, everything*, few, little*, many, much, naught*, neither, nobody, none, nothing*, one, other, own, same*, several, some, somebody, some one, something*, such, sundry*.** Those marked by asterisks are less commonly used as indefinites than the others. Many of these words are used as nouns, especially **anything, everything, something;** many are used as pure adjectives, particularly such as may be compared—**few, little, many, much;** some are used even as adverbs and conjunctions, such as **else, either, neither.**

Any one, every one, no one, some one are sometimes classified as phrasal indefinites; all but **no one** are frequently seen as single words but the two-word form is as yet preferable. **No one** has long since been reduced to **none** in most usage, but the two-word **no one** is frequently used for emphasis and clarity. **Each, every, either, neither,** are sometimes called **distributive indefinites** because they serve to separate some beings or objects from others in the same expression. **Each other** and **one another** are sometimes called **reciprocal indefinites** because they are interdependent in their meanings, that is, they imply that any action or state pertaining to one being or thing affects some other. The first—**each other**—should be used of two only; the second—**one another**—of more than two; thus, **Brother and sister should help each other** and **The members of the team respect one another.** Do not hyphenate phrasal and reciprocal pronouns; they are written as independent words.

Indefinite pronouns are the same in nominative and objective cases, in both singular and plural, and their possessives, when used at all, are formed regularly—**ones, one's, ones'; others, other's, others'.** **Else** is an adjective, an adverb, a conjunction, a pronoun; when used as the last in association with **anybody, any one, everybody, every one, somebody, some one, nobody, no one, none, what, who,** it takes the sign of possession; the preceding indefinite pronoun does not; thus, **any one else's,** not **any one's else; somebody else's, none else's (none other's), who else's.** The tendency is to regard **none** as plural, even though it is **no** plus **one.** When it is equivalent to **no one** or **not one,** it should, however, be treated as singular; when it is equivalent to **no ones** or **not ones**—that is, to two or more— it should be treated as plural. The antecedence will often help to decide. The answer to **How many men have arrived,** for instance, should be **None have arrived,** for **none** refers to plural **men** in the question. The answer to **Which car has been stolen** should be **None has been stolen,** for **none** refers to the singular **car.** In most colloquial usage, however, these distinctions are not made, and **none** is more or less loosely regarded as plural. If in the second example only two cars were considered, **Neither has been stolen** would be the correct answer.

Note that the distributives **each, either, every, neither,** and their compounds are used with singular significance; that **all, both, many, several** are used with plural significance; that **any, same, some, such** are more dependent upon context for the decision of number than are most other indefinites. **Any** is really an extension of **an,** and therefore has **one** in it; but it is used in both singular and plural modification, as **any book** and **any books.** Not followed by **one** or the idea of singleness, it is usually plural and pertains to three or more; thus, **any boys** implies more than two boys. You say **any of three or more**, not **any of two**. In two particular uses **many** is used with singular significance though it is customarily used as plural, as **many animals** and **many men**. But followed by **a—many a**—it precedes a singular noun in the sense of multiplication, as **many a man** and **many a day**, the meaning actually being **a man multiplied** or **a man many times over**, and so on. In the old ballads this expression appears in normal order as **a many man** equivalent to a great many men. In the idiom **Many is the time I've watched him**, **many** is inverted and predicative and collective. Such singular use of **many** is usually referred to by a plural pronoun, especially if the reference occurs in a different clause, as in Scott's

> In Hawick twinkled many a light,
> Behind him soon they set in night.

Little, less, least refer to quantity; **few, fewer, fewest** to number (page 93). But note that as an indefinite pronoun, and also as an adjective, **few** has idiomatic uses that are sometimes difficult to understand. In general use it means not many; preceded by **a—a few**—it means some or more than few; preceded by **the—the few**—it means not many, but all of a specific group. **Little, a little, the little** are used with the same distinctions in regard to quantity.

Note again that in **Each of the workmen took his tools**, **his** is singular because it refers to **each**, and that in **All of the workmen took their tools**, **their** is plural because it refers to **all**. But **all** may be used collectively, and thus take a singular verb, as **All's (All is) well**. In **Either is going** and **Neither likes the other**, the subjects **either** and **neither** are singular indefinites and must have singular verbs. But in answer to **Are horses or oxen to be used for this pull**, you correctly say **Either are**, for the antecedent of the indefinite **either** is plural **horses or oxen** (see **none** above).

One of the central problems of contemporary American English grammar study, however, involves the question of whether distributive compounds like **everybody** must invariably be used with singular significance. In the spoken language this is certainly no longer the case; on this particular point the influence of speech is increasingly making itself felt in the written language. At this time it seems most prudent to say that in informal usage considering these words as having plural significance is acceptable, but that in formal usage they ought still to be taken as singular.

INTERROGATIVE

An **interrogative pronoun** is one that is used to ask a question. The interrogatives are **who, which, what**—**who** having the same declension that it has as a relative (page 71), and **which** and **what** having no declension. **Whether** was once an interrogative—**Whether is the greater, the gold or the temple** —but is no longer used as such. The possessives of **which** and of **what** are formed by the use of **of. Who,** as both interrogative and relative, refers to persons only; **which** refers to lower animals, to things, and also to persons. But there is this difference between the interrogative pronouns **who** and **which** in their reference to persons; **who** is general or universal; it asks for any one of all; **which** is limited or selective; it asks for any one out of a given group or number. When you ask **Who did this** your question is universal, and the answer you receive may indicate any one or more of all living (and even dead) persons. When you ask **Which of you did this,** you address a group or a certain number, and the answer you receive is drawn from that limitation. **Which,** therefore, narrows interrogation to a particular scope; **who** does not. A noun or a pronoun may usually be supplied after **which;** never after **who.**

The interrogative **what,** like **which,** refers to persons and to lower animals and to things; like **who,** it is general or universal in its application, rather than selective. Used in reference to persons, **what** evokes explanation or description, as **What does he do, What is she like, What is his character.** Both **what** and **which** are used in direct modification of a noun, as **What kind do you have** and **Which boy do you mean; who** is never so used.

In indirect questions the interrogative pronouns are frequently mistaken for relatives. The interrogation remains in indirect question, don't forget, even though it is followed by a period; thus, in **Ask him who she is, who** is an interrogative pronoun in indirect question, for the sentence still asks **Who is she,** in spite of its being in imperative form. The same is true of **He asked who she is** and **She inquired which I wanted** and **They inquired what our business was.** But note that in **They guessed what our business was,** the factual quality of the verb makes **what** a relative clearly equivalent to **that which;** moreover, no part of this sentence is easily convertible into direct-question form, whereas the preceding one unmistakably says **What is your business.**

Note that the antecedent of an interrogative pronoun resides very often in the answer to the questions asked (page 52), but the answer may not contain the antecedent. The answer to **Who said that** may be **Shakespeare said it** or **We don't know.** If it is the former, **Shakespeare** is the antecedent; if the latter, there is no antecedent.

PERSONAL

A **personal pronoun** is one used of persons, showing by its form whether it denotes the person speaking, the person spoken to, or the person spoken about. The following paradigm contains all the personal pronouns in all genders, persons, numbers, and cases:

	Nominative Case	*Possessive Case*	*Objective Case*
FIRST PERSON SINGULAR	I	my **or** mine	me
SECOND PERSON SINGULAR	you	your **or** yours	you
THIRD PERSON SINGULAR MASCULINE	he	his	him
THIRD PERSON SINGULAR FEMININE	she	her **or** hers	her
THIRD PERSON SINGULAR NEUTER	it	its	it
FIRST PERSON PLURAL	we	our **or** ours	us
SECOND PERSON PLURAL	you	your **or** yours	you
THIRD PERSON PLURAL ALL GENDERS	they	their **or** theirs	them

One, regarded by some authorities as a personal pronoun, is here treated chiefly as an indefinite pronoun and as an adjective. It is often used, however, as a personal pronoun, as **One sees many interesting sights at the fair,** and it is called the indefinite personal. The affected use of **one** for the sake of avoiding **I,** by which first person **I** becomes subordinated as indefinite third person, has nothing to recommend it, especially when it is over-done in such expression as **One sees many interesting sights as one travels through one's native land.** The repetition may be obviated by using indeterminate **he** and **his** for **one** and **one's,** as **One sees many interesting sights as he travels through his native land.** As adjective, one means cardinal numeral 1, and also a certain one, as in **One Edward, the Black Prince.** Use it sparingly as a personal pronoun, if at all (page 64).

No other part of speech has so many inflections as the personal pronoun; no other, that is, has such extended declension. It is the only part of speech that independently changes form to indicate person. The verb changes form to indicate person, but not independently; it takes its person through the influence of another word (subject). Perhaps it is because of the unexpectedly complete case forms of pronouns that beginners in the study of English make the mistake of using the nominative case instead of the objective in such constructions as **Bill will play with you and I** and **Between you and I there are three girls,** which should, of course, be **Bill will play with you and me** and **Between you and me there are three girls.** Objective case **me** is required in both sentences, for the one is object of the preposition **with** and the other of the preposition **between.**

The forms of these highly inflected pronouns must be watched again in such expressions as **It is I** and **It is she** and **I am he** and **We are they** and **It is we.** While it is clear that the final pronoun in each of these sentences is a predicate pronoun (or attributive complement or subjective complement) and thus should be in the nominative case, the authority of usage is obviously altering this. It is not unusual to find **It is me** defended as good informal usage and even as perfectly acceptable formal usage by contemporary grammarians. It is, however, less usual to find **It is her** or **It is us** either urged or defended, especially in formal writing. This situation furnishes an interesting opportunity for the layman to determine whether a grammarian who maintains his belief in usage as the determinant of correctness is sincere or not. Those who live by the rulebook are upset by the inconsistency of **It is me** side by side with **It is he;** others seem able to bear up under the strain.

Case must be watched, again, in comparative expressions. In **He is older than I,** the nominative **I** rather than the objective **me** is required after **than** because the predicate of the degree clause is understood, that is, **He is older than I (am).** But this kind of comparative construction, while usually requiring the nominative after it, varies with context. Note that **She likes Jim better than I** and **She likes Jim better than me** may both be correct, the former really being **She likes Jim better than I like him** and the latter **She likes Jim better than she likes me.** In all such ambiguous constructions, the only safe plan is to complete the comparative expression, as in the second illustrations here, rather than leave them hanging or suspended. In the so-called as comparatives—**She is as tall as I** and **They are as far as we**—the ambiguity does not occur. Nevertheless, here too the nominative—**I** and **we**—must be used as subject of an understood verb—**I am** and **we are. As tall as me** and **as far as us** are incorrect forms.

One of the most illiterate misuses of the personal pronoun forms is that of substituting the objective for the possessive in such an expression as **them books** for **these** or **those books,** this being the substitution of a personal objective for a demonstrative or adjective plural. Even worse, if possible, is the misuse of the possessive forms **hers, his, ours, theirs, yours,** as **hern, hisn, ourn, theirn, yourn.** These, needless to say, are vulgarisms. The **you-all** of Southern United States is not a vulgarism but a provincialism or colloquialism. It is used in addressing two or more persons or in addressing one as a representative of many others. **We-all** and **they-all** are far less commonly heard. **Youse** for **you,** and **yousens** or **you-uns** for plural **you** or **your** or **yours,** are sometimes used by people who are under the impression that they stand for **you-all.**

The first person singular personal pronoun **I** is always capitalized. Used co-ordinately with a series of nouns and pronouns, both **I** and **we** should be given last position, as **She, Jane, Mary, and I are promoted** and **The Browns, the Joneses, the Smiths, and we are neighbors,** not **I, she, Jane,** and Mary or We, the Browns, the Joneses, and the Smiths are neighbors. But when I or we takes on disadvantage or fault, it may by "courtesy placement" stand first, as **I and Bill broke the windows.**

The first-person forms **we, our, us** are still conventionally used (with corresponding plural constructions) by rulers and editors and corporate bodies in place of **I, my, me,** in a collective or covering sense, as **We shall order our armies to the frontier** and **We notify our readers of a new journalistic policy** and **We shall distribute to our stockholders an extra dividend.** The first is sometimes called the royal or imperial plural. But all are regarded now as either archaic or affected, or both, except in such instances as are really plural. Any governing body or board may, for instance, like a jury or a committee, correctly speak of itself as **we** when it refers to collective action or opinion. The pronoun **we** is not capitalized in these collective uses. Personal pronouns used in reference to the Deity are capitalized, as **He** used to refer to Jesus Christ, and **Her** used to refer to Mary Mother of Jesus.

These pronouns of the first person, singular and plural respectively, should not be omitted as result of hasty or clipped or "stenographic" expression. In telegrams many words are, of course, omitted, pronouns as well as others, for obvious reasons. But to write **Received your letter** for **I** or **We received your letter** is to be incorrect and discourteous at one and the same time. The omission of a first-person identifying pronoun to accompany a noun meant to be of the first person, may result in serious misunderstanding. No noun may be used in the first person without such pronominal identification. You say **I, Harry, want you to go** and **We, the directors, make the rules** and **You must talk to us, your advisers,** if you want the respective appositives **Harry** and **directors** and **advisers** to be in the first person. It is possible that in the first example **Harry** may be construed as second person by direct address, and that the better placement of **Harry** would be at the beginning or at the end, as **Harry, I want you to go** or **I want you to go, Harry.** If you omit the identifying pronoun in such constructions as these, your expression may make nonsense or it may convey second or third person meaning rather than the desired first.

This pronominal identification is not required in the second person; as a matter of fact, in commands (the imperative) **you** is usually omitted. You may say **Follow me** or **You follow me** or **You, my constituents, follow me** or **Constituents, follow me.** All are correct, the last two being formal and emphatic and the first being the most colloquial of the four. In certain idiomatic expressions the second-person pronoun and its appositive noun are used in such close relationship as to make commas unnecessary, as **You girls do that, please** and **Will you girls do that, please.** This doubling of the person makes again for emphasis and directness. Omit **you** and the nouns may become third person as far as the printed page is concerned. The third-person pronouns rarely have or require the appositive or identifying noun; **he** is superfluous in **John he came** and **Harry he fell,** though this sort of repetition was used for emphasis in folk language and in the old ballads (page 24).

A pronoun, like a noun, used in apposition should be in the same case as the noun or pronoun that it explains. In such expressions as **We men are asking for our rights** and **Grant us men what we ask for,** we in the first must be nominative to agree with **men,** and **us** in the second must be objective to agree with **men,** inasmuch as **we** and **men** are in apposition, as are **us** and **men.** In customary usage, nouns are placed in apposition with pronouns, as in these examples. But the pronoun may be appositive to a noun, as **That man, he with the red whiskers, has offended her,** in which the pronoun **he** is in apposition with **man.** Observe, though, that, since reflexive pronouns do not occur in all cases, an objective reflexive may sometimes stand in apposition with a nominative noun; thus, in **This is the man himself, man** is predicative nominative and **himself** has to be in the objective case inasmuch as there is no nominative form (**heself**).

The second person **you,** be it noted, is the same in both numbers and always requires a plural verb, as **You are** and **You go,** never **You is** and **You goes.** It was formerly plural only, and the plural quality is still retained in the verb. In English the second person singular was formerly used when close friends spoke together, when one wished deliberately to be rude, when one spoke to another of a lower class. German, French, Italian, Spanish still use the second person singular in these ways. In formal speech the German uses the third person plural, as **Haben Sie den Hund,** that is, **Have you the dog** (though **Sie** is literally **they**). The Frenchman uses the second person plural (as we do really), as **Avez-vous le chien,** that is, **Have you** (plural) the dog. The Italian uses the feminine third person singular, as **Ha Ella il cane,** that is, **Have you the dog** (though **Ella** stands for some feminine noun of rank, such as **Vossignoria** or **Vostra Eccellenza**—**Your Grace** or **Your Excellency**). **Lei** (singular) is more common in polite address than **Ella. Loro** is used for polite address in plural. The Spaniard says **Tiene usted el perro** in addressing one person; **Tienen ustedes el perro** in addressing two or more persons. **Usted** is a contraction of **vuestra merced** meaning **Your Grace; ustedes** is **Your Graces.** All of these may be called polite modes of address. Note that German uses **Sie** with a third person plural verb in addressing one or more persons, and that Italian and Spanish have singular and plural forms and use always a third-person verb which is singular or plural to correspond. The latter differ, therefore, from German and French, and all are vastly more complicated than the English **you** forms.

The forms **thou, thy, thine, thee, ye** are now archaic except in religious expression. The last—**ye**—is, strictly speaking, nominative only, and is consistently so used in poetical and religious documents, but it occurs occasionally in literature as objective also. In Isaiah 61:6 it is written **Ye shall be named the Priests of the Lord; men shall call you the Ministers of our God.** But Shakespeare, as well as many writers since, uses **ye** also as objective. Don't confuse this archaic plural with the equally archaic particle **y^e** which once stood for the article **the** and is still sometimes affected, as **Y^e Old Coffee Shoppe.** That was once represented by the corresponding form **y^t.**

Observe in the paradigm on page 58 that gender is definitely fixed by only three forms—third person singular **he, she, it**—and that the first and second persons, both numbers, and the third person plural, are indeterminate in gender. It has been indicated above that there would be no point in having gender forms for **I** and **we** and **you** inasmuch as these are the direct or "face to face" pronouns, and genders require no distinctions in their use.

Like **it** (page 51) the second person **you** is sometimes used generally and indefinitely, as **You can't believe half you hear** and **Be good and you'll be happy.** Of course, such expressions may be focused upon some particular **you,** but all personal pronouns (with the possible exception of **I**) are used in this generic sense. In **They are putting up a building** and **He who runs may read** and **We can never tell what the Fates have in store for us** the subject pronouns defy particularization as these expressions are customarily used.

In this connection, as well as elsewhere, it is important for the sake of unity and coherence, not to violate the principle of pronominal sequence. It makes for quicker grasp and clearer understanding to maintain throughout a sentence the same person in the use of pronouns. Say **You can't believe half you hear** and **We can never tell what the Fates have in store for us**, not **We can't believe half you hear** and **You can never tell what the Fates have in store for us**. It is even worse to intermix nouns and pronouns in this confusion of person, as **If a fellow wants a friend you must be a friend**. Here the indeterminate **he** (page 65) must be used for **you**, or (less preferably) **fellow** may be repeated. Perhaps **one** is the greatest offender in the violation of pronominal sequence (page 59). It may correctly be followed by another **one**, as **One never knows what one may come to;** or by indeterminate **he**, as **One never knows what he may come to.** But pronouns of first and second persons should not be used to refer to it, as **One never knows what you** or **we may come to.**

The pronoun **it** is sometimes called the utility personal pronoun, for the reason that it is used in so many general ways over and above its pronominal offices. In such expressions as **It is the Smiths that you mean** and **It is the cats and dogs about which I am concerned**, **it** is sometimes called the expletive or the introductory or the anticipatory **it**. Though it is neuter singular, it refers in the first instance to the plural **Smiths**, and in the second to the plural indeterminates **dogs** and **cats**.

It is frequently used to anticipate an appositive clause that follows a predicate, as **It is probable that he will succeed**, in which the clause **that he will succeed** is anticipated by **it** and is in apposition with **it**. This neuter singular pronoun is similarly used to refer to and include a whole clause, expressed or understood, in such expressions as **Maybe you're right but I don't believe it** and **When they raze the building at the rear, it will give us better light**. These constructions are colloquial and idiomatic rather than strictly correct and desirable. The antecedence of **it** in the first is either **you're right**, or your implied opinion about something; of the second, it is obviously the open space that will be left after the building has been pulled down. Such indefinite uses of **it** are ruled out altogether by some authorities, especially when **it** is used to refer to a clause or a phrase that is implied or understood. But used to refer to a clause or even to an adjective idea in a clause, as **She is beautiful and she knows it** and **He wants me to go but I won't do it**, this two-letter, third singular neuter pronoun is too convenient and too firmly entrenched in good writing and speaking to be objected to successfully. Another indefinite (and provincial) use of **it** still persists in such expressions as **Let's walk it to town** and **Let's hoof it to the camp** and **Let's hike it over the mountain** and **Come and trip it as you go**, in which **it** may be regarded as an extra or supplementary object.

It is used idiomatically when it refers to a noun of indeterminate gender and when the gender of that noun is unimportant in the expression, as **The child cries for its bottle** and **The bird is shedding its feathers.** Here both **child** and **bird**, denoting living beings, have gender, but it is not known and it really does not matter. The neuter pronoun **its** in this idiomatic use does not imply that they have no gender. This usage carries over very often to nouns which clearly indicate masculine or feminine, and it is accepted; thus, **The horse has its pace** and **The cow has kicked over its milk.** **His** and **her** respectively are to be preferred, of course, but **horse** and **cow** are colloquially used indeterminately.

Personal pronouns are sometimes used to determine the gender of nouns. If you say **The citizen has voted,** the noun **citizen** is indeterminate in gender (page 19). If you say **The citizen has cast her vote,** the gender of **citizen** has been determined temporarily by **her.** The isolated noun **citizen** has undergone no change; it remains a common noun of indeterminate gender. The determining personal pronoun might have been **his,** and it is the pronoun that has gender, not its antecedent. When the antecedent denotes specific gender, then, of course, it influences the following pronoun, as **The man has cast his vote,** and is itself the determining factor.

The personal pronoun **he** (with its inflected forms) is sometimes used as of common or indeterminate gender for the sake of economy and convenience of expression; thus, in **Everybody takes his share, his** refers to **everybody** which is indeterminate, and **his** may itself be regarded as indeterminate, therefore, though as a rule it is masculine. If this provision were not made, the sentence would have to read **Everybody takes his and her share.** In **Boys and girls must do their work,** the pronoun **their** is plural in number and common in gender, and thus meets the requirements of reference. But in **The boy and the girl must do his work,** indeterminate **his** must again be used. Note further, **If any husband or wife wishes a reservation made, he must say so now** in which **he** is regarded as an indeterminate masculine. If you care to take the trouble you may say **If any husband or wife wishes a reservation made, he or she must say so now.** It will be easier always to make the subjects plural—**If any husbands or wives wish reservations made, they must say so now.** But **they** must not be used in the first instance, though this is an error that is commonly made—**If any husband or wife wishes a reservation made, they must say so now.**

A pronoun used in reference to two or more singular antecedents of different persons, takes the first person in preference to the second and third, and the second person in preference to the third; thus, **Harry, you, and I have been assigned our room** and **You and he have had your examination.** This rule holds for connections made by correlative conjunctions as well as for those made by single ones, as above. But the pronoun may be required to separate or distinguish antecedents; thus, **He and I are going in my car** (or **his car**) and **You and she will go in your car** (or **her car**).

A collective noun is referred to by a singular pronoun or a plural pronoun, in accordance with its use. In **The committee has made its choice,** the collective noun **committee** is singular, takes a singular verb, and is referred to by **its;** in **The committee are in disagreement in regard to their choice, committee** is plural, takes a plural verb, and is referred to by **their** (pages 38 and 158).

It must be noted that pronominal reference depends upon the manner in which a subject is considered. In **The uncle and guardian has done his best for his wards,** for instance, **uncle and guardian** represent the same person, and the third person singular **his** is correct. In **Uncle and guardian are doing their best,** two persons are represented, and **their** is correct. The pronoun is singular when two or more singular antecedents

connected by **and** are modified by **each, every,** or **no,** as
Every player and every spectator wears his token and **No
aim and no hope was without its idealism.** This rule applies
also when singular antecedents are markedly set off one from
another, as **Hard work, and misfortune also, has had its
damaging effects** and **John as well as Bill has received his
award** (page 207).

Singular antecedents connected by **either—or** and **neither
—nor** are referred to by singular pronouns, as **Neither the boy
nor his brother will express himself** and **Either Clara or Ida
will carry her coat.** But as pointed out above, if two or more
subjects so connected are of different genders, two or more
separate pronouns must be used. The safest course in such
reference is to change construction completely; thus, **Either
Helen or Bob will bring her or his sled** or (better) **Either
Helen will bring her sled or Bob will bring his** or (still better
and usually sufficient) **Either Helen or Bob will bring a sled.**

If two or more antecedents connected by **either—or** and
neither—nor are of different numbers, the plural antecedent
should be placed last in the series and the pronoun should
agree with it, as **Neither the horse nor the cows have been
turned out to their pasture** rather than **Neither the cows nor
the horse have been turned out to their pasture.** But when
such antecedents are connected by **and** the order makes no
difference and the pronoun is always plural, as **The horse and
the cows** or **The cows and the horse have been turned out to
their pasture.**

Those forms in the second vertical column in the paradigm
on page 58, are sometimes classified separately as possessive
pronouns, and those that require a following noun for modification—**my, your, his** (not always), **her, its** (not always),
our, their—are sometimes called possessive adjectives (page
86). The possessive forms **mine, yours, thine, hers, ours,
theirs,** and sometimes **his and its,** are called the **independent
possessives** because they may stand alone (hers, ours, theirs,
yours always do) without a following noun to modify. But
they may themselves be modified appositively, as **Mine, the
set in the corner, is not for sale** and **That box, his of the ex-
porting firm, is hand carved,** though these constructions are
not usual (page 62). These independent forms, like the possessives of nouns, may stand alone in place of subject or ob-

ject or other construction with the modified word clearly
understood or implied, as **Yours has been signed but mine has
not** and (possessive nouns) **Mary's has been signed but Kate's
have not,** the number being decided by the antecedent outside
the sentence—perhaps **your (book)** and **my (book)** in the first,
and **Mary's (book)** and **Kate's (books)** in the second.

A possessive form, it should be observed, never takes its
gender from the word it modifies, that is, from the name of
the thing possessed, but, rather, from its antecedent. It is
pointed out above that if an antecedent is indeterminate, a
pronoun may assign temporary gender; thus, **The pupil loves
her book** and **The ship has cleared her port,** in the first of
which **her** makes indeterminate **pupil** feminine and modifies
neuter **book,** and in the second **her** makes neuter **ship** feminine. **His** was formerly the possessive of both **he** and **it,** and
he, his, him were all three applied to neuter things, as **If the
salt have lost his savor. Its** did not come into general use until
the seventeenth century and is thus comparatively young; it
appears once in the Bible (Leviticus 25:5) and but rarely in
Shakespeare.

The double possessive (page 48) is as common in the use
of pronouns as in that of nouns. But as with nouns, it is
idiomatic rather than entirely logical. You may say **this boy
of mine** and **that heart of his** rather than **my boy** and **his
heart,** the former being somewhat more emphatic and dramatic than the latter. Only those possessives that do not require a noun to follow them are so used.

The possessive is required, as a rule, before a participle
used as a noun, because in expressions containing such a
participle preceded by a pronoun the emphasis is usually upon
the participial form rather than upon the pronoun. But this
does not always follow. In **They approved of his speaking,** the
meaning is that **speaking** is approved of and **speaking** is properly, therefore, object of the preposition **of,** and the possessive
his modifies it. This is customary usage. But it is possible (not
probable) that when he speaks he himself appears to merit
approval, that is, he may appear especially likable or "ap-
provable" while he is in the act of speaking, regardless of what
he actually says. In such situation the reading should be **They
approve of him speaking,** in which **him** is object of the
preposition **of** and is modified by **speaking,** that is, **They ap-**

prove of a speaking him. If any doubt exists as to such construction, test the meaning as is here done. Do you object to the act or to the person **speaking?** Do you object to his speaking really or to him while he is in the act of speaking? In nine cases out of every ten, it is the former, and the rule may be taken that participial forms in such constructions are preceded by the possessive case (pages 47 and 144).

Like the noun, the pronoun may be used as nominative absolute. But since nouns are the same in nominative and objective cases, and not all pronouns are, the question sometimes arises as to what case the nominative absolute construction of a pronoun should be. The answer is that the pronoun should be in the nominative case (page 39). Do not make it objective and call it objective absolute. In **Other things being equal I prefer this one,** the noun **things** in the absolute construction may, from a merely technical point of view, be either nominative or objective. Grammatical convention makes it nominative and calls it nominative absolute. Similarly, in **She having been elected, we shall now proceed to other business** and **We having returned on time, the party began as scheduled, she** and **we** are in the nominative absolute construction; **her** and **us** respectively would be wrong.

But note carefully that the same distinction between the nominative and the possessive in absolute construction has to be made as is made above between objective and possessive. In **His (the cashier's) having defaulted, the bank closed its doors,** the emphasis is upon the defaulting (as it is upon **speaking** above) and the pronoun is in the possessive case, as a noun would be in similar construction. But it is possible (not probable) that the pronoun may be in the nominative, as the noun would be. In **He showing himself unruly, the teacher conferred with his parents,** the emphasis is upon **he,** presumably the boy who showed himself unruly. The boy himself is important, the unruliness being merely a symptom or manifestation of some quality inherent in the boy.

By adding the noun **self** (plural **selves**) to certain of the forms in the paradigm on page 58, compound personal or reflexive pronouns are formed—**myself, ourselves (ourself** rarely), **yourself, thyself, yourselves, himself, herself, itself, themselves, oneself. One's self** is a regular possessive phrase— **one's** modifying the noun **self** just as in **boy's book, boy's** modifies **book**. **Oneself** is the regular reflexive or emphatic form in which **one** may be regarded as in apposition with **self**, just as **him** is in apposition with **self**, and **them** is in apposition with **selves**, and so on.

Reflexive pronouns are used for emphasis or intensification, as **She caught the man herself**, and for reference to a noun or another pronoun for the sake of fixing or clarifying, as **He trained himself** and **The players outdid themselves**. The two latter examples illustrate the true reflexive or "turning-back" pronominal use. The first shows one means of emphasis; **own** and **very** are frequently used in the same way, as **To thine own self be true** and **I bid my very friends farewell**. **I saw the very man** means **I saw the man himself; This is my own book** means **This book belongs to me myself**. The true reflexive is an idiomatic form devised for convenience, and is learned largely by ear. It is awkward and misleading to say **John hurt him** or **John hurt John** when you mean **John hurt himself**. Use of the reflexive in such expression avoids clumsiness and ambiguity.

But do not use reflexive pronouns in expressions in which the simpler forms are clear and easy. **I am going with yourself** is wrong because the reflexive has neither clarifying nor emphasizing function to perform; **I am going with you** is sufficient and correct. Do not use such vulgar reflexive forms as **meself, mineself, youself, hisself, theirself, theirselves, themself, ourself, my own self, your own self, their own self, his own self, her own self, our own self**. The introduction of **own** between the pronominal form and **self** is a weakening attempt to overemphasize. **Very** is sometimes used similarly for the sake of "emphasizing emphasis," as **my very self** and **your very self**, but this usage, while not substandard, cannot be recommended. The use of the simple personal in a reflexive sense, as **I do repent me**, was common in Elizabethan times. A somewhat similar provincialism still persists in **I have got me a new coat**. Do not use either of these constructions.

It is especially important to observe that there are no apostrophes used in any of the possessive forms on page 58. The apostrophe is used with pronouns only for the purpose of verb-pronoun contractions, and for no other, such as **I'm** for **I am**, **I'll** for **I will** or **I shall**, **I'd** for **I would** or **I had** or **I should**, **you're** for **you are**, **you'll** for **you will**, **you'd** for **you** would (preferably not for you had or you should), I've for I have, you've for you have, that's for that is (preferably not for that has), who's for who is (preferably not for who has), what's for what is (preferably not for what has), they're for they are, they'll for they will (not shall), they'd for they would (see you'd), they've for they have, he'd for he would (see you'd), she'd for she would (see you'd), it'd for it would, we're for we are, we'll for we will or shall, we'd for we would (see you'd), we've for we have, he's for he is (preferably not for he has), she's for she is (preferably not for she has), it's for it is (preferably not for it has), he'll for he will, she'll for she will, it'll for it will, 'tis for it is, 'twas for it was, 'twill for it will, 'twon't for it will not (preferably not used), 'twould for it would.

It has been pointed out on page 24 that the figures of speech known as apostrophe and personification arbitrarily assign gender to inanimate things through the agency of pronouns. In ordinary literal usage the moon and the earth, a ship and a train, are spoken of as neuter and referred to by it. In figurative language—apostrophe and personification in particular—they are spoken of as feminine and referred to by she (her, hers). There are many biblical instances, however, in which both figures are expressed by means of neuter it.

RELATIVE

A relative pronoun is one that refers to a noun or a pronoun and at the same time serves as a conjunctive or connecting agreement in a sentence. The relatives are who, which, what, that, and occasionally as and but. These sentences illustrate: He at last found an instructor who helped him, She asked his help which he gladly gave, There is the cabin that I want to buy, They gave us such blankets as they had, There is no one but thinks her talented. The last two uses—as and but—are disputed by some authorities. As used as a relative is correlated with such and same; but used as a relative occurs only in such negative expressions as the above; so used it means who does not, that is, There is no one who does not think her talented.

Note how the use of the relative serves the double purpose of connective and relating agent, and at the same time makes expression easier and more graceful. You may say We met a man. The man directed us, and thus make use of two independent or almost independent sentences (they may be separated by a semicolon). But there is clearly a connection between the two, and the relative pronoun exists for the purpose of establishing that connection. It may be established by **and,** but **and** indicates a connection only, whereas here there is something more than mere connection to be established, namely, the relationship between **man** and **man.** The relative pronoun exists also for the purpose of establishing that relationship. Thus, you say **We met a man who directed us,** and are saved the trouble of punctuation and the awkwardness of the repeated **man.**

Of these relative pronouns, **who** is the only one with complete case declension—nominative **who,** possessive **whose,** objective **whom. Whose** is frequently used also as the possessive of **which,** as **the building whose management is incompetent.** This is not, however, a recommended usage (see below). The possessive forms **of whom, of which, of what, of that** are commonly used, but usually with the possessive of separated from and following its object, as **We asked a man whom we were doubtful of** for **We asked a man of whom we were doubtful.** This transposition of the preposition always occurs when it is used with **that,** as **This is the car that I spoke of** and **Here is the man that I told you of.** If you transpose **of** to its true grammatical position before **that,** an awkward and unidiomatic expression results. Moreover, in informal usage **that** is frequently understood in such expressions as, **This is the car I spoke of** (see next page).

That is used in reference to beings and things; **who** in reference to persons only; **which** in reference to lower animals and to things. **As** and **but,** when used, may refer to persons, animals, or things. **What** refers to things without life and without possibility of personification; it is sometimes called the neuter relative. **Which** was formerly used of persons, and **Our Father which art in heaven** is a remnant of such use. It used to be considered preferable not to use the possessive **whose** with animals and inanimate things. Because the alternative form **of which** is so cumbersome, however, **whose** is now accepted as correct in this instance, even in formal usage. You may therefore say **The cat whose fur is thick** or **The house whose roof leaks.**

Relatives, like personals, take nominatives and objectives as antecedents, not possessives. It is incorrect to say **The girl's** speech, who gave the valedictory, was inspiring, for who may not have girl's as antecedent. You should say, rather, **The girl who gave the valedictory made an inspiring speech** or **An inspiring speech was made by the girl who gave the valedictory.** In the former, **who** refers to the nominative **girl;** in the latter, to the objective **girl.**

The natural placement of antecedent is before the pronoun that refers to it. But this general rule is more frequently violated by relatives than by other pronouns; thus, in **Whom I love, her I work for** and **No matter what I do, it will be wrong, her** is the antecedent of **whom** (I work for her whom I love) and **it** is the antecedent of **what** (It will be wrong no matter what I do).

The relative pronoun is sometimes omitted when it anticipates a final preposition, as **This is the man (whom) I gave it to.** This sort of omission is not recommended, but it is common in colloquial expression. The omission of the relative—especially the relative **that**—when it is object of the verb in a dependent clause is even more common, as **The boy I want was sitting there** for **The boy that I want was sitting there,** in which **that** understood or expressed is object of **want.** But note that this liberty of omission cannot be taken when the relative pronoun is in the nominative or the possessive case, as in **The girl who met me was about sixteen** and **The woman whose work is of national importance has been seriously ill.** And do not omit the relative or the relative phrase when it is necessary for connection in a sentence, as **They are still in the same predicament you found them.** This is too loose and disconnected, as result of the omission of **in which,** to be called anything but illiterate. The sentence should read **They are still in the same predicament in which you found them.**

The relative **that** very often has a limiting or restrictive force in a sentence. If you say **This is the man that I want,** you point out or limit the first part of your statement by the second part or **that** clause, the latter specifying some particular man. But if you say **I met Jane yesterday who told me about the party,** the **who**-clause simply adds or continues and in no way places limit or restriction upon the preceding clause. For **who** you may as well say **and she,** for the relative indicates merely a co-ordinate connection between the two

clauses. **Which** is sometimes used, like **it** and **that**, in this continuing or co-ordinating way when it refers to a whole preceding clause, as **They won the medal at last, which delighted
the school.** Here **which** has for an antecedent, not any single
preceding noun, but rather the entire preceding clause; **and
this victory** could be substituted for **which.**

But a relative pronoun may refer to any group of words—
a phrase or a clause—used in the capacity of a noun; thus, in
**They requested me to manage the subscription, which prom-
ised to be no easy job** and **She insisted that she had failed,
which I doubted, which** refers to a noun phrase in the first
and to a noun clause in the second.

Confusion of antecedence sometimes occurs in expressions
in which a personal pronoun follows a relative. If the personal
pronoun refers to the same antecedent as the relative, it has
the same person and number and gender as that antecedent, as
A man lives there who is known for his generosity. Here
man is the antecedent of both **who** and **his,** and both are,
therefore, third person, singular number, masculine gender.
But note that in **I know the man, and also the woman who
works in his office,** the relative **who** refers to **woman** and the
personal pronoun **his** refers to **man.**

A relative pronoun should not be used to represent an idea
indicated by an adjective, as **Be patient without which no one
can succeed.** Here the adjective **patient** is really the antecedent
of the relative **which,** and the expression is incorrect. Say,
rather, **Be patient, for without patience no one can succeed** or
Have patience, for without it no one can succeed. A proper
name used in a generic way to denote quality or characteristic
is referred to by **which** rather than by **who,** as **Napoleon,
which is but another name for madness.**

The relatives **who** and **that** may be used in first, second, or
third person, as **I, Robert, who assist you** and **You who know
me well** and **I that exhort you** and **you that I exhort** and **he
that (or who).**

The relatives **which** and **what** are used only in the third
person. It is worthy of note that **what** as a relative pronoun is
really equivalent to two relatives, namely, **that which** (or,
rarely, **those which**); that is, contains its own antecedent.

When this is not the case it must not be used. In **Accept what I assign you, what** means **that which**—**Accept that which I assign you** or **that thing which** (see below). But no such equivalence exists in the illiterate **The boy what was hurt has been taken to the hospital;** substitution of **that which** for **what** does not help an already ungrammatical expression.

Note again that **what**, as a relative, was formerly synonymous with **which**. It is always neuter, and rarely plural. Its antecedent as a relative is **the thing which** or **that which**, never expressed but always implied, as **This is what you asked for,** that is, the thing you asked for. But in **This car and that robe are what we want, what** is used in the plural referring to **car** and **robe,** or **the things.** And observe that in **He asked me what I did, what** is an interrogative pronoun, not a relative (page 57). **What** is sometimes used as both adjective and relative or interrogative in the same construction, as **What work he did is lost.** In this sentence **What work** means any or all work. The compounds **whatever** and **whatsoever** may be similarly used, as **whatsoever a man doeth,** that is, anything that a man doeth. This peculiar construction, or one very similar to it, occurs in connection with **who** in such expressions as **as who shall say** and **as who would dare** and **as who should tell,** in which **who** really means **any one.**

The use of a co-ordinate conjunction before a relative pronoun presupposes the use of a preceding relative of similar construction. Just as **and the boy** implies a preceding noun co-ordinate with **boy,** as **the girl and the boy,** so **and who** or **and whom** or **and which** or **but that** or **but what** implies and must have a preceding relative of co-ordinate construction. You say **The boy who received the medal and who is an all-round athlete will make his mark in the world;** you do not say **The medal-winning boy and who is an all-round athlete will make his mark in the world.** The omission of **and** in the latter would make it correct. You say **The box that was so beautifully carved but that was so badly broken is the one I wanted** or **The beautifully carved box that was so badly broken is the one I wanted;** you do not say **The beautifully carved box and that** (or **which**) **was so badly broken is the one I wanted** (page 205).

The same relative pronoun should be used in each of several successive relative clauses having similar reference or dependence, as **He is the person who came, who saw, who conquered, and who was glorified in his victory.**

Relative pronouns should be placed as closely as possible to their antecedents in order that ambiguity or confusion of reference may be avoided. In **She that is without charm has nothing,** that refers to **she** and the clause that it introduces pertains to she. In **She has nothing that is without charm, that** seems to refer to **nothing** inasmuch as it stands close to it. But this makes an absurd or, at least, an unusual reading.

In all instances in which you are in doubt as to whether **who** or **which** should be used, you may as a rule safely fall back upon **that.** Collective or group nouns sometimes cause doubt in regard to pronominal reference. **The team that I liked** is better than **the team whom** (or which) **I liked. The corps of workers that I paid** is better than **the corps of workers whom** (or which) **I paid; the committee that made the decision** is better than **the committee who** (or which) **made the decision.**

The relative **that** is also used, in spite of the foregoing rules, to obviate repetition, as **who that has seen it** rather than **who who has seen it.** It is used, again, to cover joint reference of men and objects, as **He told of great men and great sights that he had seen.** It is used after an antecedent that follows introductory or expletive **it,** as **It is he that did it** and **It is I that wish it** (this is usually restrictive that). This restrictive use of **that** is also required after any generalized or unlimited subject, as **passions that destroy** and **words that inspire.** It is preferable to **who** or **which** in such expressions as **He is the greatest that I have ever seen** and **She is the last that we can accommodate,** in which a superlative is followed and modified by a relative clause. **That** is preferable to **as** after **same** used as an adjective, as in **This is the same man that I met yesterday.** Note that in this expression the relative clause is descriptive or explanatory, and, therefore, adjective, but in **I did the same as he** the clause **as he (did)** is strictly adverbial; that is, we acted alike.

When the relatives are used indefinitely or in a generic way, they have no antecedents expressed. The implied or understood antecedent in such construction is **any one** or **anything,** as **Tell him what you please** and **Call whomever you wish** and

Take which you please and **I don't care who says so. What,** used in the idiomatic **I tell you what,** means **something or one thing** but nevertheless remains an indefinite relative.

Who, which, what may take the suffixes **ever** and **soever**—whoever, whosoever, whichever, whichsoever, whatever, whatsoever. These forms, subject to the instruction given above for the simpler ones, are used distributively to make the pronoun apply without restriction to any or all beings or things. Note the declension of **whoever** and **whosoever**—whoever, whosever, whomever; whosoever, whosesoever, whomsoever. The combinations are sometimes called the intensive relatives. Such forms as **whoso** and **whatso** are now archaic.

Perhaps more errors are made in the use of **who** for **whom** (or **whom** for **who**) than in the use of any other word in the language. An expression that ends with a preposition has somewhere in it, expressed or understood, an objective case to "fit" after the preposition, unless of course the final preposition belongs to a verb phrase (page 191). **He is the man whom I am going with** requires the objective **whom** for it is object of the preposition **with.** In similar constructions, if there is doubt in your mind as to whether you should use **who** or **whom,** you will probably be helped by turning your sentence around so that words will fall into their conventional grammatical relationships, no matter how awkward this may be; thus, **He is the man I am going with whom** has grammatical sequence if not idiomatic sequence. Note that **You did give it to whom** is the grammatical order of **Whom did you give it to. Who did you give it to** is, therefore, wrong. In **Whom do you take me to be** the objective form **whom** is used because the verb **to be** takes the same case after it as before it. The transposed reading is **You do take me to be whom; me** is objective case, subject of the infinitive. (For **than whom** see page 211.)

Note that in **Who did you suppose was coming, Whom** would be wrong, for by restoring strictly grammatical order you get **You did suppose who was coming** in which **who** is seen to be subject of **was coming.** But you may express the same idea by saying **Whom did you suppose to be coming,** that is, **You did suppose whom to be coming.** This same sort of "case predicament" may confront you in the use of the personal pronouns, as, for instance, **I took it to be him—him** because **to be** takes the same case after it as before it, and **it** is objective, subject of the infinitive **to be.** But you say **I think (that) it is he,** for here **he** is predicate pronoun or attribute complement (page 105). Note again **Who do you think she is** in which **who** is the attribute complement, as **You do think she is who.**

Here there is a somewhat more complicated problem since a pronoun has to be understood to clarify it: **I shall reward (him) whoever finishes first.** The error of using **whomever** in this kind of sentence is commonly made. But **whoever** is the subject of **finishes** and as such should be in the nominative case. An analogous problem exists where a parenthetical expression is present, as **He is the man who I believe will win the election.** So common is the use of **whom** in spoken sentences of this type that some consider **who** as close to a hypercorrection. In written English, however, **who** must still be regarded as correct.

Chapter Three

ADJECTIVE

DEFINITION AND CLASSIFICATION

An adjective is a word or a term used to describe or limit the meaning of a noun or a pronoun; it is an adjunct of nouns and pronouns. If it describes, it is called a **descriptive adjective,** as *gorgeous* view and *white* house. If it limits or bounds or confines, it is called a **limiting adjective,** as *four* apples and *double* line. The former is sometimes called a qualitative adjective; the latter a definitive or quantitative adjective. Adjectives always, as in these examples, change or modify or qualify or define the meanings of words to which they pertain; and both kinds may be used before the same noun to bring its meaning to a focus or make it more specific, as **six white houses.**

The use of a single adjective to do the work of a phrase very often makes for economy, as **a courageous man** for **a man of courage.** But this must not be taken to mean that the shorter form is always desirable. Sometimes the phrase yields detail or emphasis or rhythm that the adjective alone cannot convey, as **a thing of beauty** rather than **a beautiful thing;** for **beauty** is the idea to be accented, and the noun **thing** is weak and colorless and general. **Bars of steel** is stronger than **steel bars,** and **land of enchantment** is more rhythmic and emphatic than mere **enchanting land.**

Inasmuch as English is one of the most facile or "elastic" of languages, adjectives may be devised or "built" in various ways. The words **hard** and **new** and **white** may, for instance, be called **pure adjectives,** but they may easily be merged with other parts of speech to form such **derived adjectives** as **hard-hearted** and **hard-won, new-found** and **new-mown, white-headed** and **white-hot.** And such derivatives may be made in almost any way, and with parts of speech that are not adjectives except in such derived combinations as **lily-white, awe-inspiring, well-tried, down-and-out, free-for-all, ill-omened, pay-as-you-go.** No other language, with the possible exception

79

of German, is so fluid and convenient in this respect. Most
such combinations are metaphorical. They were originally put
together because of their appropriateness and their pictorial
values. And they stick for the same reasons, undergoing a try-
out period very often as hyphened terms, and later becoming
solid ones.

Many adjectives are formed from other parts of speech by
means of different suffixes, as believable, choral, irritant,
fortunate, comical, wretched, silken, provident, eastern, hope-
ful, sensible, fragile, divine, civilizing, glorious, brackish,
favorite, restive, faithless, godly, verbose, vigorous, quarrel-
some, virtuous, thirsty. There are few suffixes in the language
that may not be used in the formation of adjectives, those
here presented being the merest illustrations. Adjectives are
sometimes given prefixes in order to change their meanings, as
graceful and disgraceful, happy and unhappy, active and in-
active, operative and co-operative, religious and irreligious,
limitable and illimitable, moral and immoral, irritant and non-
irritant, fine and superfine. It will be observed that such prefixing is used to negative or neutralize or intensify the meaning of the basic adjective. The adjective that is already
suffixed is the one that frequently takes a prefix. The so-called
participial adjective—a participle used adjectively, as known
results and relenting fate—is the adjective that is most easily
influenced by either prefixing or suffixing, or both, as un-
known results, unrelenting fate, distinguished presence, un-
distinguished record. The final participial inflections of the
verb always carry over to the adjective form, never the imperfect-tense final inflection. But in regular verbs the two are,
of course, the same (page 114).

A proper adjective is a descriptive adjective that is derived
from a proper noun, as *American* scene and *British* campaign. It is capitalized, as the proper noun is, except in special
and technical practice such as library forms and advertising
copy. The proper geographical adjective may be used as a
noun, of agent as a rule, as American and British, and it is
usually formed simply by the addition of a letter (n very
often) or two at the end of a geographical name. But note
that, while the change from America to American or from
Britain to British is a comparatively simple one, that from
Halifax to Haligonian or from Norway to Norwegian is by
no means so simple. The dictionary may be depended upon

to give correct proper adjective forms in alphabetical order with other forms, even though proper place and personal names may be listed in an appendix.

Adjectives may, in general, be used substantively. An **abstract adjective**, like an abstract noun (page 18), represents quality, as **the good, the true, the beautiful, the right, the wrong.**

A **concrete adjective** is one used substantively with a concrete noun clearly understood after it, as **The good (people) die young** and **The poor (people) you have always with you.**

On the other hand, any word in the language may be used adjectively, though such use may sometimes be highly special or irregular. You may say **The top of the desk is scratched** or **The desk top is scratched** and **The phrase introduced by** *of* **is correct** or **The** *of* **phrase is correct.** In the first you have used a noun **(desk)** as an adjective, in the second a preposition **(of).** But the commoner transferences, as a **boys school** instead of **a school for boys** and **a shoe lace** instead of **a lace for a shoe,** are everyday colloquialisms and are additional proof of the facility of English usage.

This may, however, be a troublesome and bewildering facility for those who are not fully acquainted with the way (and waywardness) of the English tongue. Since a **work-horse** is a horse that works, they may quite logically but, of course, wrongly assume that a **workhouse** is a house that works; since a **gas oven** is an oven heated by gas, they may think a **gas mask** is a mask heated by gas. It is only after one becomes acquainted with the habits of English, especially with such combinations as these, that he may hope to use the terms **sitting room, dining car, ironing board, clotheshorse, clothespin, clothespress, hardpan, hard sauce, hard-shell, hardship,** and a host of similar compounds, with understanding and accuracy.

In French, the **adjective adjunct** usually follows its noun, as **le cheval noir,** the horse black. In English, it usually precedes its noun, as **the black horse** and **the new moon.** In this natural English order the adjective is said to be used attributively. When the attributive adjective is "happily paired" with its noun, so as to be felt as an inseparable part of it, it

is called **epithet adjective**, as **black mood** and **sour grapes**.
When the epithet is a title, however, it usually follows its
noun, as **Ivan the Terrible** and **Peter the Great** and **Paul the
Fourth**, this reversed order yielding emphasis and distinction.
The is used before such adjective when the epithet is written
out; when expressed by Roman numerals, **the** is omitted, as
Paul IV and **Elizabeth II**. It should be observed, too, that the
title epithet, while appositive in nature (see below) is, as a
rule, not set apart by commas because the relationship between noun and adjective is too close to be so broken. When
titles are stated in general terms rather than specific, they are
not preceded by **a, an,** or **the,** for they are then abstract; thus
you say **They call him governor,** not **a governor,** and **The
position of mayor is most trying,** not **position of a** or **the
mayor.**

The epithet adjective may come to have special or unusual
meanings. If you say **He made a sorry spectacle of himself,**
sorry means pitiful; if you say **I am sorry, sorry** means regret-
ful. In **glad tidings, glad** pertains to exciting or causing glad-
ness; in **glad hearts, glad** means cheerful or happy. Note,
again, the difference between **lofty ambition** and **lofty mountain,** between **feverish pulse** and **feverish times,** between **happy
days** and **happy speeches.** While the natural placement of the
adjective is before its noun, it may, for the sake of emphasis,
be wrenched completely away from it, as **Great was the
acclaim he received.** This is a much more striking or arresting expression than **He received great acclaim.**

Aside from its uses as title, the adjective is frequently used
in appositive position and with appositive significance; thus,
in **Alice, sweet and twenty, was sitting on the porch, sweet
and twenty** is an appositive adjective phrase. It may, of course,
precede **Alice** but much would be lost by way of grace and
force of expression.

While in normal usage the adjective precedes the noun that
it modifies, as **a cruel blow** and **the fearless and indomitable
leader,** it may in many instances follow, especially when it
closely qualifies or characterizes or, so placed, adds to grace
and emphasis of expression. When it follows its noun it is
sometimes called **poetical adjective,** because the poets so often
follow this style, as **Douglas tender and true, sorrow un-
fathomable, wisdom infinite, depth immeasurable, joy un-**

speakable. But in certain everyday expressions, also, the adjective follows its noun, as in the legal damage **irreparable**, libel **unbelievable**, notary **public**, court **martial**, malice **aforethought**, malice **prepense**, heir **apparent**, sign **manual**, and in the commercial bills **payable**, bills **receivable**, month **past**. The old terms knight **errant** and retort **courteous** show the French influence in noun-before-adjective arrangement.

The **modified adjective** requires special classification because it is, as a rule, transposed for grammatical and expressional reasons rather than for such as are given above. It is usually very awkward to place an adjective before its noun when the adjective is modified by a phrase of any kind; thus, **A man anxious about his child entered the hospital** is correct form, whereas **An anxious about his child man entered the hospital** is the ultimate in awkwardness if, indeed, not downright incorrect. The use of hyphens before such delayed nouns by no means always helps; **a-never-to-be-repeated experience is** bungling compared with **an experience never to be repeated.** In most cases when the adjective is modified by a single adverb, placing it before the noun is customary, as **very satisfactory results** and **greatly exaggerated reports.** Occasionally, when the modifier-group is long and cumbersome, transposing it after the noun makes for smoother reading and easier understanding; thus, **The gadget, extraordinarily fantastic and uniquely displayed, caused a sensation** is better than **The extraordinarily fantastic and uniquely displayed gadget caused a sensation.**

Adjectives modify nouns more often than they modify pronouns. Such expressions as **all ye** and **whether of the twain**, in which the adjective and the pronoun stand in apposition, are now archaic. And such as **that indescribable she** and **what an incorrigible he** are unusual and irregular, to say the least, though they may be used for humorous effect. **She is indescribable** and **He is incorrigible** or **Mary is indescribable** and **Bill is incorrigible** represent natural order. In such constructions the adjective is said to be used predicatively, and it is called **predicate adjective** (page 105).

The predicate adjective occurs after copulative verbs (page 105)—**appear, be, become, feel, look, seem, smell, sound, taste,** and the like. Be sure not to confuse the predicate adjective with the adverb. **She looks bad** is correct if the meaning is (and it probably is) that she appears to be ill or troubled, for **bad** is a predicate adjective belonging strictly to she. But if it means that having lost something she is careless or unthorough in looking for it, then **She looks badly** is correct, for **badly** is an adverb of manner modifying **looks**. Note the difference, then, between **They arrived safe** (They were safe on arrival) and **They arrived safely** (They had no difficulties in arriving); similarly, **The music sounds sweet** and **She sang sweetly**, **Alice feels sad** and **She called sadly**, **The milk smells sour** and **She turned sourly upon him**. The predicate adjective may pertain to a phrase or a clause, as **To hurt his feelings was unworthy of you** and **That he should come so early is ridiculous** (pages 228 and 233).

But regardless of what is said above, certain adjectives are customarily used predicatively rather than attributively, or at least they follow rather than precede nouns, such, for instance, as **afraid, akin, alert, alike, alive, alone, ashamed, askew, asleep, athirst, averse, awake, aware, awry, else, enough, extent, extinct, fraught, plenty** (page 169), **pursuant;** and participial adjectives are frequently predicative, though not necessarily so. The phrase **lady alone** is better than **alone lady, man alive** than **alive man, ribbon askew** than **askew ribbon, The man is afraid** than **He is an afraid man, The child is ashamed** than **He is an ashamed child,** and so on. **Plenty** is preferably a noun, but it may be an adjective used predicatively in the sense of plentiful or abundant. Used in direct modification of noun or adjective or adverb it is an impropriety, as **He is plenty champion, She is plenty beautiful, I am plenty sincerely yours** (page 169).

It will be noted that many of the adjectives here listed may likewise be adverbs; it is because of this double capacity or divided allegiance that idiom expediently places them after their nouns as a rule. It is similarly fortunate and expedient that such indefinite pronominals as **any one, anything, every one, everything, nobody, no one, nothing, some one, somebody, something** are always followed, often predicatively, rather than preceded, by their adjectives, as **Something wonderful has happened** rather than **A wonderful something has happened.**

The adjective is used as objective complement, that is, to complete the predicate and explain or describe the object (pages 41-42), as **Joe painted the fence white.** This is by no means the same as saying **Joe painted the white fence. White** finishes the idea of painting and pertains to the thing painted, namely, **fence.** It even more emphatically does both if **fence** is given an attributive adjective, as **Joe painted the brown fence white.** Do not mistake adverbial modification in this construction. In **She furnished the house beautifully, beautifully** is an adverb of manner modifying **furnished.** To use the adjective **beautiful** in this relationship would be incorrect. But in **She made the house beautiful, beautiful** is objective complement completing **made** and describing **house.**

A limiting adjective that indicates number is called a **numeral adjective.** A **cardinal adjective** is a numeral that answers the question how many, and indicates number as absolute, as **one, three, five, fifteen, twenty, hundred.** An **ordinal adjective** answers the question how many and indicates number serially or relatively, as **fourth, eleventh, thirtieth, hundredth.** Both cardinals and ordinals (like proper and abstract and concrete adjectives) are used as nouns, as **Seven is a lucky number** and **I'll take the sixth from the end.** Both may be used in the plural, as **We are at sixes and sevens** and **How many thirds have you.** The cardinal is used to indicate the numerator of a fraction; the ordinal, to indicate its denominator, as **four-fifths** and **ten-twelfths.** The names of fractions used as unit adjectives and nouns are usually hyphenated, as **one-fourth of an acre;** used as separate words, the first attributively and the second as noun, they are not hyphenated, as **John has one third and I have two thirds.** If the denominator of a fraction is two, the partitive (see below) **half** is used, as **one-half.** Used as a noun, the ordinal is generally preceded by **a** or **an** or **the,** as **A third will be dropped** and **The fourth is yet to appear.** The cardinal is usually not so preceded but it may be, as **Ten are coming early** and **The ten who are coming early will be prepared.**

In so-called straight copy, cardinals and ordinals should be written out, as in the examples above; in special or technical copy, they should always be indicated by figures. The ordinals are sometimes suffixed with **d** or **rd** or **st** or **th,** as **3d** or **3rd** or **1st** or **5th.** These are hybrid forms and have nothing logical to recommend them. They are always read **third** and **first** and **fifth,** and context may always be relied upon to distinguish cardinals from ordinals. Use these combined figure and letter forms sparingly if at all.

A limiting adjective that indicates addition, division, multiplication, subtraction, and the like, answering the question how many folds or layers, is called a **multiplicative adjective,** as **double, duplicate, fivefold, hundredfold, octuple, quadruple, single, triple.** These indicate, in other words, the number of times a thing spoken of exceeds something else.

A limiting adjective that indicates repetition, answering the question how often or how many times, is called an **iterative adjective,** as **once, twice, thrice, four-score, daily, weekly, monthly, quarterly, yearly, annually.**

A limiting adjective that indicates a part or a fraction, answering the question what part or fraction of, is called a **partitive adjective, as a half, a quarter, a tenth.**

As was pointed out on page 79 an adjective that definitely signifies number, quantity, direction, and the like, is a limiting adjective. All pronouns used as adjectives—pronominal adjectives or adjective pronouns—may be called limiting adjectives without doing too much violence to classification. The personal possessive pronouns **my (thy), his, her, its, our, your, their** (page 58) may be possessive attributive adjectives, and **mine (thine), ours, yours, theirs** may be possessive predicative adjectives. The reflexive pronouns **myself, yourself, herself, himself,** and so on, are sometimes called emphasizing adjectives. **This, these, that, those, yonder, the** are demonstrative adjectives. **Each, every, either, neither** are distributive adjectives. **Whose, which, what, that** are relative adjectives; **whose, which, what** are also interrogative adjectives; and the compounds of both of these groups—**whoever, whosever, whichever, whatever**—are similarly relative or interrogative adjectives according to use. **All, any, both, certain, divers, else, enough, few, former, first, latter, last, little, less, least, much, many, more, most, never, no, none, one, only, other, own, same, several, some, such,** and their compounds (if any), are indefinite adjectives. **A** and **an** belong to this list as adjectives, not as pronouns. All of these bold face words, that is, are pronouns or adjectives according to their use. Officiating or substituting for nouns, they are pronouns; limiting or defining nouns and pronouns, they are adjectives. Rules pertaining to these words functioning as pronouns may in part apply to them functioning as adjectives, but there are many distinctions such as naturally belong to individual parts of speech (page 54). The personal pronoun **them**, for instance, must not be used as an attributive adjective. **Them boys** for **those boys** is a vulgarism. The distributives **each, every, either, neither,** as adjectives, influence for singular number as they do as pronouns. But **either** and **neither,** as adjectives, modify both singular and plural nouns, and **each** and **every** as adjectives modify singular nouns only, though such nouns may be collectives as **army, few, group, mass, people, rout, school** (page 17).

Never, **no, none** are classified as negative adjectives as well as negative adverbs. **No** is the most commonly used as both adjective and adverb, as, respectively, **No man knows** and **I have no small regard for him.** Never and **none** are used little as adjectives, the former being principally an adverb and the latter a pronoun. But in **He is never the man to say no,** never is an adjective modifying **man,** and in **I mean none other than you, none** is an adjective modifying **other.** Used in direct modification of a noun, **none** is now regarded as archaic, as **None assurance doth he give.**

The limiting adjectives **a, an, the** are sometimes separately classified as articles, **a** and **an** being called the **indefinite articles** and **the** the **definite article.** Many authorities classify all three as demonstrative adjectives, **a** and **an** indicating one or any one or some one or a certain one, and **the** specifying a definite person or object. **An** is original Anglo-Saxon meaning one; **a** is an abbreviated form of **an.** (Up to the beginning of the eighteenth century the form **an** was also used as a subordinate conjunction meaning **if.**) Clearness and nicety of meaning very often depend upon the exact use of these three little parts of speech, and the best writers and speakers observe the following rules pertaining to them:

An is used before words beginning with a vowel sound, no matter what the initial spelling of such words; **a** is used before words beginning with a consonant sound, no matter what the initial spelling of such words; thus, you say **an appetite, an error, an entrance,** and **a man, a dog, a field.** If between an indefinite article and its noun there is an adjective, **a** or **an** is used in accordance with the initial sound of the adjective, as **a good appetite** and **a serious error, an errant dog** and **an extensive field.** It is the sound immediately following the indefinite article, that is, which decides whether or not the **n** is to be pronounced. Note, now, that while some words begin with a consonant, they are nevertheless pronounced with an initial vowel sound; **honor,** for instance, and **hour** and **heir** begin with the consonant **h,** but it is silent and the words are pronounced as if they begin with a vowel; hence, **an honor (onor), an hour (our), an heir (air)** are correct. Conversely, some words begin with a vowel but are pronounced with initial consonant sound; **unit,** for instance, and **union** and **university** begin with the vowel **u** but are pronounced as if they began with **y;** hence, **a unit (yunit), a union (yunion), a university (yuniversity).** But in England the last is likely to be preceded by **an.** There was once a strict rule, still observed in England but generally disregarded in the United States, to the effect than **an** should be used before unaccented **h,** as **an hotel** and **an historian** and **an heroic act,** and before any word beginning with unaccented **u** as **an university** and **an universal truth.** But the indefinite **a** is now preferably used before all of these words, **h** being distinctly heard in the first three and **y** in the last two, thus making them comply with the general rule above given.

The articles **a** and **an,** implying one as they do, make non-sense if used after **fashion of, kind of, manner of, sort of, style of, type of,** or any other such classifying phrase. Say **What manner of man is he,** not **What manner of a man is he,** for what manner of one man is absurd. Say **That is a new type of car,** not **new type of a car,** for the latter is similarly absurd (page 198). Be especially careful when such words as these are followed by a pluralizing phrase, as **Those kind of people disturb me.** Here the subject **kind** is wrongly preceded by **Those** and is wrongly given a plural verb, chiefly because of the plural attraction of **people.** Inasmuch as the subject of the thought is **people** (though **kind** is the grammatical subject) this sentence is better as **People of that kind disturb me.** This is better even than **that kind of people** or **those kinds of people,** both of which are awkward though grammatically correct.

The definite article **the** was once a demonstrative pronoun. It is pronounced with neutral **e** before consonant sounds, with long **e** before vowel sounds, as **thǝ boy, thǝ girl, the art, the orb.** In ordinary usage **the** merely signifies or points out what (that who or that which) requires no further identification, as **The desk has come** and **This is the ticket,** in which there is the indication that the thing designated by **the** is known as result of previous description or explanation. It is also used in anticipation—**anticipatory the**—to point out something that is to be described or explained, as **The poem that I am going to read was written only last year** and **To ease the pain he took a narcotic before cutting.** This use of **the** commonly occurs in the topic sentence of a paragraph, enabling the reader to anticipate a little of what is to follow.

Sometimes **the** is used to emphasize or distinguish or make unique, and so used is usually accented in speech and italicized in writing, as **He is *the* man** and **This is *the* Mr. Jones.** The definite article is used, again, to generalize—to make generic—a group or class or species, as **The fish of the sea are mysterious** and **The lilac is the loveliest of early spring blooms** and **The cat is a miniature tiger.** But note that this usage is not permissible unless the class thus indicated is inclusive. You may say **The human being is mortal** but not **The man is mortal.** You must say **Man is mortal** or **Woman is mortal,** unless, of course, you are pointing out some particular man or woman, as **The man I mean is standing there.** The is likewise omitted before **man** and **woman** when these two words are used in reference to the two great divisions of the human race, as **Man is magnificent; woman is magnanimous.** If **the** were used here it would seem to indicate that there are still other divisions.

Note further that in **Iron is useful, iron** is used inclusively and generally and is not preceded by **the,** but that in **The iron of the Rockies is considered best for the manufacture of machinery,** it is not generalized but is specialized, and **the** is accordingly used. This principle applies likewise to **a** and **an.** You do not say **A generosity is a fine quality,** but you do say **A discriminating generosity characterized all his giving** and **The generosity of the man has been impressive.** Similarly, you say **Charm may be cultivated,** not **The charm** or **A charm may be cultivated.** When you say **The dahlia is a dazzling flower** you specify class; when you say **There is a kind of plant called dahlia** you generalize. **A** before **dahlia** in the latter would be wrong; the omission of **the** before **dahlia** in the former would likewise be wrong.

The is used also to render an idea abstract, as **the living and the dead;** to give distributive meaning, as **a dime the**

copy and a dollar the package (equivalent to each); to denote
possession, as He raises the hand (his hand).

[In such terms as **The Bronx** and **The Crimea** and **The
Hague,** the definite article is official but quite unnecessary.
The section of Greater New York north of Manhattan was
settled by a colony of Danes headed by Jonas Bronck. Their
settlement early became known as **The Broncks,** that is, the
place where The Broncks live, just as we may say today **The
Smiths live here** and **The Joneses live there.** Strangely enough,
when the last three letters—**cks**—were simplified to **x,** the
definite article "stuck" to the surname **Bronx.** You may omit
it from your Bronx (your **the Bronx?**) envelope address, and
delivery of your letters will be in no way delayed. **The Crimea,**
like the **West Indies** and the **British Isles** and the **Mediter-
ranean Sea,** and a host of other "articled" titles, has remained
through persistence of usage rather than for any other reason.
The Hague may have a somewhat more logical hold upon its
prefatory **the:** It meant originally the enclosure or park surrounded by a hedge in which the princes of Orange hunted.
The word itself meant **hedge** and it was, indeed, **the hedge**—
the royal hedge—the pointing out its uniqueness or unusual-
ness. But all three of these proper nouns, and others to which
the stubbornly attaches, are listed in directories and geogra-
phies, not under **t,** but under the first letter of the name proper.
And the omission of the article in the general use of such
names makes little or no difference today.]

The demonstrative values of the articles in such expressions
as these must not be overlooked: **A secretary and treasurer
was elected** (one official was elected); **A secretary and a treasurer were elected** (two officials were elected); **I like the red
and blue shawl** (one shawl of mixed colors); **I like the red
and the blue shawl** (two shawls, one red, one blue). The article thus repeated before each of two or more connected adjectives modifying a singular noun individualizes and separates
them; the article used before the first only, merges or com-
bines them. **I like the red and blue shawls** really means that
I like two or more shawls each of mixed red and blue, but it
may be taken to mean either that I like two shawls, one red
and the other blue, or that I like two shawls of mixed red and
blue. So I must say **I like the red and the blue shawl** or **I like
the red shawl and the blue one** or **I like the two** (or more)
shawls of mixed red and blue. Note, too, that if I say **I like**

the red and the blue shawls, I mean more than two shawls—
a group of reds and a group of blues.

When there is no likelihood of ambiguity or misunderstanding, the article may be repeated with the singular noun or it may be used only once with the plural noun, as **The Old and the New Testment** or **The Old and New Testaments**. And for the sake of emphasis, when there is no likelihood of misunderstanding, you may say **a far and a distant future** or **the far and the distant future**, since there is only one future. But **the or a far and distant future** is correct also.

It will have been seen that the article influences the number of its following noun in the foregoing examples. **The right and left hand** means one hand and is, therefore, obviously absurd, but **the right and the left hand** means two hands as result of the repeated article, **hand** being understood after **right**. But **the right and left hands** is correct, as are **the eastern and the western hemisphere** and **the eastern and western hemispheres**, and the two forms are equally good. But do not say **the right and the left hands** or **the eastern and the western hemispheres** for, expanded, these really read **the right hands and the left hands** or **the eastern hemispheres and the western hemispheres**, inasmuch as the understood noun is assumed to be of the same number as the expressed one. It is conceivable, of course, that the latter type of construction may be correct, the substance of the thought deciding. **The right ribs and the left ribs** and **the right and left ribs** and **the right and the left (set of) ribs** are correct. But in such instances it is better always to use the separative term—**set, series, group, order,** and the like.

The rule may be stated again in somewhat different form: The article should be used before each adjective in a connected series when the adjectives pertain to different beings or objects. Conversely, the article is used before only the first of a series of connected adjectives pertaining to the same being or object or the same kind of being or object. The article may be repeated for emphasis in instances that offer no likelihood of misunderstanding, as **John is a serious and a diligent student.** Again, the article is used before only the first of a series of nouns that pertain to the same person or office and are thus really appositive, as **He was made the captain and manager,** which means two different kinds of work but one office and one officer (page 90).

It is again pointed out on page 159 that a singular noun modified by two or more adjectives that denote widely different qualifications of that noun, may be given a plural verb by virtue of the distinctions emphasized by the adjectives: thus, **Greek and Latin literature are basic to culture** and **Classic and modern music were played at the concert.**

In such expressions as **the sooner the better** and **the more the cheaper, the** is not an adjective at all but an adverb of degree meaning **by that** or **by so much.**

It has also been seen that the normal order of modification is article, adjective, noun, as **a good man** and **the fine speech.** But there are certain usages in which the article does not have the same unifying or combining power that it has in these, and which require its placement between adjective and noun or between adjective and adverb; thus, you say **many a boy, too severe a strain, how excellent a view, so sweet a story, too great a sacrifice, all the more, all the greater reason.** Ear is the deciding factor in most such idioms; **a so sweet story** and **a too severe strain** and **a how excellent view** sound awkward and ridiculous, though the order is grammatical. Such expressions as **a too great sacrifice** and **a too severe sentence** are heard and seen, but they are not idiomatic. The phrase **many a boy** requires a singular verb but it is really plural in significance; it means many boys but it singles boys out as individuals. In such expressions as **twice a day, fifty cents an hour** and **a dime a dozen,** the article is equivalent to **each** or **every.** Do not substitute the Latin **per** except in commercial listings and the like; **per** is a bookkeeping term, not, strictly speaking, an English term.

Though **a** and **an** mean one, they may nevertheless modify nouns of plural significance, as **a dozen** and **an army, a great many days** and **a thousand years** (page 35). In the last two the adjective or adjectives and the plural noun following are regarded as a single unit, and are thus modifiable by **a** or **an.** Cardinals should, as a rule, be in agreement with the nouns they modify, but usage is confused and hard pressed in regard to such combinations, and idiom has arranged some strange bedfellows. The dictionaries say, for instance, that **dozen** is a preferred plural before another noun and following a plural, that is, **five dozen** and **five dozen eggs;** that **head** and **hundred** and **sail** (to name a few of the most common of the kind) are preferably the same in both singular and plural, as **fifty head of cattle** and **fifteen hundred** and **thirty sail**. But in regard to the last two, usage will be found about evenly divided among these forms and the regular plural. **Thirty sails** is not wrong, but it is not the choicest idiom; **fifteen hundreds of dollars** is unusual and affected. Note again that in **This hundred dollars is all I need** the entire amount is taken as a unit and, therefore, as singular; even though **hundred** implies plurality and **dollars** is plural, **this** and **is** are correctly singular. **Twelve bushels** and **five tons** and **thirteen loads,** and many other similar numeral plurals, are considered by many authorities as more elegant than **twelve bushel** and **five ton** and **thirteen load.** Call all of this inconsistent, if you please; language, like the human being that it serves, exercises the prerogative of inconsistency sometimes.

Note that **A few were there** and **A great many are going** follow **a great many days** and **a thousand years** as treated above. Yet, while the latter may take singular or plural verbs, the former take plural verbs only. The term **a few** means somewhat more than **few**, and it is invariably plural, as are also **quite a few** and **a great many**. The best authorities say that **quite a few** means more than **a few, few** itself meaning the least number represented by these three terms. **Few** refers to number—to numbered units; **little** refers to quantity. **A little** and **quite a little** follow the same instruction as that given for **a few** and **quite a few** except for the fact that **little** and **a little** and **quite a little** are invariably singular (page 56).

The articles are, in the main, applied to nouns only, but in occasional special uses they may apply to other parts of speech also. **The *shall* in that sentence is plural** and **Insert an *it* there and your sentence will be complete** are correct though unusual.

COMPARISON

Most English adjectives have no gender, number, person, case; that is, there is no declension of adjectives. Adjectives in many other languages do have declension, are inflected for gender, number, person, case; that is, adjective endings have to be adjusted to these inflections in the nouns they modify. Numeral adjectives do, of course, represent number, but it is absorbed by or transferred to the nouns they modify; thus, in **Five hundred is the total amount,** **five** loses its plural identity in the singular collective **hundred,** and in **Five hundreds of** dollars have been spent the term **five hundreds** is a unit plural. Used before a noun, a numeral adjective bears no sign of plural, as **ten thousand soldiers**. But used without a following noun, as a noun itself, it may bear such sign, as **tens of thousands of soldiers**. In addition, many adjectives to which s is added become nouns in usage but nevertheless retain their qualifying nature, as **betters, blues, brilliants, doubles, eatables, empties, grays, greens, incapables, irons, italics, liberals, particulars, reds, rights, seniors, thirds, unmentionables, valuables, vitals**; and the proper adjectives, it has been seen (page 80), undergo the same modification in meaning if not in form when they are used as nouns. Some of the pronominal adjectives, too, have inflections, but their modifications may be regarded as belonging to their pronominal nature rather than to their adjective nature. The so-called pure adjectives—**able, beautiful, good, much, sincere, white,** and the rest—are inflected for the purpose of indicating more or less of a given quality. This change in form in an adjective is known as **comparison.**

There are three degrees of comparison—positive, comparative, superlative. The positive degree denotes simply that the quality exists but is not stated in relation to a similar quality in any other being or thing, as **the high ceiling** and **the good man** and **the valuable chair.** The comparative degree denotes that the quality exists to a greater or a less degree than in another being or object, as **the higher ceiling** and **the better man** and **the more or less valuable chair.** The superlative degree denotes the greatest or the least amount or intensity of the quality existing among all beings and objects compared, as **the highest ceiling** and **the best man** and **the most or least valuable chair.**

From the foregoing illustrations it may be seen that comparison of adjectives is made by three different devices; namely, **er** and **est** are added to the positive to form the comparative and the superlative respectively, the adverbs **more** and **most** are used to modify the positive to form the comparative and the superlative respectively in ascending or increasing comparison, **less and least** to form them in descending or decreasing comparison. Monosyllables and some dissyllables form their comparatives by adding **er** and their superlatives by adding **est**. Most adjectives of more than one syllable are compared by the use of **more** and **most** or **less** and **least** before the positive forms, to form comparatives and superlatives respectively.

The two methods are interchangeable with some words, as **commoner** or **more common (less common) commonest** or **most common (least common).** Sometimes, for the sake of euphony or emphasis, especially in poetical and religious expression, monosyllabic adjectives are compared by means of the modifying adverbs, as **more true** and **less true, most true** and **least true.** But this usage is special rather than general. If two or more adjectives are connected by **and**, expressed or understood, the modifying adverb may be used before the first only and be understood before others, as **the most savage, vicious, and unruly beast,** which means **the most savage, the most vicious, and the most unruly beast.**

It should be observed that while the suffixes **er** and **est** are usable in ascending comparison, there are no corresponding suffixes in the descending scale; thus, **higher** and **highest** must have as comparative antonyms either **less high** and **least high** or **lower** and **lowest;** that is, descending or diminishing comparison is possible only by the use of **less** and **least,** whereas ascending comparison may be made by **er** and **more, est** and **most.** Do not be misled by such forms as **smaller** and **smallest, thinner** and **thinnest.** Here the **er** and the **est** mean respectively **more** and **most** of the qualities mentioned, additions of the qualities of **smallness** and **thinness.** Participial adjectives are invariably compared by the use of the adverbs, though in early times **worrieder** and **worriedest, tireder** and **tiredest, learneder** and **learnedest** were not uncommon. There are many dissyllabic words the comparatives and superlatives of which have to be learned from the dictionaries and the best writers. The rule, as above indicated, is at best variable. Both **tenderer** and **tenderest,** and **more tender** and **most tender** are used, and this variability is true of such adjectives as **bitter, clever, cruel, happy, likely, lovely, silly, tame, true.** The tendency is—and ought to be—to make them comply with rule.

But do not make the mistake of using both the adverbial form and the suffix form of comparison with the same word. Again, it was customary in Elizabethan times to say **more lovelier** and **most unkindest.** This is no longer true, however, and the double comparative and the double superlative are regarded as improprieties.

The formation of suffix comparison follows the final consonant spelling rule. The comparative and superlative of **red**, for instance, require doubling the final consonant before adding a suffix beginning with a vowel; thus, **redder** and **reddest**. The final silent **e** rule is also followed in the formation of suffix comparison—final silent **e** is dropped before a suffix beginning with a vowel; thus, **grave** becomes **graver** and **gravest**, and dissyllables ending with **le** follow suit, as **gentler** and **gentlest**, **littler** and **littlest** (though adverbial comparison is also correct for both of these). There are many adjectives that end with **ly**, and they must not be mistaken for adverbs. Such adjectives, for instance, as **cleanly, costly, cowardly, deadly, friendly, gentlemanly, kindly, likely, lonely, lovely, mannerly,** change final y to i before the suffixes **er** and **est;** thus, **costlier, costliest; deadlier, deadliest; lovelier, loveliest**—and another spelling rule applies. But all of these may be formed also by **more** and **most,** and some of them have to be; you do not, of course, say **mannerlier** and **mannerliest** or **cowardlier** and **cowardliest,** any more than you use (though you may form) an adverb of **lovely**—**lovelily**—or of **friendly**—**friendlily** (page 163).

There are some old comparatives and superlatives that are very irregular as result, principally, of historical changes in words and of composite forms resulting from intermixture of adjective forms. Some are now archaic in one degree or another. The chief of these irregular comparisons are

Positive	*Comparative*	*Superlative*
aft[1]	after	aftermost
bad, evil, ill	worse or worser (page 98)	worst
far[1]	farther	farthest
fore	former	foremost or first
forth[1]	further	furthest or furthermost
good	better	best
hind	hinder	hindmost
	hither[2]	hithermost
in[1]	inner	inmost or innermost
late[1]	later or latter	latest or last
little	less or lesser	least

Positive	Comparative	Superlative
low	lower	lowest **or** lowermost
many⎫ much⎭	more	most
near[1]	nearer	nearest **or** next
	nether[2]	nethermost
nigh[1]	nigher	nighest **or** next
old	older **or** elder	oldest **or** eldest
out[1]	outer **or** utter	⎧ outmost **or** outermost ⎨ utmost **or** uttermost
	thither[2]	thithermost
	under[2]	undermost
up[1]	upper	upmost **or** uppermost

[1] These are also adverbs or prepositions, or both.
[2] These have no positive.

In addition, the following, with superlative in **most,** have no comparative degree form:

bottom	bottommost
eastern	easternmost
end	endmost
front	frontmost
head	headmost
left	leftmost
mid **or** middle	midmost **or** middlemost
north	northmost
northern	northernmost
rear	rearmost
right	rightmost
south	southmost
southern	southernmost
top	topmost
western	westernmost

There is sometimes a difference in meaning and use between the two forms given for the same degree.

Farther and **farthest,** it should be noted, are used as a rule to pertain to physical distance; **further** and **furthest** to progress of thought or condition. But the two are increasingly used interchangeably by the best writers.

Later and latest, for instance, pertain to time only; latter and last to succession or order of arrangement.

Elder and eldest pertain to relative age or to superiority of age, as within a family; they are used of persons only. Older and oldest are more frequently used in reference to actual advance of years as this affects unrelated beings or things. You say He succeeded to the title on the death of his elder brother and Franklin was older than Washington. Elder and eldest are decreasingly used (page 100).

While first and last are listed above as superlatives, and really are superlatives, they are as frequently used with detached or independent meaning as with comparative significance, as one of our first citizens and the last word, meaning respectively our leading citizen and the decisive or climactic word.

Worser is now archaic, and lesser, while disappearing, is used interchangeably with less. Lesser is still preferred by many authorities as the substantive. A common colloquial error has it that a thing goes from worse to worse or from worst to worst. Either is ridiculous, for it means going exactly nowhere since both members of each group are of the same degree—comparative or superlative. The correct form is from worse to worst, that is, from comparatively bad to superlatively bad.

Note that while the comparative of mere is easily formed —merer—it is practically never used, though the superlative merest is common; and that sheer is usually compared sheer, more sheer, and sheerest, the comparative sheerer rarely being used for reasons of euphony.

Articles, numerals, pronominals do not admit of comparison. Adjectives that denote measurement or quantity or general geographical position or an invariable quality (silken, wooden, woolen) are not compared. Proper adjectives are, strictly speaking, not to be compared but they nevertheless frequently are, as American, more American, most American (which may easily be both ridiculous and dangerous). In the main, adjectives that in themselves denote the absolute are not compared, such as absolute, boundless, circular, complete, definite, empty, eternal, enough, favorite, final, full, illimitable,

inevitable, mutual, perfect, perpendicular, round, square, sufficient, supreme, total, triangular, unique, universal, vacant. But used in a relative or approximate sense, many of them are compared by the best writers and speakers. If you say that a thing is more complete or more perfect than another, you may quite properly mean that the one has more of the elements that make for completeness or perfection than the other, that neither is absolutely complete or perfect, but that one is more nearly complete or perfect than the other. **More than enough** or **more than sufficient** are, like **more complete** and **more perfect** and **more supreme,** and so on, sometimes called **superfluous comparisons,** but they are nevertheless idiomatically fixed and are not entirely illogical.

It must be remembered, moreover, that comparatives and superlatives are used to emphasize or intensify meaning as well as merely to indicate literal differences of degree. In conversation especially, such forms as **chiefer** and **chiefest, completer** and **completest, rounder** and **roundest** are by most authorities given sanction as examples of relative comparison. It is neither poetic license alone nor period characteristic that justifies Longfellow's **most perfect harmony,** Milton's **divinest melancholy,** Shakespeare's **perfectest herald of joy,** to mention the minimum of such usage.

The adjective **preferable** should be given no comparative or superlative forms. Do not say **more preferable** or **less preferable, most preferable** or **least preferable.** It is correctly followed by the preposition **to,** not by **before** or **over.** Say **This book is preferable to that,** not **before** or **over that.** But as with **complete** and **perfect** discussed above, there are instances—rare perhaps—in which **more preferable** and **most preferable** may be justified. If, for instance, you are asked to select three things in preferred order from a group of five, you naturally select a first choice, a second, and a third; that is, a first preference, a second preference, a third preference. This, in turn, looks very much like justification for **most preferable, more preferable, preferable.**

The superlative is sometimes used to indicate a very high order of quality, without the slightest suggestion of comparison. When you write **my dearest girl** or **my dearest boy** you may mean that there are other girls or boys less dear to you than the one you address, but the probability is that you think of only one girl or boy beyond any possible comparison with others. The parent who addresses one child as **dearest** cannot be said to be slighting his other children. **Dearest** in these uses is independent, and is sometimes called the **absolute or independent superlative.**

The comparative degree has an exclusive quality that must be carefully regarded. When you say that one thing is better than another, you imply that the "one thing" is separate and apart from "another"; that is, the comparative degree used with separative **than** (as it usually is) never permits the latter term of comparison to include the former. So, if you say **This one is better than any,** you make the mistake of not separating the compared things into the two necessary hard and fast groups; **any** is all-inclusive, and therefore includes **this one,** and **this one** is thus to some extent compared with itself. The two units compared must be distinguished by a separating term, such as **else** or **other.** If you say **This one is better than any other** or **Mary did better than any one else,** you place **this one** in a class by itself and compare it with all others, and **Mary** in a class by herself and compare her with all others. Note further the difference between **I like this instrument better than any** and **I like this instrument better than any other,** between **This sketch is worse than any I have seen** and **This sketch is worse than any other I have seen.**

The comparative is generally followed by **than,** or, stated oppositely, the object of comparison is generally preceded by **than,** as **I like English better than any other subject.** Do not substitute **as** for **than** in such comparison as this; **I like English better as any other subject** is an error sometimes made by those of foreign extraction. But note that there are some comparatives that take **to** or **of** or some word other than **than** after them, such as **anterior, elder, exterior, former, hinder, inferior, inner, interior, junior, latter, major, minor, nether, outer, posterior, prior, senior, superior.** After such as these **than** does not idiomatically fit. You say **older than** but not **elder than,** elder being used chiefly as a substantive; **anterior, exterior, hinder, inferior, interior, junior, major, minor, nether, posterior, prior, senior, superior** *to;* **former, inner, latter, outer** *of.*

The superlative degree, on the contrary, implies that the thing compared is one of the group regarding which comparison is made; that is, the superlative degree, usually introduced by **of** or **in** or **among** or **within,** never permits the latter term to exclude the former. It therefore has an inclusive quality. You do not say **This is the best of all other books I have read,** for the book referred to by **this** must be kept in the same class or group of **all books read.** In such superlative statements as this **other** or **else** must be studiously avoided; thus, **This is the best of all books** (or **all the books**) **I have read** or **This is the best among all the books I have read** or—using comparative form—**This is better than any of the other books I have read.** You cannot logically say **best of all other** because **this book** is not one of the others. Note that in a superlative statement **among** may, as a rule, be substituted for **of** in completing the comparison.

The superlative refers to more than two, as a rule; the comparative to two only. **Bill is the better of the two** and **John is the best of the three** illustrate correct usage. In much colloquial expression **best of two** and **worst of two** and **finest of two,** and the like, are frequently encountered, but such phrases are not to be recommended. The superlative, however, represents a being or thing as the highest in its group or order or class. Now, if the group or order consists of only two units the superlative may conceivably be correct, for use of the comparative might imply that there are more than two members in the group. Some grammarians thus justify **This is the best one of the pair** or **of the couple,** and in cases in which totality does not exceed two, the superlative is not absurd, and **best half** and **youngest twin** cannot be regarded as absurd. But the point does not come up so very much in general usage, and the rule of two for comparative and three or more for superlative may safely be followed in the vast majority of comparative expressions.

Two or more adjectives modifying the same noun or pronoun are usually arranged from short to long, that is, the shortest and simplest is placed first, the longest and most difficult last. This represents a general principle in the world of things at large. Thus, you say **a new and extraordinary service** and **a weak and inexcusable answer.** But the conjunction is not used between such modifying adjectives when one of them modifies the complete idea represented by the other and the noun following. If you say **a good old friend,** the adjective **good** modifies the unit idea expressed by **old friend,** these two

words forming a closed epithet that stands as a single term. So
closely knitted is the phrase that no comma is used between
good and **old**. Again, in **a clever young man**, **clever** modifies
the inseparable unit idea **young man**, that is, **a young man who
is clever**. But make sure that the order of adjectives is correct
in such double-adjective phrases. If you say **the first two men
in line**, you mean the first man and the second man in a single
file. If you say **the two first men in line**, you mean the two
head men standing abreast, probably in a double file. There
can be no such arrangement as **the two first pages**, for pages
are not arranged abreast as men in marching lines may be.
You must say **the first two pages**, that is, the first page and
the second page. Similarly, **the three next garages** and **the five
last lessons** should be, except under very extraordinary circumstances, **the next three garages** and **the last five lessons.**

The adjective is sometimes used indefinitely, especially after
an infinitive or participle; thus, in **Generosity is the quality of
being able to give without stint**, **able** pertains to no specific
word but to some one or something implied or understood.

Always place an adjective as closely as possible to the word
it modifies. Such errors as **a cold glass of lemonade** and **a hot
bottle of water** are commonly made, and are ridiculous when
analyzed. They should, of course, read **a glass of cold lemonade** and **a bottle of hot water.**

Do not use an adjective to modify an adverb or another
adjective, as **that there, this here, this much, that high, half
dead, real good, near through** (though **near** is adverb as well
as adjective, the adverb **nearly** is preferable here). **Here** and
there are usually regarded as adverbs, but in such expressions
as **this book here** and **that man there** they are called **locative
adjectives. Real** is an adjective; **really** an adverb. The use of
this or **that** for **so** (**that sleepy** for **so sleepy**) is colloquial but
incorrect (page 54).

Do not use adjectives inappropriately and extravagantly.
Wonderful and extraordinary soup and **colossal and stupendous artistry** are typical of the many youthful and over-en-
thusiastic expressions that are "too much with us." Soup may
be delicious and artistry may be skillful, but neither is wonderful, extraordinary, colossal, or stupendous. The adjectives

awful, marvelous, wonderful are probably the most thought-lessly and loosely used of all.

The phrases **in general** and **in particular,** composed as they are of a preposition and an adjective, are by some authorities considered not quite so good as the single adverb equivalents **generally** and **particularly.** But they are firmly established in standard usage.

Do not confuse closely related adjectives and substantives so that the more important idea is expressed by adjective and the less by noun. The tailor who advertised **Baggy trousers removed** meant **Trouser bagginess** or **Bagginess in trousers removed,** though **Trousers pressed** would have said all that he wished to say and would have said it vastly better.

Said and **aforesaid** are adjectives meaning before-mentioned. They are appropriate and correct in legal and technical phraseology, but not in general usage. You may properly write **The vagrant entered said premises during the absence of the lessee,** but you may not write **The boy has failed and said boy cannot therefore have a diploma.** Like **above-mentioned, foregoing, same, such,** these adjectives are sometimes called fixed-point adjectives, inasmuch as they point out or limit or fix on the basis of something gone before.

Chapter Four

VERB [1]

DEFINITION AND CLASSIFICATION

A verb is a word or a term with which one may make an assertion in regard to action or in regard to state or condition. In the main, the simpler definition—a verb is a word that expresses action—is sufficient to cover the majority of uses of this part of speech. In **The officer struck the thief,** the verb **struck** denotes action and the expression itself makes an assertion in regard to action. But in **The young man was successful,** the verb **was** denotes a state or condition and the expression itself makes an assertion in regard to state or condition; there is no action indicated.

The verb is the most important part of speech. Without the verb there can be no assertion or statement of fact and condition in a sentence; there can be only naming of action and condition. Other parts of speech—even nouns (subjects)—are frequently understood or implied. The verb may be but it is understood far less frequently. A single intransitive verb may constitute a sentence, as **Go,** that is, **You go.** A single noun may not be made to do this without already established connections.

Sometimes a verb—as in the second illustration above—does nothing more than connect what goes before it with what follows as **predicate nominative** (page 39). Such verb is called a **copula** which means link or bond. The verb **be** in its various forms is the most commonly used copula verb, but **appear, become, seem,** are also copulative verbs, and **come, continue, feel, get, go, grow, keep, lie, look, prove, remain, run, sit, sound, stay, turn, wax** are frequently used copulatively, as, in order,

They appear eager	They lie dormant all winter
We became weak	You look gay

[1] The conjugation paradigms on pages 122 to 132 must be consulted in connection with much of the material in this chapter.

He seems ready	That will prove unsatisfactory
It will come true	She has remained constant
The weather continued cold	The boy runs wild
We feel sad	We sat enthralled
He gets weary	It sounds plausible
They go mad	She stayed rigid
It grew crooked	We turned purple
They keep happy	He waxed eloquent

A copula takes the same case after it as before it. A noun or a pronoun following a copula is variously called **predicate nominative** or **attribute complement** or **subjective complement** or **predicate noun** or **predicate pronoun** (page 39). An adjective used after a copula to describe or explain a subject is called a **predicate adjective** or **predicative adjective**. These constructions have still other names—**noun attribute** (I am the *man*), **pronominal attribute** (I am *he*), **adjective attribute** (I am *good*).

Care must be exercised not to confuse such attribute with a pure adverb that modifies a verb. In **The old lady went insane,** insane clearly belongs to **lady,** the subject, and has nothing whatever to do with the verb; but in **The old lady groped insanely at the lamp, insanely** clearly belongs to the verb **groped,** telling the manner in which she groped at the lamp. In **She became a lawyer, lawyer** is attribute complement; it explains and belongs to the subject **she.** In **Her new dress becomes her,** her is direct object of the verb; it receives the action of the verb. Again, in **The candidate's speech was eloquent, eloquent** describes and belongs to **speech,** and it is thus predicate adjective. But in **The senator spoke eloquently, eloquently** is an adverb modifying **spoke.**

Sometimes the action of a verb is so asserted that it passes over to or is directed toward a receiver or object, as in the above **The officer struck the thief.** The officer's action passes over to **thief,** that is, **thief** is the object of the action taken by the officer, asserted of the officer. In such construction the verb is said to be **transitive.** The simple definition of a transitive verb as a verb that takes an object is good in the vast majority of uses but it is not always sufficient. Suppose you say **The officer struck,** meaning that he struck out wildly with his fists hitting nothing; **struck** is in such use not transitive for there is no receiver of the action. And in the use of **struck** in the sense of stopped work, the verb is usually used intransitively, as in **The workers struck,** although a transitive use is possible, as in **The union voted to strike the electronics factory.** In **They are playing,** the verb **are playing** is intransitive; in **They are playing football,** the verb **are playing** is transitive. In **The car stalled,** the verb **stalled** is intransitive; in **I stalled the car,** the verb **stalled** is transitive.

A **transitive verb,** then, **is** one the action of which "crosses over" to a receiver; an **intransitive verb** is one the action of which does not pass over to a receiver, or one that indicates a state or condition. Copulas are intransitive verbs. It is obvious that transitiveness and intransitiveness are dependent upon the relation of words in a sentence, and that, as above explained, the same verb may sometimes be transitive, sometimes intransitive, according to such relationship. These, for instance, are transitive uses: **She stretches the taffy, He slams the window, He flies the flag, She opens the cabinet, He walks the dog;** these are intransitive uses, **The taffy stretches, The window slams, The flag flies, The cabinet opens, The dog walks.** Some authorities say that in the latter group a reflexive pronoun—**itself, himself, herself**—is understood after each verb and that it is thus transitive. But if this were true there would be few intransitive verbs indeed, for it is possible, as a rule, to devise some receiver of action.

Some authorities, on the contrary, contend that cognate verbs (page 41)—verbs that are followed by objects that repeat their meaning—are intransitive. However, the verbs in such expressions as **He slept a peaceful sleep** and **He lived a useful life** are by the majority of grammarians regarded as transitive verbs. But observe that verbs followed by adverbial modifiers (page 42)—nouns denoting measure, weight, distance, space—are intransitive, as **They hiked a mile** and **We stayed a year.**

Intransitives may sometimes be made transitives through prefixed prepositions or adverbs, as **I stand here alone** and **I understand the problem, He has grown tall** and **John has outgrown him, They looked everywhere** and **They overlooked the closet, They tread lightly** and **They retread the tire.** Sometimes an idiomatic preposition—**to trifle with, to speak to, to be taken in, to look at, to pretend to, to laugh at**—following an intransitive verb makes it transitive, as **I laugh** (intransitive) and **I laugh at John** (transitive). In the latter **at** is really a part of the verb **laugh**, not a preposition with **John** as object. **Laugh at** denotes an action; it is asserted of **John**, that is, John receives the action. Change the voice and you must get **John was laughed at**, not **John was laughed**. **Attend to, arrive at, come to** are other verb-preposition combinations that make for transitiveness (page 191).

A **causative verb** is a derivative that indicates causing or producing an action that is named in the original verb, as **darken** (from **dark**) to cause darkness; **frighten** (from **fright**) to cause fright; **drench** (from **drink**) to cause wetness; **raise** (from **rise**) to cause to rise. Most such verbs have the suffix **en** which is sometimes called the causative suffix—**blacken, brighten, shorten, tighten, whiten,** and so on.

An **impersonal verb** is one that is indefinite in regard to subject and thus in regard to source of action, as **It rains** and **It is said** (page 51). The now archaic **me** verbs—**meseems, methinks**—are impersonal verbs.

A **verb of incomplete predication** is one that makes no sense used as a predicate unless it is followed by a complement, that is, unless its predication is completed by a word or phrase or clause that makes it meaningful. Thus, **The boy is** and **The girl became** and **The audience feels** are all expressions of incomplete predication, the predicate in each calling for a completing term—**The boy is bad** and **The girl became successful** and **The audience feels enthusiastic.** Of course, in an abstract sense these sentences may be complete. The first may mean the boy exists; the second, the girl grew or developed; the third, the audience is moved. But in customary usage **is** and **became** and **feels** above would be nonsensical intransitives calling for completion.

The omitted objective complement (page 42) very often makes even greater nonsense by way of incomplete predication. **They made Victoria** is ridiculous until the predicate is completed, as **They made Victoria queen** or **They made Victoria a great city.** True, **They painted the barn** may be complete as it stands, but it is incomplete if the expressional intention is to tell what color, as **They painted the barn red.** Similarly, **They elected John** may be complete, but it may not be if the intention is to indicate the office, as **They elected**

John secretary. In **The Huns destroyed** there may or may not be complete predication. If the meaning is that the Huns were generally destructive and made a campaign of destruction, the predicate is complete. If definite reference is intended, then there is incomplete predication—destroyed what? In **The Huns laid waste** the same ambiguity of predication exists— laid waste what? In **The Huns laid waste the land** (or the territory or the city or the government buildings, and so on) predication is completed by supplying a definite object (**laid waste** may be regarded as a single verb phrase, similar to **laid hold of** and **laid siege to,** or **waste** may be regarded as a noun used as object of **in** or **to** understood).

A **principal** or **notional** verb is a verb that in and of itself expresses act or state, or, in a verb phrase, that part of the phrase that does so. In a verb phrase it is usually the last member of the phrase. For instance, in **(They) shall have been seen, seen** is the principal or notional verb, the part of the verb that conveys the main notion or idea. In **I ran, ran** is principal. In **I shall run** and **I have run, run** is principal. The terms **principal** and **notional** are used interchangeably.

An **auxiliary verb** is one that is used with a principal verb in order to specify certain time or manner of action or state; it is thus a helping verb, a verb that helps another to focus its meaning in regard to time and manner. In **He will have been seen, will have been** are auxiliary verbs, **will** making the verb phrase future, **have** making it perfect, **been** making it passive. In **He will run, will** is auxiliary; in **I have run, have** is auxiliary.

In Latin, verbs denote time and manner by undergoing inflection—**amo** means I love; **amabam** means I loved; **amare** means to love; **amari** means to be loved. Auxiliaries are implied in verb endings. In English this is true to only a very limited degree (page 122), various auxiliaries being used to indicate shades of meaning. To make the subject more confusing, auxiliaries may themselves be used sometimes as principal verbs, as **I have a car (have** is notional) and **I have driven a car (have** is auxiliary).

The auxiliary verbs are **be, can, do, have, may, must, shall, will,** with their various forms **am, are, is, was, being, been, were** from **be; could** from **can; did** from **do; had** from **have;**

might from **may; should** from **shall; would** from **will.** As above indicated some auxiliaries have meanings of their own and may be used as notional verbs. This may be true on occasion even when they precede other verbs in a verb phrase and seem to be auxiliaries only. For instance, in **You may take this one if you wish, may** has notional force meaning permission, but in **Open the door so that I may go,** or **you may go,** or **he may go,** it is merely an inflection in the present tense of the potential (or subjunctive) mood, and really has no meaning of its own, its identity being absorbed by notional **go.**

Note in the conjugations on pages 122 to 132 that **be** with its various forms is an auxiliary in forming the passive voice, and in forming tenses that denote progressive or continuous action. It has been pointed out above that **be** may be used also with the meaning of **exist** and that it is the most frequently used copula.

Can (imperfect **could**) is used chiefly as auxiliary; when it stands alone, a notional verb is usually understood after it; it means to possess power, to be able to do. Although the use of **can** to denote permission is still frowned on by grammatical conservatives, it is nonetheless widespread (see **may**). In **I can do it, can** is really notional and do is an elliptical infinitive, that is, **I am able to do it.**

Do is frequently used as a principal or notional verb, as **He does well** and **He has done it. Do** as auxiliary is used only for emphasis in the present and imperfect tenses, as **I do believe** and **I did believe,** both stronger than merely **I believe** and **I believed.** It is used in interrogative sentences; instead of saying **Think you so,** we say **Do you think so.** It is used similarly in negatives, as **Do not go** and **Do not believe** instead of **Go not** and **Believe not** (the latter are poetic, dramatic, biblical). But in certain questions and negatives **have** is preferable to **do;** thus, **Has he any money** is better than **Does he have any money,** and **He hasn't any** is better than **He doesn't have any. Do** is not used as auxiliary with any form of the verb **be** except the imperative, as **Do be patient;** but note **Do try to come. Do** is used, again, as a substitute for other verbs to prevent repetition, as in **We think as you do** and **You think and so does my brother** and **I haven't seen that play yet but I shall do soon.** The last is less common in this country than in

England; we insert **so** after **to do.** In **How do you do, do** is both auxiliary and notional—**You do do how.** Do is provincially used in both countries in the sense of I should like, as **I could do with some bread** meaning **Pass the bread** or **I should like some bread. Do** is idiomatically used to mean suitable or satisfactory, as **This will do** and **Will mine do.** Note that **doest** and **doeth** are notional, and that **dost** and **doth** are auxiliary; thus, **He doeth best who loveth best** and **He doth beseech us, Thou doest what thou wishest** and **Thou dost have thy gods.** These archaic forms, and sometimes also the forms **do** and **did,** are used for the sake of euphony.

Have means to own or possess. It is always a sign of perfect tenses, and its imperfect **had** is a sign of pluperfect (past perfect) tenses. The archaic **hath** and **hast** are respectively third person and second person plain forms. Note that **have** may be auxiliary to **had,** as **I have had a good time,** but **had** may never be auxiliary to **have.** In illiterate usage both **have** and **of** are encountered after **had;** thus, **If I had have** or **had of known** for **If I had known.** Note also that in certain verb phrases—the pluperfect tense of **have**—**had** may be auxiliary to **had,** as **After he had had his midnight snack he went to bed.** Observe that **have** as auxiliary loses all meaning of ownership or possession, and merges with its notional verb (a past participle) to bring out the meaning that the action or state of that verb is complete at some specified time, as **I have accepted his resignation. Have** may be auxiliary to **be** and **do** as well as to **had.** In **I have had** and **I have done, had,** the imperfect of **have,** and **done** are notional verbs. In **I have been ill, been** is notional; but both **have** and **been** may be auxiliary, as **I have been weeping. Have** or **had** cannot be used as auxiliary to **can, may, must, shall, will, ought.** Do not use **had ought** or **We'd ought.** The two idioms **had rather** and **had lief** mean respectively **should prefer to** and **as soon,** as **I had rather be a doorkeeper in the house of my God than to dwell in the tents of wickedness** (Psalms 84:10) and **I'd as lief not be as live to be in awe of such a thing as I myself.** The **be** after **rather** and after **lief** is an idiomatic elliptical infinitive (page 138). A third idiom occurs less often, namely, **had best,** as **We had best start again;** that is, it is best for us or our best course is to start again. **Had best** should be used sparingly; **had liefer,** not at all. But **had better,** that is, **had preferably, had as lief, had as well, had rather**—followed by an infinitive or by a clause introduced by that—are commonly and correctly used to denote preference or advisability.

It used to be maintained that may (imperfect might) as notional verb denotes either permission or possibility, as respectively, You may have my car and He may win the prize. In its use to indicate permission it is rapidly being supplanted by can, especially in the interrogative form, as Can Johnny go to the movies with us. Either may or can is now acceptable in such sentences. As an auxiliary it is subjunctive or potential resultant, as Let us go so that we may get there on time.

Must as a notional verb connotes necessity; as an auxiliary it carries imperative quality to its accompanying notional verb. In archaic usage the notional verb is sometimes omitted after must, as I must onward and I must away for I must move onward and I must go away. Must is really an enforced or emphasized may; it originally meant may. Do not use must of for must have.

Shall is from Anglo-Saxon sceal meaning I am obliged or compelled. Will is from Anglo-Saxon willan meaning I intend or purpose or will. Used as a principal verb, will means decree or resolve, as in God wills it; as such it may be used with any of the auxiliaries listed above. Do not confuse this future tense verb will with the regular verb will meaning bequeath. It was formerly maintained that, used as notional verbs, *where the emphasis falls upon them,* shall indicates external and will indicates internal forcing or compulsion, that is, You or He shall go means one of you is going as a result of outward forcing, whereas I will go means that I am going as a result of inner force, namely, my own will. In other words, it used to be held that will used in the first person indicates purpose or intention; shall used in the second and third persons indicates command or threat or promise or compulsion. To some degree this distinction is breaking down, with will being used in the second and third persons to indicate external forcing; in such cases it is usually italicized in writing, as You *will* stay home tonight. Thus either shall or italicized will may be regarded as correct in sentences of this type. As auxiliaries, shall used to be regarded as necessary in the first person, and will in the second and third persons to express simple future happening. In this usage, the distinction is no

longer observed in speech and rarely in writing; **will** is therefore correct in any person to express simple futurity. Used as
principal verbs, **shall** and **will** form what is sometimes called
the **purposive future;** used as auxiliaries, they form what is
sometimes called the **declarative future** (page 150).

In questions, **will** is not used in the first person, for it would
be absurd to ask **Will I do my work** or **Will we take a walk.**
Both of these should begin with **shall,** for **shall** here denotes
consent or approval. In the second and third persons **will**
should be used in questions.

Because of the blurring of the distinction between **shall**
and **will,** the distinction formerly made between **should** and
would has analogously become less marked. For all purposes,
would is now considered correct in all persons. In addition,
should is used in the sense of ought, as **You should not eat
that;** and **would** is used in the sense of habitual action, as
Helen would sob whenever he left the house.

A **defective verb** is one that lacks one or more parts needed
to form a complete inflectional listing or conjugation of it. All
of the auxiliaries above discussed are defective with the exception of **do** and **have.** These two may be used in every form
in which verbs may be conjugated; each may, therefore, have
complete parts—**do, did, doing, done** and **have, had, having,
had**—and each may be completely notional. But **must** has no
other form; **shall** and **will** have the respective imperfects
should and **would;** you cannot say **shalled** or **shalling,** though
you may say **willed** and **willing** using the verb in a strictly
notional sense. Similarly, you have **may** and **might,** and **can**
and **could; canned** and **canning** and **maying (a-maying)** are
again different words. The parts of **be** are **am, was (were),
being, been,** but **be** has no passive voice.

Dare, let, and **ought** are called semi-auxiliaries by some
authorities. In most usage they do not express a complete or
independent idea, yet they are not necessary for fixing time
and manner of verbs in conjugating. They are usually followed by the infinitive with **to** expressed or unexpressed, and
thus appear to have auxiliary quality.

Dare was once imperfect; usage converted it into present
and set up **durst** as imperfect. Meaning **challenge, dare** is

regular; meaning **venture, dare** is spelled as here in the third person singular, present indicative, in negative statements, with **to** usually understood before the infinitive; thus, **He dare not try it,** that is, **He dare not to try it.** The **to** is more likely to be expressed in affirmative statements, as **He dare to try it.** But **He dare try it** is also correct. The imperfect tense today may be either **dared** or **durst,** as may the past participle, the former preferably since it is desirable to make language regular and uniform.

Let is not to be taken as an auxiliary in such imperative expressions as **Let me go** and **Let me see,** that is, **Let me to go** and **Let me to see.** The imperfect is **let** as is the past participle, whether it is used in the old sense of **hinder** or in the modern sense of **allow; letted** is now obsolete. Do not use **leave** for **let** in such expressions as **Let the dog alone** and **Let me be** and **Let go.** Though **leave** is frequently encountered in these usages, it is less correct than **let.** Neither **dare** nor **let** is defective.

Ought is a defective verb; it is used only in present indicative, and is followed by the infinitive to express obligation or necessity, or expectation, as **I ought to come** and **He ought to have tried. Ought** has no other form, though it was originally the imperfect of **owe.** It never takes an auxiliary, least of all **be** or **do** or **have. You don't ought** and **You had ought** are substandard. The plain or solemn style of **ought,** found in literature, is **ought'st** or **oughtest.** In early writings **ought** is sometimes found as **aught,** and **aught** and **ought** are nouns meaning anything or any least part, and adverbs meaning at all or to any extent. Do not confuse with **naught** or **nought;** a cipher is a **nought** or a **naught,** not an **ought** or an **aught.**

The old verb **wit** to know, is **wot** in the present, and **wist** in the imperfect. There are no other forms; all appear in the Bible and Shakespeare and elsewhere in early literature. **Beware** is a defective causative (page 112) verb, combination of **be** and the old adjective **ware,** meaning conscious or cautious or wary. It has this imperative form only. There are no other defective verbs—**beware, can, may, must, ought, shall, will, wit**—and it has been pointed out that at least two of these are little used today.

A **redundant** verb is one that has more than the required parts for a complete conjugation; the word **redundant** is, therefore, the special antonym of **defective** in grammatical use. The verb **light**, for instance, may be either **lighted** or **lit** in the imperfect tense and the past participle; the verb **mow** may be **mowed** or **mown** in the past participle; the verb **rap** may be **rapt** or **rapped** in the past participle. The lists below reveal others. Just as defective verbs tend to fall out of use with time, so redundant verbs tend to drop superfluous parts; thus, of the two imperfects of **break** and **speak**—**brake** and **broke, spake** and **spoke**—the former of each has fallen out of use, though it is, of course, found. Defective verbs are irregular verbs; redundant verbs may be both regular and irregular.

A **regular** or **weak** verb is one that forms its imperfect tense and past participle by the addition of **ed** to the simple form of the verb as **walk** and **walked, laugh** and **laughed;** by adding **d** only if the simple form ends with **e**, as **despise** and **despised, love** and **loved.** Some authorities prefer to say that in the latter instance mute **e** of the simple verb is dropped, and **ed** is added. Since the result is the same, either explanation is acceptable. When the **ed** occurs after the sounds **ch, f, k, p, s, sh, x,** it is pronounced **t.** If this final sound is preceded by a double consonant in the same syllable, one consonant is dropped if the **t** spelling is used, and the verb is still regarded as regular. Among the most commonly encountered **t** spellings today are **dealt, leapt, slept, swept** and **wept.**

An **irregular** or **strong verb** is one that forms its imperfect tense and past participle by means of an internal change—change of root vowel, as a rule—and thus without the addition of **d** or **ed** or **t**, as present **take**, imperfect **took**, past participle **taken**; and present **stick**, imperfect **stuck**, past participle **stuck.** All told, there are a few more than two hundred irregular verbs in English, the most commonly used of which are here given in the present, the imperfect, and the past participle:

Present	Imperfect	Past Participle
abide	abode	abode
arise	arose	arisen
be	was	been
bear (carry)	bore **or** bare	borne
bear (bring forth)	bore **or** bare	born

Present	Imperfect	Past Participle
beat	beat	beat **or** beaten
become	became	become
befall	befell	befallen
beget	begot **or** begat	begot **or** begotten
begin	began	begun
behold	beheld	beheld **or** beholden
beseech	besought	besought
beset	beset	beset
bid	bid **or** bade	bid **or** bidden
bide	bode	bode
bind	bound	bound
bite	bit	bit **or** bitten
bleed	bled	bled
blow	blew	blown
break	broke	broken
breed	bred	bred
bring	brought	brought
broadcast	broadcast	broadcast
burst	burst	burst
buy	bought	bought
cast	cast	cast
catch	caught	caught
chide	chid	chidden **or** chid
choose	chose	chosen
cleave (adhere)	cleaved **or** clave	cleaved
cleave (split)	cleft **or** clove **or** clave	cleft **or** cloven **or** cleaved
cling	clung	clung
come	came	come
cost	cost	cost
creep	crept	crept
cut	cut	cut
deal	dealt	dealt
do	did	done
draw	drew	drawn
drink	drank	drunk **or** drank
drive	drove	driven
eat	ate	eaten
engrave	engraved	engraved
fall	fell	fallen
feed	fed	fed
feel	felt	felt

Present	Imperfect	Past Participle
fight	fought	fought
find	found	found
flee	fled	fled
fling	flung	flung
fly	flew	flown
forbear	forbore	forborne
forbid	forbade	forbid or for-bidden
forget	forgot	forgot or for-gotten
forsake	forsook	forsaken
freeze	froze	frozen
get	got	got or gotten
give	gave	given
go	went	gone
grind	ground	ground
grow	grew	grown
have	had	had
hear	heard	heard
hide	hid	hid or hidden
hit	hit	hit
hold	held	held or holden
hurt	hurt	hurt
keep	kept	kept
know	knew	known
lay	laid	laid
lead	led	led
leave	left	left
lend	lent	lent
let	let	let
lie	lay	lain
lose	lost	lost
make	made	made
mean	meant	meant
meet	met	met
outdo	outdid	outdone
pay	paid	paid
put	put	put
read	read	read
rend	rent	rent
rid	rid	rid
ride	rode	rode or ridden

Present	Imperfect	Past Participle
rise	rose	risen
run	ran	run
say	said	said
see	saw	seen
seek	sought	sought
sell	sold	sold
send	sent	sent
set	set	set
shake	shook	shaken
shed	shed	shed
shoe	shod	shod
shoot	shot	shot
shred	shred **or** shredded	shred
shrink	shrunk **or** shrank	shrunk **or** shrunken
shut	shut	shut
sing	sang **or** sung	sung
sink	sank **or** sunk	sunk
sit	sat	sat
slay	slew	slain
sleep	slept	slept
slide	slid	slid **or** slidden
sling	slung	slung
slink	slunk	slunk
smite	smote	smitten **or** smit
speak	spoke	spoken
spend	spent	spent
spin	spun	spun
spread	spread	spread
spring	sprang **or** sprung	sprung
stand	stood	stood
steal	stole	stolen
stick	stuck	stuck
sting	stung	stung
stink	stank **or** stunk	stunk
stride	strode	stridden **or** strid
strike	struck	struck **or** stricken
strive	strove	striven
swear	swore	sworn
sweep	swept	swept
swim	swam	swum
swing	swung	swung

Present	Imperfect	Past Participle
take	took	taken
teach	taught	taught
tear	tore	torn
tell	told	told
think	thought	thought
throw	threw	thrown
thrust	thrust	thrust
tread	trod	trodden or trod
wear	wore	worn
weave	wove	woven
weep	wept	wept
win	won	won
wind	wound	wound
wring	wrung	wrung
write	wrote	written

The following verbs are regarded by most grammarians as being both regular and irregular, though those asterisked are placed by some as regular verbs under the t-imperfect rule (page 114). Some authorities regard all t-imperfects as irregular. Some hold that when t is substituted for as many as three letters at the end of a verb, this constitutes a radical change in the root. But the distinction is too fine. The definition of weak verbs and strong verbs on page 114 is authoritative.

awake	awaked or awoke	awaked or awoke
belay	belayed or belaid	belayed or belaid
bend	bended or bent*	bended or bent
bereave	bereaved or bereft	bereaved or bereft
bet	betted or bet	betted or bet
blend	blended or blent*	blended or blent
bless	blessed or blest*	blessed or blest
build	builded or built*	builded or built
burn	burned or burnt*	burned or burnt
clothe	clothed or clad	clothed or clad
crow	crowed or crew	crowed
dare	dared or durst	dared (rarely durst)
dig	digged or dug	digged or dug
dight (adorn)	dight or dighted	dight or dighted
dream	dreamed or dreamt*	dreamed or dreamt
dress	dressed or drest*	dressed or drest

dwell	dwelled **or** dwelt*	dwelled **or** dwelt
gild	gilded **or** gilt*	gilded **or** gilt
gird	girded **or** girt*	girded **or** girt
grave	graved	graven **or** graved
hang	hanged **or** hung[1]	hanged **or** hung
heave	heaved **or** hove	heaved **or** hoven
hew	hewed	hewed **or** hewn
kneel	kneeled **or** knelt	kneeled **or** knelt
knit	knitted **or** knit	knitted **or** knit
lade	laded	laded **or** laden
lean	leaned **or** leant*	leaned **or** leant
learn	learned **or** learnt*	learned **or** learnt
light	lighted **or** lit	lighted **or** lit
mow	mowed	mowed **or** mown
pen (coop)	penned **or** pent*	penned **or** pent
plead	pleaded, plead, **or** pled	pleaded **or** pled
prove	proved	proved **or** proven
quit	quitted **or** quit	quitted **or** quit
rap	rapped **or** rapt*	rapped **or** rapt
reave	reaved **or** reft	reaved **or** reft
ring	ringed, rang **or** rung	ringed **or** rung[1]
rive	rived	rived **or** riven
saw	sawed	sawed **or** sawn
seethe	seethed **or** sod	seethed **or** sodden
shape	shaped	shaped **or** shapen
shave	shaved	shaved **or** shaven
shear	sheared **or** shore	sheared **or** shorn
shine	shined **or** shone	shined **or** shone
show	showed	showed **or** shown
slit	slitted **or** slit	slitted **or** slit
smell	smelled **or** smelt*	smelled **or** smelt
sew	sewed	sewed **or** sewn
sow	sowed	sowed **or** sown
speed	speeded **or** sped	speeded **or** sped
spill	spilled **or** spilt*	spilled **or** spilt
spit	spitted, spit **or** spat	spitted **or** spat
split	splitted **or** split	splitted **or** split
spoil	spoiled **or** spoilt*	spoiled **or** spoilt
stave	staved **or** stove	staved **or** stove
stay	stayed **or** staid	stayed **or** staid
strew	strewed	strewed **or** strewn

[1] These are two different verbs.

string	strung	stringed **or** strung
strow	strowed	strowed **or** strown
sweat	sweated **or** sweat	sweated **or** sweat
swell	swelled	swelled **or** swollen
thrive	thrived **or** throve	thrived **or** thriven
wake	waked **or** woke	waked **or** woken
wax	waxed	waxed **or** waxen
weave	weaved **or** wove	weaved **or** woven
wed	wedded **or** wed	wedded **or** wed
wet	wetted **or** wet	wetted **or** wet
whet	whetted **or** whet	whetted **or** whet
wont	wont	wonted **or** wont
work	worked **or** wrought	worked **or** wrought

Most irregular verbs are of Anglo-Saxon origin. Newly introduced verbs are usually adopted as regular verbs, as **radioed, telephoned, televised.** Old irregulars tend to be dropped or to be brought into line. **Climbed,** for instance, was once **clomb, helped** was **holp.** The **en** participial form increasingly becomes an adjective form exclusively. **Beholden,** for example, is now almost always used as an adjective rather than as the past participle of **behold; molten** has largely given way to **melted, shapen** to **shaped, shaven** to **shaved, swollen** to **swelled,** the **en** forms remaining as adjectives. We say **sodden** (not **seethed**) **earth,** rotten (rarely **rotted**) **wood,** molten (not **melted**) **metal** (but **melted butter, melted snow**), drunken (not **drunk**) **man,** bounden (not **bound**) **duty,** ill-gotten (not **ill-got**) **gold,** a **sunken** (not **sunk**) **ship,** a **proven** (rarely **proved**) **proposition, forgotten** (not **forgot**) **man, begotten** (not **begot**) **son, stricken** (not **struck**) **man, foughten** (not **fought**) **field, downtrodden** (not **downtrod**) **man.** But observe **cleft palate** and **cloven foot.** And contrarily enough, the weak verb sometimes drops its **ed** when used as an adjective, as **roast** (not **roasted**) **beef, dread** (not **dreaded**) **enemy, link** (rarely **linked**) **chain, push** (not **pushed**) **cart.** But practically any past participle in **ed** may also be used adjectively (page 147).

It has been explained that verbs forming the imperfect tense by **d** or **ed** or **t** are by most grammarians regarded as regular or weak verbs; those that have past participles with **en,** as irregular or strong verbs. Verbs that are the same in present, imperfect, and past participle are regarded as irregular. The following old monosyllabic verbs, however, are also irregular verbs, the **d** or **t** at the end not being inflectional but part of the root: **beat, bid, bind, bite, burst, fight, find, get, grind, hold, let, shoot, sit, slit, slide, stand, tread, wind** (but see lists above).

The final consonant rule in spelling applies primarily to verbs—**planning, rubbing, webbing;** so, too, does the final silent **e** rule—**breathing, biting, seething.** Pluralization of certain nouns applies also, as pointed out on page 25, to the inflection of verbs in third singular present indicative—**He** key**s, He** tri**es, It** perch**es, She** reach**es.**

INFLECTION

Verbs are inflected for voice, mood, tense, number, person. They also undergo changes of form, as has been explained above, when they are converted from present to imperfect or to past participle (or both). But the latter is a change of form made in the verb itself, regardless of its relationship to other words. Voice, mood, tense, number, person are inflections that are made because of the relation of a verb to other words in an expression. English verbs have no gender. They have no case, but they cause case.

The systematic arrangement of all forms of a verb by which these inflections are shown, is called its **conjugation.** The principal parts of a verb are the three (or four) forms that key the entire conjugation. When these parts are known, that is, all other forms are easily devised from them. The first part is the infinitive, usually preceded by **to.** This, in English as in other languages, is called the root form of the verb; it is also the form of all verbs except **to be** in present tense active indicative with the exception of third singular. The second part is the imperfect tense; the first radical change of form may occur here, such as the addition of **d** or **ed** or **t,** or some change of internal vowel. The third part is the past participle in which again there may be, as has been explained, some radical change of form. The present participle always ending with **ing,** is sometimes added to make a fourth principal part. But this part is not important inasmuch as it is always of the same final -**ing** formation; thus, the principal parts of **flow** are **present tense indicative** or **present infinitive** *flow,* **imperfect tense indicative** *flowed,* **past participle** *flowed* **(present participle** *flowing***).**

Inflections of the English verb are, as a rule, indicated by using other verbs—principally the verbs **be** and **have**—called auxiliaries (page 108). A few inflections are indicated by changes in the verb itself, as **flows, flowest, floweth, flowed, flowed'st, flowing.** Here are six variations from the original **flow,** a small number indeed when it is considered that a Latin verb, for instance, often has ten times as many inflectional changes, made for the most part in the word itself rather than by means of auxiliaries (page 156). Most regular verbs have only four forms, as **walk, walks, walked, walking,** and most irregular ones have only four or five, as **come, comes, came, coming,** and **rise, rises, rose, rising, risen.** Even our most irregular verb—**be**—has but eight forms—**be, am, is, are, was, were, being, been.**

Before these inflections are discussed seriatim, a picture of typical conjugations may be presented so that in what follows easy reference may be made for the illustration of points. In each instance, the conjugation of indicative, subjunctive, and potential moods is given first according to the pattern based on Latin and then in a form more favored by present-day students of English structure. Imperatives, infinitives, and participles are listed only once.

Simple conjugation of the verb *be*

Principal parts: present **be;** imperfect **was;** past participle **been**

Indicative Mood
Present Tense

Singular	Plural
1 I am	1 We are
2 You are	2 You are
3 He[1] is	3 They are

Imperfect or Past Tense

1 I was	1 We were
2 You were	2 You were
3 He was	3 They were

Future Tense

1 I will be	1 We will be
2 You will be	2 You will be
3 He will be	3 They will be

[1] Or **she** or **it** throughout.

Perfect or Present Perfect Tense

Singular	Plural
1 I have been	1 We have been
2 You have been	2 You have been
3 He has been	3 They have been

Pluperfect or Past Perfect Tense

1 I had been	1 We had been
2 You had been	2 You had been
3 He had been	3 They had been

Future Perfect Tense

1 I will have been	1 We will have been
2 You will have been	2 You will have been
3 He will have been	3 They will have been

Subjunctive Mood

Present Tense

1 If[1] I be	1 If we be
2 If you be	2 If you be
3 If he be	3 If they be

Imperfect or Past Tense

1 If I were	1 If we were
2 If you were	2 If you were
3 If he were	3 If they were

Future Tense

1 If I should[2] be	1 If we should be
2 If you should be	2 If you should be
3 If he should be	3 If they should be

Perfect or Present Perfect Tense

1 If I have been	1 If we have been
2 If you have been	2 If you have been
3 If he have been	3 If they have been

Pluperfect or Past Perfect Tense

1 If I had been	1 If we had been
2 If you had been	2 If you had been
3 If he had been	3 If they had been

[1] Or lest, that, though, till, unless (see page 136).
[2] Or shall, will, would.

Future Perfect Tense

Singular	*Plural*
1 If I should have been	1 If we should have been
2 If you should have been	2 If you should have been
3 If he should have been	3 If they should have been

Potential Mood

Present Tense

1 I may[1] be	1 We may be
2 You may be	2 You may be
3 He may be	3 They may be

Imperfect or Past Tense

1 I might be	1 We might be
2 You might be	2 You might be
3 He might be	3 They might be

Perfect or Present Perfect Tense

1 I may have been	1 We may have been
2 You may have been	2 You may have been
3 He may have been	3 They may have been

Pluperfect or Past Perfect Tense

1 I might have been	1 We might have been
2 You might have been	2 You might have been
3 He might have been	3 They might have been

Imperative Mood

Present Tense

Singular	*Plural*
2 Be (you or thou)	2 Be (you or ye)

Infinitives

Present	*Perfect*
To be	To have been

Participles

Present	*Past*	*Perfect*
Being	Been	Having been

[1] Or can or must.

Principal parts: present **be;** imperfect **was;** past participle **been**

Indicative Mood
Present Tense

I am
You,[1] we, they are
He[2] is

Imperfect or Past Tense

I, he was
You, we, they were

Future Tense

I, you, he, we, they will be

Perfect or Present Perfect Tense

I, you, we, they have been
He has been

Pluperfect or Past Perfect Tense

I, you, he, we, they had been

Future Perfect Tense

I, you, he, we, they will have been

Subjunctive Mood
Present Tense

If[3] I, you, he, we, they be

Imperfect or Past Tense

If I, you, he, we, they were

Future Tense

If I, you, he, we, they should be

Perfect or Present Perfect Tense

If I, you, he, we, they have been

Pluperfect or Past Perfect Tense

If I, you, he, we, they had been

---

[1] Both singular and plural throughout.
[2] Or she or it.
[3] Or lest, that, though, till, unless (see page 136).

Future Perfect Tense

If I, you, he, we, they should have been

Potential Mood

Present Tense

I, you, he, we, they may be

Imperfect or Past Tense

I, you, he, we, they might be

Perfect or Present Perfect Tense

I, you, he, we, they may have been

Pluperfect or Past Perfect Tense

I, you, he, we, they might have been

Simple conjugation of the verb *see*

Principal parts: present **see**; imperfect **saw**; past participle **seen**

Active Voice

Indicative Mood

Present Tense

Singular	Plural
1 I see	1 We see
2 You see	2 You see
3 He[1] sees	3 They see

Imperfect or Past Tense

Singular	Plural
1 I saw	1 We saw
2 You saw	2 You saw
3 He saw	3 They saw

Future Tense

Singular	Plural
1 I will see	1 We will see
2 You will see	2 You will see
3 He will see	3 They will see

[1] Or **she** or **it** throughout.

Perfect or Present Perfect Tense

Singular	*Plural*
1 I have seen	1 We have seen
2 You have seen	2 You have seen
3 He has seen	3 They have seen

Pluperfect or Past Perfect Tense

Singular	*Plural*
1 I had seen	1 We had seen
2 You had seen	2 You had seen
3 He had seen	3 They had seen

Future Perfect Tense

Singular	*Plural*
1 I will have seen	1 We will have seen
2 You will have seen	2 You will have seen
3 He will have seen	3 They will have seen

Subjunctive Mood

Present Tense

Singular	*Plural*
1 If[1] I see	1 If we see
2 If you see	2 If you see
3 If he see	3 If they see

Imperfect or Past Tense

Singular	*Plural*
1 If I saw	1 If we saw
2 If you saw	2 If you saw
3 If he saw	3 If they saw

Future Tense

Singular	*Plural*
1 If I should[2] see	1 If we should see
2 If you should see	2 If you should see
3 If he should see	3 If they should see

[1] Or lest, that, though, till, unless.
[2] Or shall, will, would.

Perfect or Present Perfect Tense

Singular	Plural
1 If I have seen	1 If we have seen
2 If you have seen	2 If you have seen
3 If he have seen	3 If they have seen

Pluperfect or Past Perfect Tense

Singular	Plural
1 If I had seen	1 If we had seen
2 If you had seen	2 If you had seen
3 If he had seen	3 If they had seen

Future Perfect Tense

Singular	Plural
1 If I should have seen	1 If we should have seen
2 If you should have seen	2 If you should have seen
3 If he should have seen	3 If they should have seen

Potential Mood

Present Tense

Singular	Plural
1 I may[1] see	1 We may see
2 You may see	2 You may see
3 He may see	3 They may see

Imperfect or Past Tense

Singular	Plural
1 I might see	1 We might see
2 You might see	2 You might see
3 He might see	3 They might see

Perfect or Present Perfect Tense

Singular	Plural
1 I may have seen	1 We may have seen
2 You may have seen	2 You may have seen
3 He may have seen	3 They may have seen

[1] Or can, must.

Pluperfect or Past Perfect Tense

Singular	*Plural*
1 I might have seen	1 We might have seen
2 You might have seen	2 You might have seen
3 He might have seen	3 They might have seen

Imperative Mood

2 See (you)	2 See (you)

Infinitives

Present	*Perfect*
To see	To have seen

Participles

Present	*Past*	*Perfect*
Seeing	Seen	Having seen

Principal parts: present **see;** imperfect **saw;** past participle **seen**

Active Voice
Indicative Mood
Present Tense

I, you, we, they see
He sees

Imperfect or Past Tense

I, you, he, we, they saw

Future Tense

I, you, he, we, they will see

Perfect or Present Perfect Tense

I, you, we, they have seen
He has seen

Pluperfect or Past Perfect Tense

I, you, he, we, they had seen

Future Perfect Tense

I, you, he, we, they had seen

Subjunctive Mood
Present Tense

If I, you, he, we, they see

Imperfect or Past Tense

If I, you, he, we, they saw

Future Tense
If I, you, he, we, they should[1] see

Present or Present Perfect Tense
If I, you, he, we, they have seen

Pluperfect or Past Perfect Tense
If I, you, he, we, they had seen

Future Perfect Tense
If I, you, he, we, they should have seen

Potential Mood

Present Tense
I, you, he, we, they may[2] see

Imperfect or Past Tense
I, you, he, we, they might see

Perfect or Present Perfect Tense
I, you, he, we, they may have seen

Pluperfect or Past Perfect Tense
I, you, he, we, they might have seen

By **synopsis** of a verb is meant its orderly arrangement or conjugation in one person and number only. From a synopsis of a verb it is easy to imply the associated forms in every tense, once you have the complete conjugation (such as above) to guide you. Below are two conjugational paradigms of different types from the foregoing conjugations, presented in synopsis only. One is the passive voice of the simple conjugation of see, **simple conjugation** meaning the conjugation containing all those verb forms most generally used. The second is the **progressive** or **continuous conjugation** of the verb see, the conjugation that denotes continuing state or action. The former, the passive voice, you get by adding the past participle of any verb to every form of the verb be. Look at the conjugation of be on page 122; add seen to it, and you have the following passive forms.

[1] Or shall, will, would.
[2] Or can, must.

Synopsis of *see* in the simple conjugation in the passive voice, first person singular number

Indicative Mood

Present Tense: I am seen
Imperfect Tense: I was seen
Future Tense: I will be seen
Perfect Tense: I have been seen
Pluperfect Tense: I had been seen
Future Perfect Tense: I will have been seen

Subjunctive Mood

Present Tense: If I be seen
Imperfect Tense: If I were seen
Future Tense: If I should be seen
Perfect Tense: If I have been seen
Pluperfect Tense: If I had been seen
Future Perfect Tense: If I should have been seen

Potential Mood

Present Tense: I may be seen
Imperfect Tense: I might be seen
Perfect Tense: I may have been seen
Pluperfect Tense: I might have been seen

Imperative Mood

(Second person present only)

Singular	Plural
Be (you) seen	Be (you) seen

Infinitives

(No person or number)

Present	Perfect
To be seen	To have been seen

Participles

(No person or number)

Present	Past	Perfect
Being seen	Being seen[1]	Having been seen

[1] Some of the passive forms are technical merely, formable but rarely usable. The past participle is really the same in both active and passive.

Synopsis of *see* in the progressive conjugation in the active voice, first person singular number

(This is formed, you will observe, by adding the present participle of *see* to every form of the verb *be* on pages 122 to 124.)

Present Tense: I am seeing
Imperfect Tense: I was seeing
Future Tense: I will be seeing
Perfect Tense: I have been seeing
Pluperfect Tense: I had been seeing
Future Perfect Tense: I will have been seeing

Subjunctive Mood

Present Tense: If I be seeing
Imperfect Tense: If I were seeing
Future Tense: If I should be seeing
Perfect Tense: If I have been seeing
Pluperfect Tense: If I had been seeing
Future Perfect Tense: If I should have been seeing

Potential Mood

Present Tense: I may be seeing
Imperfect Tense: I might be seeing
Perfect Tense: I may have been seeing
Pluperfect Tense: I might have been seeing

Imperative Mood

(Second person present only)

Singular	Plural
Be (you) seeing	Be (you) seeing

Infinitives

(No person or number)

Present	Perfect
To be seeing	To have been seeing

Participles

(No person or number)

Present	Past	Perfect
Being seeing[1]	Been seeing	Having been seeing

[1] Some of the progressive forms are technical merely, formable but rarely usable.

This progressive or continuous conjugation is used principally in the active voice. But note that the passive voice can be formed throughout. If you conjugate the verb *be* as progressive, as **I am being,** and add to it the past participle of the principal verb you wish to use in the passive progressive, you may easily enough form the passive voice of this conjugation; thus, **I am being seen, I was being seen, I will be being seen, I have been being seen, I had been being seen, I will have been being seen.** Though most passive progressive forms are not used in everyday communication, all may be and some have to be if precision of expression is to be achieved. **I am being hurt** and **I was being hurt** and **At this time tomorrow I will be being initiated** are correct and intelligible, though labored. It is similarly accurate and not too troublesome to say **The garage is being built** though some grammarians have scorned this passive progressive form and have sanctioned the idiomatic **The garage is building** to mean the same thing, that is, **The garage is going up** or **They are erecting the garage.**

The verb **going,** used in the progressive conjugation, has come to have an idiomatic use. In **I am going** it is future in significance, as **I will go.** In three other tenses it denotes future time in reference to the past, as **I was going** and **I have been going** and **I had been going,** and thus has the quality of a future perfect. It is completely negatived in meaning in such expressions as **I am going to remain** (I shall remain) and **I am going to stand still** (I shall stand still), the meaning being the very opposite of proceeding—I am not really going anywhere.

The **emphatic conjugation** is formed in the present and imperfect active indicative and in the imperative by using **do** as an auxiliary, as **I do see, I did see,** and (imperative) **Do see.** The **negative conjugation** is formed by the insertion of a negative form, usually **not,** as **I see not, I saw not, I will not see.** The insertion of **do** in the negative forms of the present and imperfect indicative and in the imperative makes for smoother and more idiomatic expression, as **I do not see, I did not see, Do not see. Do** is used for similar reasons in the formation of the so-called **interrogative conjugation,** as **Do I see,** rather than **See I,** and **Did I see,** rather than **Saw I.**

VOICE

Voice is that inflection of a verb that shows whether its subject is the doer of the action indicated or is acted upon.

If the subject performs the action, the verb is in **active voice,** as **Jerry won the race.** If the subject is acted upon, the verb is in **passive voice,** as **The race was won by Jerry.** A verb that is generally without voice, such as the copulative verb **be,** is sometimes called a **neuter verb,** that is, a neutral verb **(neuter** in this use has nothing to do with gender). In the formation of the passive voice in the simple conjugation, and of both voices in the progressive conjugation, **be** is such an important agent that some authorities assign voice to it in these functions. But it decides or identifies voice in these forms; it does not itself have voice.

Note in the above illustrations of active and passive verbs, that the change from active to passive is made by using the object of the active verb as the subject of the passive; that is, the active-voice expression **John hit Bill** becomes **Bill was hit by John.** The action in the second, therefore, does not pass over to a receiver, and the verb is necessarily intransitive. Transitive verbs only may be thus converted into passive use. But if a sentence has an active verb followed by both direct object and indirect object, it may be changed into passive form in two ways; thus, **He gave me a car** may become either **I was given a car by him** or **A car was given me by him.** In the first of these passive forms, **car** is **retained object** (page 43); in the second, **me** is **retained indirect object (to me).** The indirect object or the direct object may become subject in such conversion of voice.

Those who are confronted with the inconsistencies of grammar for the first time are sometimes puzzled by such expressions as **The building rented easily** and **The pudding tastes good** and **The book reads slowly,** in which, while the verbs are active, the meaning is passive. They are sometimes called false or idiomatic passives. Logically expanded the expressions, of course, mean that the building was rented easily, that the pudding is good when it is tasted, that the book is one that forces slow reading.

Difficulty also sometimes arises in the use and understanding of the apparent passive of the present tense in such expressions as **They are come** and **Timothy is arrived** and **Christ is risen.** These are of course not actual passives, but survivals of older Germanic perfect active forms. Compare **Sie sind gekommen** and **Er ist angekommen** in German, which are exact parallels. It is true, however, that quite apart from the archaic flavor of these expressions in English, they do differ semantically from their perfect active counterparts in that they indicate a kind of continuing action that the perfect forms do not have, while the participles contribute more to the subjects really than to the predicates.

It should be noted by the way that passive verbs may sometimes be regarded as copulative (page 104), as **He is considered a hermit** and **She is thought a genius** and **The girl is named Isabella** and **Johnson was elected president**. These are objective-complement constructions (page 42) turned around as direct object and indirect object were turned around above. Since all copulas take the same case after them as before them, **hermit, genius, Isabella, president,** are in the nominative case.

MOOD

Mood means manner. Applied to the verb, it means the manner in which an action or a state is expressed or is to be regarded. Some grammarians prefer **mode** to **mood,** but the majority use the latter because **mood** has connotations of a certain mental state which gives a clue to the use of the particular mood of the verb. But either word may be used to indicate the four or five different ways or styles or manners of verb expression.

An expression that indicates action or state as real or factual, or as not real or factual, or that asks a question about it, is said to be in the **indicative mood.** It should be noted from this definition that a supposition or condition that is treated as if it were a fact is also expressed by the indicative mood. Observe **He is going to college** (affirmative statement) and **He is not going to college** (negative statement) and **Is he going to college** (question) and **He is going to college if he passes his examinations** (supposition or condition that may be taken as a fact inasmuch as his general standing is high and he has never yet failed in examination). The conjugational paradigms above show that there are six tenses in the indicative mood.

A predicate that indicates action or state as supposed or imagined, or as contingent or contrary to fact is said to be in the **subjunctive mood. Subjunctive** means joined under—**subjoined.** This formerly meant (and still does to a degree) that the subjunctive mood is used in subordinate or subjoined clauses. But it is used in simple sentences also and in main clauses, and the indicative is often used in subordinate clauses.

Observe these illustrations of the various uses of the subjunctive mood: **Thy heart be comforted** (wish or prayer); **If he had done as advised, he would now be a free man** (condition contrary to fact); **If the day be rainy, we will stay at home** (doubt or uncertainty, since clear weather has been prophesied); **He ordered that I be deported** (command); **Strive lest you fail** (purpose or contingency); **They are frightened lest they be struck by lightning** (fear or imagined state). Note that, with the exception of the first example, the subjunctive is used in dependent clauses. Note also that the subjunctive is usually indicated by **except, if, lest, that, though, till, unless, whether.** But these are not required if the verb or its auxiliary is transposed before the subject, as **Had I gone** instead of **If I had gone** and **Were I you** instead of **If I were you.** It will be seen from the foregoing examples that when the verb introduced by **if, though, lest,** and so forth, is in the subjunctive, the other verb in the sentence is usually in the indicative.

Except for its use in certain almost ritualistic phrases and in sentences indicating condition contrary to fact, the subjunctive mood has almost disappeared from English. In part this has happened because in many instances the indicative serves equally well. In subordinate clauses of concession, for example, there is no particular advantage to writing **Even though it hurt me, I will still do it** rather than **Even though it hurts me, I will still do it.** Actually it may even be contended that the subjunctive in the former sentence is redundant, since the notion of concession is perfectly well expressed by the subordinating conjunction. Similarly, in sentences involving doubt or uncertainty, the conjunction **if** may be sufficient to convey the idea of doubt; that is to say, **If this is treason, make the most of it** is equally expressive of uncertainty as **If this be treason, make the most of it.** The retention of subjunctive forms in conditional sentences results from the value in being able to distinguish between real and unreal conditions. There is certainly value in being able to make the distinction between **If she was here, you noticed her** and **If she were here, you would notice her.** Even in subordinate clauses of real conditions, however, the indicative is sometimes encountered, the justification for its use presumably being that the quality of the condition is determined by the verb of the main clause. And in contrary-to-fact conditions in the past like **If Susan had been here she would have enjoyed herself, had been** is subjunctive, true, but since in form it is similar to the indicative, its mood can actually be ignored except in parsing exercises.

The present subjunctive is preferably used to indicate future contingency, as **Speak slowly that you be not misunderstood.** The imperfect subjunctive is preferably used to indicate mere indefinite supposition, as **I should try it if I were he.** Except for the always exceptional verb **to be,** the subjunctive has only two forms that are distinct from those of the indicative, namely, the third person singulars of the present and the perfect tenses. In the future tenses of the subjunctive the auxiliary **should, shall, would,** or **will** may be used (page 123).

An expression that indicates action or state as possible or probable or necessary, or that is placed in the form of entreaty or wish, is said to be in the **potential mood.** This mood is expressed by use of the auxiliaries **can, may, could, might, must, would, should.** Many grammarians do not treat the potential as another mood, but classify all potential forms as subjunctive. The potential mood has four tenses; the future and the future perfect are omitted from its conjugation, inasmuch as the auxiliaries imply future, and refuse to blend with **shall** and **will.**

An expression that indicates command or wish or permission is said to be in the **imperative mood,** as **Leave the room** and **Bless my soul** and **Go if you wish.** It is most frequently used to give orders or commands. It has but one tense, the present; usually but one person, the second; and is both singular and plural, active and passive. While the imperative is customarily used in the second person, it sometimes occurs (idiomatically) with first or third, as **Stand we all together** and **Come one, come all.** The verb **let** is used, as a rule, with imperative first and third person expressions, as **Let us assemble in the chapel** and **Let every one sign his name.**

An expression in which state or action is merely named without the limitations of definite person and number as vested in a subject, is said to be in the **infinitive (mood).** When you say **I drive** or **He drove,** you use a verb that is limited by the person and number of a subject; whereas, when you say **to**

drive or **to have driven** you merely name or indicate action
without in any way confining it. The action in the latter is, in
other words, infinite; in the former, finite or limited. All forms
of the verb but infinitives and participles are called finite verbs
or verbs proper. Infinitives and participles are preferably
known as **verbals** rather than as moods. The present infinitive
is thus the root form or the natural or name form of the verb.
The term **infinitive,** as generally used in grammar, means the
present tense, not the perfect tense, the only two tenses in
which it exists. The perfect infinitive really has little or nothing
to do with time, but rather with completing or perfecting, and
with manner. The sign of both the infinitives is **to;** it is now
for the most part a sign only, though it formerly had prepositional value. It still retains the force of **to** of the old dative
case in **They are more to be pitied than scorned** and **Here is
food to eat** and **Her burdens are hard to carry,** for in these it
conveys the meaning of purpose or fitness or oughtness. But
in the main it is meaningless. It is, indeed, omitted after such
auxiliaries as be, do, have, may, can, shall, will, must, as **I
shall (to) go** and **We can (to) stay.** And it is usually omitted
after the active verbs **behold, bid, come, dare, feel, find, have,
hear, help, let, mark, make, need, observe, please, see, watch,**
but not after these verbs when they are passive, as **We saw
him (to) fall** and **They helped us (to) pack,** but **He was seen
to fall** and **We were helped to pack.** The infinitive with **to**
omitted but clearly understood is called the **pure** or **elliptical
infinitive.**

The infinitive may be used in most ways in which a noun
is used, as

> **To sympathize is to understand** (subject and predicate
> nominative)
> **They tried to exercise** (direct object)
> **It is educative to read** (appositive—It—to read—is educa-
> tive)
> **She made him (to) accept** (objective complement)
> **There was nothing for him to do but** (or **except** or **save**) **to
> go** (object of a preposition)

The infinitive may be used like an adjective, as

> **He had his tasks to perform** (**to perform** modifies **tasks**)
> **This claim is to be taken seriously** (predicate adjective)

The infinitive may be used as an adverb is, to express condition, degree (or comparison), manner, reason or purpose, result, as

To speak freely I think your work is bad (condition; that is, on condition that I may speak freely)
He was too excited to understand (degree)
He knows better than to attempt that (comparison)
He will strive to please you (manner)
They are trying to finish before night (reason or purpose)
She has managed to become a good player (result)

The infinitive of purpose is frequently the object of the preposition **for**, with a regular objective-case subject, as **For them to come is imperative** and **They have planned for him to visit us,** in which the one **for** phrase is subject of **is,** and the other is object of **have planned. In the plan for him to visit us,** the **for** phrase may be an adjective adjunct of **plan** or it may stand in apposition with **plan.**

In **These, to be sure, are very beautiful** the infinitive is used independently or absolutely. In such expression as **a desire to travel,** some authorities regard the infinitive **to travel** as an adjective modifying **desire,** and some regard it as in apposition with **desire.** The active infinitive, like certain progressive forms, is sometimes used in a passive sense, as **a loft to let,** that is, **to be let; an employe to blame,** that is, **to be blamed.** But note **this building to be sold,** not **to sell;** and **the employe to be dismissed,** not **to dismiss.**

It will be seen in the above illustrative sentences that the infinitive, whatever its own construction, may be modified by an adverb, as **He attempted to run rapidly;** that it may take an object, as **He tried to throw the ball;** that it may take an objective complement, as **They tried to make him king;** that it may take an attribute complement, as **He is said to be good,** and that it may modify a noun, as **He had permission to leave;** a pronoun, as **It is yours to forgive;** an adjective, as **We were glad to see him;** an adverb, as **He is old enough to pay full fare;** a verb, as **They are saddened to hear it** and **He struggled to free himself.**

The infinitive may have a so-called subject, but one that in no way changes its form. This subject of the infinitive is always in the objective case (unlike the subject of a finite verb which is always in the nominative case). In **They wish me to go,** for instance, **me** is not the object of **wish;** they do not wish me, but they wish a going on my part; thus, they wish a going me or me to go (a to-go me). The **me** and the **to go** are inextricably linked, **me** having the force of subject of **to go,** and both being object of **wish.** Note, again, in **It is time for them to come,** objective **them** is subject of the idea of coming, and **to come** is object of the preposition **for.** The subject of an infinitive may be a prepositional phrase or the object of such phrase, as **For him to do such a thing is unbelievable.**

Much ink has been used in a discussion of the so-called **split infinitive,** that is, the infinitive in which an adverb stands between the preposition **to** and the verb itself, as **I decided to faithfully study** and **I urged him to again thoroughly consider.** It is better, especially in such expressions as these, not to insert modifiers between **to** and the verb because they make for awkwardness and for wrenched construction. **I decided to study faithfully** and **I urged him to consider again thoroughly** are better. **To** is always to be considered a part of the infinitive—as much a part of it as **er** is a part of the French verb **aller,** as **en** is a part of the German verb **gehen.** As a rule, the modifying adverb may be placed after or before the infinitive.

But note that ambiguity or "squinting" may occur if the adverb is placed before the infinitive, as **He tries faithfully to practice,** in which **faithfully** may modify either **tries** or **practice.** The split infinitive may occasionally be more than justified for the sake of emphasis and for the sake of avoiding awkward or labored phrasing, as in **I want you to thoroughly understand** and **I wish it to be emphatically explained** and **It is necessary to so arrange the work.** A few authorities rule it out altogether; some justify its use almost indiscriminately for the reason that it abounds in literature of all periods. Do not use the split infinitive if it in any way seems to strain or wrench or otherwise throw expression "out of joint," as in **They expect this year to again more than double the output** (page 246).

Do not substitute **and** for **to** before an infinitive. **I shall try to come** is correct; **I shall try and come** is incorrect, because the verbs **try** and **come** are not co-ordinate. Similarly, **I shall**

come and get it is ungrammatical, though a colloquialism.
I shall come to get it is correct; the **coming** and the **getting**
not being co-ordinate (except under unusual circumstances).

The three participles (page 124) are likewise infinite rather
than finite verbs. The present participle always ends in **ing,**
and always indicates action as continuing or progressing, as
Running **as fast as he could, he soon caught up.** The past
participle is the same as the imperfect indicative for regular
verbs **(ed),** but for irregular verbs it is not the same as a rule
(page 114). It denotes action that is past or that goes
backward into the past in relation to the action indicated by
the principal verb, as **Time** *lost* **can never be recovered** (really
Time that has been lost). The perfect participle is formed by
the use of the auxiliary **having,** and it denotes previous completion of state or action, as **Having been discharged he took
his car and returned home.**

The present participle is used, as illustrated on page 132,
in the formation of the progressive or continuous conjugation.
The past participle is used in the formation of the compound
tenses, after certain auxiliaries (page 123). No verb can be
conjugated without the use of the participle. The perfect participle is formed, it has been seen, by prefixing **having** to the
past participle to get the active-voice form, and **having been**
to get the passive-voice form. It is because the perfect participle is thus merely an extended or modified form of the past,
that some authorities say there are but two participles in
English, namely, the present and the past.

The participle may be used as an almost pure adjective, as
The whipping waves roared through the night. Here **whipping**
has more, however, than merely adjective quality, in that it
indicates continuous and present action. The ideas of continuity and repetition belong to the verb nature of **whipping;**
they are seldom absent from **ing** endings. Such adjectives as
fierce, harsh, angry, cruel, savage, furious do not connote
these qualities. But **whipping** in the above sentence has more
adjective nature in it than it has in **The waves, whipping the
shore savagely, roared through the night.** Here **whipping** is
an adjective, in that it modifies **waves,** but it is also pro-
nouncedly a verb, in that it takes an object **(shore)** and is
modified by an adverb **(savagely).**

Now note that in **The whipping of the waves through the night disturbed our sleep,** whipping is used as a substantive, subject of the verb **disturbed.** But it still connotes habitual or continued action, and by this token retains its nature as a verb. It is, therefore, called a **verbal noun,** or, by some authorities, a **verbal abstract noun.** It is preceded by **the;** it is followed usually by **of** with an object that pertains closely to it. But it cannot really take an object and it cannot be modified by an adverb. It may be modified by possessives and by adjectives, especially by **no, more, such, this, that;** and it may thus take an attribute (see below).

Observe again **By savagely whipping the coastline, the waves have changed geography.** Here the substantive **whipping** is called a **gerund.** It still denotes continuity and thus has verb nature; but, like a noun, it is object of a preposition **(by),** and, like a verb, it is modified by the adverb **savagely,** and takes the object **coastline.** It is thus easy to see that this form is closer to the verb than the preceding form or verbal noun. You may say **The punishing of the boy was justified by his conduct** in which **punishing** is a verbal noun; or you may say **Punishing the boy was justified** in which **punishing** is a gerund. You may not say **The punishing the boy was justified** or **Punishing of the boy was justified.**

Just by way of "clinching" these very confusing participial forms, observe that in **She is a singing Diana, singing** is a participial adjective; that in **We heard Diana singing the enchanting melody, singing** is a participle modifying **Diana,** taking **melody** as object; that in **Diana's singing of the enchanting melody made everybody gay, singing** is a verbal noun, subject of **made,** modified by **Diana's** and by the adjective phrase **of the enchanting melody;** that in **Singing an enchanting melody makes one gay, singing** is a gerund, subject of **makes,** and **melody** is direct object of **singing.** Both the gerund and the verbal noun are sometimes called **substantive participle.**

Remember that the verbal noun may take adjectives and articles as modifiers before it, and a prepositional **(of)** phrase after it; and that it expresses an action as a thing. The gerund may govern the objective case but not the possessive **(of)** case, may not be modified as the verbal noun is, and refers action to an agent or recipient.

The following illustrative uses of verbal nouns may also be helpful:

Your answering of the questions will help us (subject)
Don't permit his leaving to disturb you (object)
**Two important sports absorb them in the winter, their skating
and their skiing** (appositive)
Jim's greatest demerit is his procrastinating (attribute)
She wants to discontinue her playing (object of infinitive)
She has been applauded for her playing (object of preposition)
They could see Mary climbing the hill (objective complement)
They thought her playing to be deserving of applause (subject of infinitive)

Note in the following illustrative uses of the gerund that it is sometimes almost indistinguishable from the verbal noun:

Studying music has done much for her (subject)
She prefers practicing in the afternoons (object)
Her pet hobby, dancing on the ice, has been her fate (appositive)
She remained sitting at the window (attribute)
We found them suffering (objective complement)
They were curious about reaching the top (object of preposition)
They are going skiing (adverb—for the purpose of skiing)

A repeating possessive should not precede the gerund in a phrase, as **By his practicing he has been able to outdo the others.** Here the possessive **his** repeats **he.** It would be ridiculous to repeat a noun possessive in this way, as **By John's practicing John has been able to outdo the others. His** should not be referred to by **He,** for the antecedent of a noun or a pronoun should not be in the possessive case. The sentence should read **By practicing he has been able to outdo the others.**

The participle of a copulative verb is followed by an attribute, as **Being tired when night came, I did not go out** and **Grown weary they decided to stop for rest** and **Having been a loyal friend, he was sadly missed when he passed on.** While the participle is often a minor element in absolute constructions (page 69), it may be a major one, as **Speaking of the old** days, do you remember the time we joined the circus in which speaking of the old days is an independent or absolute participial phrase. Note the difference between **There being but three of them they decided to take the small car** in which there is an introductory adverb or expletive, and **Their being ill spoiled the party** in which **their** is a possessive pronoun modifying the participial substantive **being.** In the latter example **ill** is predicate adjective referring to the indefinite **their** or to some noun understood after it **(bodies).**

Care must be exercised to see that a participle—especially one at the beginning of a sentence—has a definite noun or pronoun to modify. A participle indefinite in modification is said to be **dangling** or **hanging** or suspended. In **Believing that the sun would come out, the picnic was planned,** the participle **believing** dangles; it has nothing to modify. It is naturally linked by position with **picnic,** but such modification is absurd. The sentence must be rewritten as **Believing that the sun would come out, they planned the picnic** or **the picnickers planned their outing.** Now the introductory participle clearly modifies **they** or **picnickers.** Recent studies in the structure of English have made it possible to state this rule of word order: when a sentence begins with a participle, the first substantive (noun or pronoun) not in the possessive case in the main clause is modified by that participle. This explains why **Strolling through the park Jack's hat blew off** and **Entering the room the lights went out,** types of errors that occur all too frequently, are considered so humorous. These should, of course, read **While Jack was strolling through the park his hat blew off** and **As I entered the room the lights went out.** Supplying a single noun or pronoun to be modified by the dangling participle in each of these is not so easy as it was in the former examples, and substitute dependent clauses are the most convenient correction.

The dangling-participle construction is not to be confused with the nominative absolute containing a participle, as **The stenographer having returned, I proceeded with my dictation.** Here there is no obvious grammatical connection intended among the first four words—the nominative absolute—and the rest of the sentence. The participle **having returned** does not dangle, but definitely modifies **stenographer.**

It has been noted (page 47) that the possessive case of a noun or a pronoun is generally required before substantive

participles, as **We approve his coming** and **Bill's playing is
hopeless.** Him in the first and Bill in the second would be
wrong, because it is the coming that is approved in the one
and it is the playing that is hopeless in the other. If you say
We approve him coming, you must mean that you approve
him under the circumstances of coming, and this would be
unusual if not absurd. Similarly, if you say **Bill playing is
hopeless,** you must mean that Bill is hopeless while he is
playing, and this would also be absurd under normal circumstances. In other words, the leading word in the sense of the
sentence should govern the construction.

The special offenders among suspended participles are
initial **being** and **seeing** followed by **as** or **that,** as **Being as
(or that) it looks like rain, I shall take my umbrella** and
Seeing as (or that) he is ill, I shall call a doctor. These sentences should begin with **inasmuch as** or **owing to the fact that**
or **since** or **because,** for **being** and **seeing** have no definite
modification; the sentences should usually be made complex
with the causal clause coming first. Such use of **being** or **seeing** or other participles is substandard usage, and should be
strictly avoided. Say **Inasmuch as it looks like rain I shall take
my umbrella** and **Owing to the fact that he is ill I shall call a
doctor.** But an introductory phrase may sometimes be substituted, as **Because of his illness I shall call a doctor.**

The dangling-gerund phrase is as studiously to be avoided
as the dangling-participial phrase (page 144). In **In conversing with the students the situation was made clear,** for
instance, the introductory gerund phrase is not logically related to the subject as it should be. It absurdly seems to
modify **situation.** In **In conversing with the students the
teacher was able to make the situation clear,** the phrase is
logically related or "tied" to the subject. The rule of making
introductory gerund (and participial and infinitive) phrases
pertain to subjects does not apply, however, when such phrases
are general in their application rather than special. In **Generally speaking, he is a satisfactory student** and **In walking,
the arms should be allowed to swing freely,** the introductory
phrases refer to general action rather than to any particular
agent, and they thus apply to the entire statement following.

All participles conjugated on pages 124 and 129 are usable
in the constructions treated above. They may very often give

to expression a less formal and more closely knit relationship of parts than do the finite verb forms, and they thus make for smoothness and coherence. **Having been promoted he was heartily congratulated** is somewhat more compact and "cosy" than **He had been promoted and he was heartily congratulated,** for the participial phrase condenses and relates the idea of the verb without the formality or stiffness of predication.

But care should be exercised not to overuse gerunds and verbal nouns for infinitives, and for phrases and substantives generally. They frequently make expression stilted and confused. **It is foolish to take such risks** is better, for instance, than **It is foolish taking such risks,** and **He began to count the returns** is better than **He began counting the returns.** In the same way **Wasteful cooking is a social evil** is simpler than **Cooking wastefully is a social evil,** and **To attain your end more quickly try this method** is better than **For attaining your end more quickly try this method. John's ambitions surge like the coming in of the tide** is improved by omitting the verbal noun construction entirely, as **John's ambitions surge like the tide at flood.** The infinitive is to be preferred, again, in such expressions as **He hated doing it** and **Inciting riot is unlawful,** that is, **He hated to do it** and **To incite riot is unlawful.**

The verbal noun is regarded by many as a more dignified form of expression than the gerund in such expressions as **My work is the teaching of English** and **The preaching of salvation is my chosen career.** These are fuller, better rounded, and less colloquial than, respectively, **My work is teaching English** and **Preaching salvation is my chosen career.** And (as noted on page 142) such variant phrasings as **My work is teaching of English** and **My work is the teaching English** and **Preaching of salvation is my chosen career** and **The preaching salvation is my chosen career** are wrong. Similarly, **I suggested my friend's writing of a novel** is clumsy, awkward, and inadequate. The preposition **of** is superfluous and the construction of **friend** is not basically possessive. Say **I suggested to my friend the writing of a novel** or **I suggested to my friend that he write a novel** or **I suggested** (apparently to another) **that my friend write a novel** (pages 141 to 143).

The perfect participle is frequently misused for the present in such expressions as **Having seen the man advance I ran** and **Having felt ill I went to bed early** for **Seeing the man**

advance **I ran** and **Feeling ill I went to bed early.** The latter
are more likely to be correct in all similar constructions. But
there is possibility that either of the former may be correct.
If, for instance, after the man advanced there was a pause or
an interim, or if the illness had been felt all day or for a
number of days previously, the perfect participle is correct.
But if immediacy of situation is indicated (as it usually is or
should be) the present participle is correct.

The present participle, as has been seen (page 132), is used
in the formation of the progressive or continuous conjugation.
Formerly this participle was sometimes prefixed by **a,** as
a-maying, a-going, a-preparing, a being equivalent to **at, in, of,**
or **on. I am going a-milking, sir** and **Forty and six years was
the temple in building** (John 2:20) means, respectively, **I am
going at my milking, sir** and **Forty and six years was the
temple being built.** While the latter is objected to by some
authorities, it remains nevertheless a useful form and is increasingly used; the former has disappeared, though still found
in old ballads. It is better to say **The work is being done** than
to say **The work is doing, The house is being built,** than **The
house is building,** even though (and this is the bone of con-
tention) the former in each example does combine a present
participle with a past, gives an active verb a passive meaning,
and may in extended use make for awkwardness. **They say
that house has been being built for five years** has, first, an
active present indicative predicate, and, second, a passive
perfect progressive, but it is nevertheless correct, though
unusual. In the more extended progressive forms, however,
some authorities insist that the simpler **They say that house
has been building for five years** is idiomatic if not strictly
logical. There is consolation in the fact that neither has to be
used very much.

The past participle, especially when it ends with **en,** always
splits allegiance between verb and adjective; it may always be
used as adjective as well as verb, and tends, as language grows
older, to become "frozen" in the adjective form (page 120).
The past participle in **ed** is also used adjectively to a large
extent. When you say **a given book** you probably do not mean
a book that has been given to some one, but, rather, a certain
book or a book specified as containing a particular thing.
Similarly, in **the driven snow, the broken harmony, the mis-
shapen figure, a grown man, the risen Lord, the frozen fruit,**

**the shorn lamb, the spun yarn, the sunken ship, the woven
thread,** the past participle has become primarily adjective,
with little of its verb nature left to it. On the contrary, observe that you may not say **the stood people** for **the standing
people** or **the sat audience** for **the seated** or **sitting audience**
or **a slept room** for **a sleeping room.**

The past participle, in relation to the time indicated by a
principal verb in a sentence, denotes past time. The action of
the past participle, that is, always begins before the time
indicated by the principal verb and may come down to the
present and go into the future; thus, **They work in this community, respected by all** and **They will work in this community, respected by all,** and so on through the remaining
tenses, the past participle phrase, **respected by all,** remaining
timeless as far as influence of the principal verb is concerned.

TENSE

Tense is that inflection of a verb which denotes action in
relation to time. It may denote time as present, time as complete, time as continuous. Just as there are three general divisions of time—present, past, future—so there are three
general classifications of tense—present, past, future. The
second is also called **imperfect** because it does not denote
completeness of action at any specific time; that is, **imperfect**
names the tense as to manner, **past** as to time. In foreign
languages this tense is called imperfect as a rule, and sometimes preterite. Just as there are three general times at which
anything may be perfected—again, present, past, future—so
there are three general classifications to signify these times of
perfection—present perfect, past perfect, future perfect. The
past perfect is also called pluperfect, **plu** being from Latin
plus meaning more, that is, more than perfect tense.

A tense expressed by a single word, as **I** *go* and **I** *went,*
is called a **simple tense.** A tense that requires an auxiliary verb
(or more than one) to complete its inflection, as **I** *have gone*
and **I** *shall have gone,* is called a **compound tense.** All tenses
but the present and the imperfect are formed by the use of
auxiliaries, the imperfect usually having some internal or
terminal inflection to indicate its time. The perfect tense always has some form of the verb **have,** and this auxiliary thus
becomes the sign of the perfect. **Shall** and **will** are signs of the

future tenses; **be** is the sign of passive and progressive forms of the verb.

Since most tense inflections in English are indicated by means of extra words called auxiliaries rather than by endings or internal changes in a verb itself, they afford niceties of distinction that are not to be found in most other languages. In Latin, for instance, **amabat** means both **He loved** and **He was loving;** the context has to be depended upon to tell which. In English, as indicated by the translations, there is a specific form for each of these expressions.

But it must not be assumed that tenses always express time with precision. Those of the indicative mood are more specific in regard to time than those of other moods. In the latter, tense very often indicates more of manner than of time. Present tense indicates action that takes place or state or condition that continues in the present, as **John runs** and **I am running** and **I do run** and **That is a fact.** But the adjective **present,** like the adverb **presently,** is a fluid term, remember. It may mean immediate, but it may extend both forward and backward in significance, as **the present age** and **the present season.** The present tense may also denote habitual action, as **He leaves at eight every morning;** it may denote a general truth, as **Time tells a tragic story;** it may be used to vivify and thus emphasize past events, as **Washington conquers hardship at Valley Forge** (this is called the **historical present**); it may denote sheer future time, as **Tomorrow he goes to Chicago, and on Tuesday he proceeds to St. Louis;** it is used of quotations (a kind of historical present), as **Milton says** and **The Bible exhorts** and **Shelley writes,** each followed by direct quotation.

Imperfect tense indicates action or condition simply as belonging to past time, as **He departed yesterday** and **We were playing cards** and **The czars were very despotic.** It also indicates action that is progressive in past time, as **We swam while they played tennis** and **We were singing while they were dining.** It may, again, be used to indicate habitual action of the past, as **They always brought two cars with them** and **They formerly ate four meals a day.**

Present perfect tense indicates action or condition as completed or perfected in the present or continued to the present. It must be remembered that the present perfect must come to the present and actually touch it, as **I have worked since early morning,** meaning I began work in the past (early morning) and continued to (touching) the present. It is wrong, therefore, to say **I have worked from day before yesterday to yesterday noon,** because the time last mentioned (yesterday noon) does not touch the present. It is similarly wrong to say **I have entered this school three years ago,** for here the action expressed is wholly in the past; **have entered** does not touch the present; thus, the imperfect must be used—**I entered this school three years ago.** The imperfect tense should not be used for the present perfect, especially the imperfect with the auxiliary **did.** Use **Have you seen the circus,** not **Did you see the circus;** use **This is the first time I have ever been late,** not **This is the first time I was ever late.** Be especially careful never to use the imperfect tense after **have** instead of the past participle, when the two forms are different. **I have came** and **He has went** and **They had saw** and **You had gave** are substandard forms.

Pluperfect or past perfect tense indicates action or condition as perfected or completed at some definite past time, usually in relation to some other past act, as **We had left the city many years before the earthquake occurred.** Note that the auxiliary **had** is the imperfect of **have,** sign of the perfect. Here, it is clear that the earthquake occurred in past time, and that our leaving the city took place even before the tragedy. Two past acts are, therefore, indicated, the first being "past past" or "more past" than the second. Note the difference between **I went to the station to meet her** and **I had gone to the station to meet her.** This relation between or among acts is the key to the proper use of the pluperfect. Kept clearly in mind it will prevent such use of the imperfect for the pluperfect as **When he finished his work, he went to the theatre.** This should read **When he had finished his work, he went to the theatre** because the first act "pre-pasts" or antedates the second.

Future tense denotes action or condition simply as happening or existing in the future, as **I shall go** and **He will go** (page 111). Some grammarians explain a subordinate future or a "past future" by which they mean an action that in the past was regarded or viewed as future; thus, if you say **I warn you I will apply for leave,** you use simple future in the second clause; if you say **I warned you I would apply for leave,** you use subordinate or past future in the second clause. When the warning took place, you used the simple future; you have now merely adapted that future to another time, and **I warn you I will apply for leave** becomes **I warned you I would apply for leave.**

Future perfect tense indicates action or condition as perfected or completed at some specified future time or before some future action, as **He will have gone before I arrive.** The meaning here is that his going will be completed before my arriving, that is, the future act of my arriving will be "prefutured" by his going. As in the simple future above, you may have in the future perfect a sort of subordinate or "past future perfect" by which is meant an action that in the past was regarded or viewed as perfected in the future; thus, suppose you say **I am certain that they will have arrived by this time** as entirely of a past time—**I was certain they would have arrived by that time.** As in the above, you have merely adapted the future perfect tense to another time by the use of **would** or **should.** Here as there, all verbs are in the indicative mode, not in the subjunctive.

By the term **sequence of tenses** is meant the logical relationship of time as expressed by tense to other words, especially to other verbs, in an expression. **Then, yesterday, formerly** naturally imply past time, and thus imperfect tense. **Now, today, at present** naturally imply present tense. When verbs indicate logical time relationships, they are in natural sequence, as **I expect he is coming.** When the verb of a subordinate clause is made to agree with a principal verb, it is said to be in **conventional** or **attracted sequence,** as **I expected he was coming.** Principal verbs in the present or the future tenses take subordinate verbs in any tense; principal verbs in the past-time tenses should be followed by subordinate verbs that denote past time; thus, **He says he had to go, He says he will go, He says he has won the prize, He will understand that he he has been in the wrong, He has tried hard in order that he may win,** and **He said he had to go, He said he would go, He said he had won, He would understand that he had been in the wrong, He had tried hard in order that he might win.** If, however, the subordinate clause expresses a general truth—a fact that is true for all time—the latter part of the foregoing rule has to be revised; that is, an imperfect tense in a principal clause may be followed by a present tense in a subordinate clause, as **John** *said* **that Washington** *is* **the capital of the United States.**

Errors are commonly made in infinitive sequence, especially in such expressions as **He hoped to win the medal** and **He hoped to have won the medal.** Ponder these two constructions a little, and the first will be seen to mean that he may or may not have won the medal, that is, **He hoped to win the medal, and succeeded** or **failed.** The second implies clearly that he did not win the medal or that the medal was won by a competitor. Note again that in **I think you ought to do it,** the meaning is you still may or may not do it; that in **I think you ought to have done it,** the meaning is that you have not done it. After imperfect-tense verbs that in themselves connote future—**expect, hope, intend, wish**—this difference between the present infinitive and the perfect amounts to a language idiom and needs to be carefully watched. In general usage, the present infinitive indicates the same time as the principal verb, as **They want to go,** in which both verbs pertain to the future; and the perfect infinitive indicates time completed at the time of the principal verb, as **He was to have gone yesterday** (he did not go) and **She was supposed to have done it** (she did not do it). But the infinitive must not be permitted to repeat the time of the principal verb that it follows, as **She had hoped to have done it** for **She had hoped to do it.** The principal verb **had hoped** tells the whole story here, namely, that she did not do it, and all that is, therefore, needed after it is a mere naming of the action without any inflection whatever. The same rule applies to **We have long been intending to go** and **I should have been required to go; to have gone** would be wrong in either expression for the reason given above.

Verbs connected by conjunctions should have subjects repeated before them if they do not agree in mood and tense and conjugation, as **I was seriously ill during the spring but I am now, according to the doctor, completely recovered** and **He fought on the field and bled in the cause and died for his country.** But there is much good usage to the contrary, especially in short expressions, as **You are and will be greater than you think.** And observe what force is lost to **I came, I saw, I conquered** when it stands **I came, saw, and conquered.** Like many other rules this one is good as a caution to young writers and speakers. Nothing can make writing and speaking more diffuse and incoherent than habitual use of verbs of different forms with a single subject, especially in long and involved sentences.

It is better always to make verbs agree in mood and tense and conjugation, provided no damage is done the thought in such uniformity. **He is studying hard and is doing well** is better than **He is studying hard and does well, He has studied hard and has done well** is better than **He has studied hard and he did well.**

The notional or principal verb must be repeated, rather than understood, when its forms differ as between or among verb phrases in related constructions. You should use **I have not done it and I will not do it** rather than **I have not and I will not do it** or **I have not done it and I will not,** for the forms of **do** are different after the auxiliaries **have** and **will.** When the forms after auxiliaries are the same, however, the repetition is not necessary, as in **He must and he shall do it** and **I haven't done it, nor has he.** The old grammars stated the rule thus: No form of a word must be understood in a sentence that has not already appeared in that sentence. When the second form occurs at the end of a sentence, most authorities rule that the repetition is unnecessary inasmuch as the required form may be more easily understood here than elsewhere. A few authorities assert that **He came to school as fast as he could come** is preferable to **He came to school as fast as he could.**

The phrasal preposition **instead of** is preferably followed by a gerund or a verbal noun, not by a finite form of the verb, as **Instead of telling the truth he deliberately lied. Instead of tell the truth he deliberately lied** is wrong. It is likewise incorrect to use **His father was disturbed to find that the boy had lied instead of told the truth.** The negative co-ordinate **and not** or the comparative subordinate **rather than** may be used in expressing such ideas as this, and the verb that follows either should be kept parallel with the verb that precedes; thus, **His father was disturbed to find that the boy had lied and (had) not told the truth** or **His father was disturbed to find that the boy had lied rather than (had) told the truth.** In both instances, **had** would be understood in the last clause. **Tell** for **told** in the last example would be incorrect. This rule is most frequently violated perhaps in the paralleling of infinitives and principles, as **Rather than going with John he decided to stay at home**

for **Rather than go with John he decided to stay at home.** In
the latter form the infinitive (elliptical) **go** parallels to **stay.**

It follows, conversely, that in such constructions as the
foregoing, **and not** and **rather not** should not be followed by
a gerund or a verbal noun. This, for instance, is wrong:
**Various aspects of a subject appear and reappear in many
chapters rather than (or and not) being developed consecutively in a single chapter.** Either of these readings is correct:
**Various aspects of a subject appear and reappear in many
chapters instead of being developed consecutively in a single
chapter** or **Various aspects of a subject appear and reappear
in many chapters rather than (or and don't) stand consecutively developed** and so forth. [But inasmuch as the parallel-
ism exists between **in many chapters** and **in a single chapter,**
this reading is best: **Various aspects of a subject appear and
reappear in many chapters rather than in a consecutively
developed single chapter.**]

Verbs must not be omitted, to be understood by the reader,
if such omission is likely to cause absurdity, as **The terrace
was filled with visitors eating cheese and beer.** The understood
verb must be a repeated preceding verb in such expression as
this. But **eating** before **beer** is absurd. The sentence must be
revised to read **The terrace was filled with visitors eating
cheese and drinking beer.**

In **Either he has been cruel, or his friends wrong,** a "blind
supply" is left after **friends,** that is, it is impossible to know
whether **are** or **were** or **have been** is to be supplied as predicate
of the alternate clause. The supplied verb here cannot be the
same as the preceding verb, for number is changed.

Verbs in parallel expressions should be kept consistent and
uniform, if clear and easily grasped construction is to be
achieved. It is irregular and confusing to say **Seeing a man
steal a purse and thus to prove him a thief are by no means
the same.** Both subject phrases should be the same in this
sentence, either **seeing** and **proving** or **to see** and **to prove.** In
He would neither study nor allowed me to, would is auxiliary
to notional **study,** and **would** is understood after **nor—He
would neither study himself nor would he allow me to study**
being the expanded reading. The verbs connected by **neither**

—nor must be kept parallel, otherwise the absurd verb phrase **would allowed** occurs.

Got is the past participle and the imperfect tense of **get. Gotten** is an old form, still frequently used by Americans. It is not archaic, however, in adjective use. **Got** means **have** or **possess** or **obtain** or **secure.** Use it sparingly if at all after **have.** Some authorities justify **have got** for the sake of emphasis, as **I have got my man.** Do not use **got** for **is** or **was; I got hit** for **I was hit** is substandard.

Changes in discourse require revolutionary changes in pronouns and verbs as a rule. **The teacher said, "I wish you would study a little harder so that you may cover the ground and have time for thorough review"** becomes **The teacher said he wished we would study a little harder so that we might cover the ground and have time for thorough review** as a student reports it after class; and as the teacher reports it to his colleagues it becomes **I told them that I wished they would study a little harder so that they might cover the ground and have time for thorough review.** There may be still other readings, but they are unimportant compared to the principles of change involved. Note the first singular **I,** the first plural **we,** the third plural **they;** note the conversion of present tenses into imperfect tenses; note again the consistent change of sequence in both pronouns and verbs.

NUMBER AND PERSON

The English verb is not highly inflected for number and person. It derives both from its subject—a finite verb agrees with its subject in number and person. With the exception of the very irregular verb **to be,** the verb undergoes a change for number and person only in the third person singular present and perfect indicative, as respectively **He, she, it loves** and **He, she, it has loved** (the latter is really a number and person inflection of the verb **have**). The **s** inflection here is the only one that still survives for number and person. All other forms of the verb are alike in the two numbers and the three persons, as **I, we, you, they love** and **I, we, you, they have loved.** This is much simpler than, for instance, the Latin which usually has a different form for each person in both numbers, as **amo** I love, **amas** you love, **amat** he loves, **amamus** we love, **amatis** you love, **amant** they love.

[In the ancient style (also called plain or solemn or elevated or Quaker style) there were, in poetical and religious expression, special inflections in the second person singular and occasionally in the third person singular, such as **Thou art, Thou wast, Thou wert, Thou hast, Thou hadst, Thou dost, Thou didst, Thou shalt, Thou shouldst, Thou wilt, Thou wouldst, Thou canst, Thou couldst, Thou mayst, Thou mightst, Thou oughtst, He doth, He hath, He saith.** The endings st and th are respectively clipped forms of **est** and **eth**, the e being dropped in the more commonly used forms, as well as the apostrophe. But **could'st** and **may'st**, and so forth, are still seen inasmuch as the apostrophe was formerly always used and still remains in plates. In the less commonly used plain forms, the e is as frequently retained as omitted, as **He loveth** and **Thou lovest.** But **doeth** and **doest, sayeth** and **sayest,** and **haveth** and **havest** are archaic forms of archaic forms. In the subjunctive, the plain form may have in the second person singular the same form of the verb as the first person singular, with, of course, the pronoun **thou.**

Singular nouns and pronouns used as subject and connected by **either—or, neither—nor, whether—or,** require a singular predicate, as **Neither Bill nor John is here,** not **Neither Bill nor John are here.** But if these conjunctions connect subjects of different number and person, there is some question in regard to predicate agreement. It is always better to avoid such constructions if they are puzzling. Most authorities contend that the predicate should agree with the last subject in these respects, as **Neither Mary nor we are coming** and **Either he or I am coming** and **Either they or I am coming.** There is much good usage to corroborate this rule. Some say that if one of the subjects is plural, the predicate should invariably be plural, as **Either the clocks or the radio are wrong.** But other authorities argue that the subject in all such instances is to be weighed generally or collectively, and a conclusion reached; thus, in the first example **none** is really the subject of the predicate, in the second **one,** in the third **some one.** So we should say **None of us is coming** (page 55) and **One of us is coming** and **Some one is coming.** The last rule is logical for the reason that we invariably write **He and I are going (Both of us are going)** even though we would never think of saying **He are and I are going.** The problem may always be avoided by using two clauses, as **Either he is coming or I am**

and **Neither Mary is coming nor I** and **Either they are coming
or I am.**

What is to be done about the subordinate predicate in such
expression as **You are he who (has, have) betrayed us?** Usage
says **has** because **who** is in the third person agreeing with its
antecedent **he,** and though **he** is attribute to the second-person
subject **you,** it nevertheless remains a third-person pronoun.
Note, however, that these sentences are correct: **I who am ill
do implore you** and **You who are ill do implore me** and **He
who is ill does implore me,** for **who** is in the first person in
the first example, in the second person in the second, in the
third person in the third, as result of its antecedence.

In **It is I, your uncle, who (advise, advises) you,** first person
I is the antecedent of third-person appositive **uncle.** Though
there is again disagreement in usage, the majority of grammarians feel that **uncle** must be regarded as first person and
that the predicate must, therefore, be **advise.**

Note that **which** in **Our Father which art in heaven** must
be in second person and have **art** for predicate, since its antecedent **Father** is nominative by direct address and thus in second person. Note again **This is one of the most interesting
books that (has, have) ever come to my desk.** The subject of
the subordinate clause is **that;** its antecedent is **books,** not
one, though the latter may seem to be because it is the subject
of the entire expression. But it would be ridiculous to say that
the antecedent of **that** is **one** for the reason that the second
clause completes a comparison, and no comparison is possible
without more than one. The verb should, therefore, be plural
have. Turn the sentence around—**Of all the books that have
come to my desk this one is the most interesting**—and the
number of **have come** becomes clear at once (page 244).

When additions are made to a singular subject by such terms
as **besides, with, along with, together with, as well as, accom-
panied by, but often, commonly, even, for instance, also, in
addition to, divided by, subtracted from, multiplied by,** the
predicate must agree in number and person with that singular
subject; thus, **He as well as I is going** and **Bill together with
Mary and Jim is coming** (pages 191 and 207). **Two and two
is four** is really **Two multiplied by two** or **Two added to two**

is four, the subject two being taken as unit quantity; that is, **The figure or number two becomes four.** This follows in all similar mathematical expressions.

Two singular subjects connected by **and** or **but** and set off in sharp contrast one with the other, require a singular verb for they really belong to separate statements or propositions, as **Hard work, and not mere luck, is the basis of success** and **Interest in the job, but also ambition, is the open secret of promotion.** And when the latter of two subjects is parenthetical or appositive or adversative, the predicate agrees with the first subject only, as **Great Britain, not we, is responsible** and **One, perhaps two, was ready** and **No one, not even the agents of the Federal Bureau of Investigation, knows how many alien propagandists, professional culture carriers, spies, and** *agents provocateurs* **the war unloosed in the United States.**

The subject of the following, like the subjects above, may be apparently plural but is in reality singular: **The secretary and treasurer has run away with our funds.** This means, of course, that two offices are held by one person. It is pointed out on page 90 that if **the** is placed before **treasurer** also, the meaning is that two persons are mentioned, and the predicate in consequence has to be plural, as **The secretary and the treasurer have run away with our funds.**

If two or more singular subjects connected by **and** are specifically emphasized by the aggregating adjectives **each, every, no,** they are taken as separate and individual, and attract thus a singular predicate, as **Every man and every woman in the room was thrilled** and **About that no word and no thought is to be entertained.**

A collective-noun subject (page 38) that indicates an aggregate, that is, a group taken as a whole or a unity, takes a singular subject, as **The audience was large.** But if separate individuals in such group are indicated by the collective noun, it takes a plural predicate, as **The audience were strongly in disagreement.** Fractions follow this rule of collective nouns. Generally, a fraction stands as a unity and takes thus a singular predicate, as **Two-thirds of the work is done.** But the idea of individual plurality may be conveyed by a fraction, and a plural predicate be thus required, as **Three-fourths of the papers are scattered around the floor.**

A singular-noun subject, modified by two or more adjectives that give it different parts or aspects or meanings or varieties, may as subject take a plural predicate, as **Renaissance and modern art represent widely different ideas.** On the other hand, when two or more subjects pertain to one person or thing, or when they denote a single idea or unity, they take a singular predicate, as **The essayist and poet was awarded the prize** and **Her love and affection and devotion remains the same.** We say **The long and the short of it is** because the two subjects **long** and **short** mean conclusion or result. We say **Not enjoyment and not sorrow is our destined end or way** because the subject is equivalent to **Neither enjoyment nor sorrow,** and two singular subjects connected by **neither—nor** or **either—or** take a singular predicate (page 156).

If a compound subject is divided so that the predicate follows one and precedes the other, it is made to agree with the first in person and number, as **The men were waiting, and the foreman too.** But this construction is not considered satisfactory by some, who feel that whatever the form of verb required in the second part—whether changed or not—it must be supplied; thus, a better reading is **The men were waiting, and the foreman was too.** (This rule is applied generally to a change of tenses that are not of the same formation, as explained on page 152.)

Impersonal and singular **it** used as subject requires a singular predicate, no matter whether its attribute is plural or singular, as **It *is* the children who demand our first attentions.**

When a predicate precedes its subject in an expression beginning with an introductory word like **such** or **there,** or with an introductory phrase, care must be exercised to adjust its number, as **Such were the ups and downs of our visit** and **There have been a boy and a girl here to see you** and **Near the door are a broom and a shovel.** The predicate does not take its number from the first of a series of subjects following it, though there is some authority for this. Say **There were food to spare and dollars to share,** not **There was food to spare and dollars to share.** Note also **There have been invited one clergyman and two lawyers** and **His chariot were the swans and the ripples of the lake** and **Death is the wages of sin** (see below).

If a compound subject consists of a singular noun and a
plural noun, the latter should be placed next to the predicate,
as **The president and the club members were most cordial.**
Make sure, however, as to whether the plural immediately
preceding the predicate is a part of the subject. In **One of the
fellows were here,** for instance, the plural **were** is attracted by
fellows which is not part of the subject but is object of the
preposition **of.** The predicate should be **was.** This is **ca**lled the
error of ear or of proximity. Similar plural attraction occurs
sometimes when a singular subject is modified by a plural noun
used as adjective, as **Six months' interest is due.** The plural
possessive form **months'** suggests **are** to the ear, which would
be wrong since **months'** merely modifies.

If a subject is plural in form but singular in meaning, its
predicate should be singular (page 34), as *Gulliver's Travels*
was written by Jonathan Swift and **News is scarce today. The
wages of sin is death** is a biblical exception. Still, wages is
used collectively in the sense of result or price, and the singular **death,** the dominant word of the sentence, is really the
subject but is placed at the end for stylistic reasons. This
rule is extended to cover the following: Two or more nouns
used as subject indicating one or singleness of meaning take
a singular verb, as **Jones, Smith, Brown and Company is having a closing-out sale,** that is, **The firm of Jones, Smith, Brown,
and Company is having a closing-out sale.**

The interrogative pronoun, used as subject, takes as a rule
a predicate in the third person singular, as **Who is going.** But
if a noun or pronoun follows the predicate in the same construction, the predicate takes the number and person of the
nominative following it, as **Who is she, Who are you, Which
are the samples, What were they.** In these constructions, the
interrogative pronoun is really the attribute complement placed
before the verb rather than after it.

The most common violation of number and person in the
predicate is probably the use of **He or She** or **It don't** for **He
or She** or **It doesn't.** This error in the third person singular,
present indicative of the negative conjugation is winked at by
some authorities these days, probably because its sheer mo-
mentum discourages all hope of reform. In the affirmative conjugation the mistake of using **do** instead of **does** is rarely made
except by children and provincials—**He or She** or **It does is**

used even by those who do not speak particularly good English. Do not use **He don't** or **She don't** or **It don't,** any more than you would use **He haven't** for **He hasn't** or **He aren't** for **He isn't.**

Ain't is an illiterate form for **am not, is not, are not, have not.** It is and always has been regarded as such wherever English speech has been attempted.

A single infinitive or prepositional phrase or a single clause used as subject of a sentence takes a third person singular predicate; but two or more phrases or clauses so used require a plural verb, as **To see is to believe** and **To see and to believe are synonymous** and **That you have broken the law and that you have done so many times before are sufficient to condemn you.**

For such verb contractions as **I'd, they'll, Mary's, Bill'd** see page 70. The placement of the apostrophe is in some contractions conventional rather than strictly logical or correct. In **sha'n't,** for instance, the omission of **ll** is indicated by the first apostrophe, of **o** by the second, but **shan't** is the customary writing. Such contractions are at best conversational merely; they should be used sparingly in formal writing, except in those instances in which verbatim conversation or dialect is reported.

Chapter Five

ADVERB

DEFINITION AND CLASSIFICATION

An adverb is a word or a term used to modify the meaning of a verb, an adjective, or another adverb; that is, the adverb is an adjunct of the verb, the adjective, and the adverb itself, as **She sang** *beautifully* and **Her hat was** *really* **unusual** and **He studied** *very* **hard.** The adverb may likewise modify a phrase, as **constantly on guard** and **always in trouble.** In the main the adverb, like the adjective, may condense or economize expression by doing the work of a phrase in much of its usage, as **He lived here formerly** for **He lived at this place in a former time, He did it grandly** for **He did it in a grand manner, He praised him highly** for **He praised him to a high degree.**

Note that certain verbs require adverbs. **Act, behave, comport, conduct, operate,** for instance, are really neutral verbs, on-the-fence verbs, that are pushed one way or the other by adverbial modification. They denote neither good nor bad action; so we say **act well, behave badly, comport becomingly, conduct wisely, operate efficiently.**

The adverb is the offending term (if there is offense) in the split infinitive, as **to honestly believe** for **honestly to believe** or **to believe honestly** (page 246).

The relation of an adverb to a verb is like that of an adjective to a noun, that is, it limits or qualifies its meaning, directs it, specializes it, makes it more pictorial, indicates action as stronger or weaker. Like the adjective again, the adverb is derived from other parts of speech, very often by means of prefixing and suffixing, principally the latter through the addition of ly to adjective forms (**ly** is a clipped form of **like,** as **womanlike** and **womanly**). But, as pointed out on page 96, ly endings do not always signify adverbs; many **ly** words are used adjectively as well as adverbially; thus, **Step lively** and **They are a lively couple, She spoke kindly to him** and **She is a kindly person.**

It is misleading and too generalizing to say that adverbs are formed by adding **ly** to adjectives, though this old but untrustworthy definition is still frequently heard. If it were strictly true, then we should have to use such awkward and inconvenient forms as **godlily** and **kindlily and manlily** and **womanlily**. These are logical and correct as forms but they are rarely used, and context very often has to decide for us whether an **ly** form is to be construed as adjective or as adverb.

The addition of **ly** to an adjective form to make an adverb sometimes has no influence whatever upon the root; it is an addition merely, as **austerely, entirely, exclusively, grandly, grimly, lonely, merely, sincerely, wisely**. Sometimes, especially if the adjective already carries a suffix ending with **e**, the final **e** is dropped, as **ably, doubly, feebly, gently, humbly, idly, nimbly, nobly, simply, singly, subtly, trebly**. But note **agilely, completely, deliberately, facilely, fertilely, futilely, hostilely, juvenilely, servilely, solely, subtilely, supplely** (otherwise it would invite confusion with **supply**). The old spelling rules may be helpful with forms such as these. Note especially **due** and **true**, adverbs of which become **duly** and **truly**. They may likewise be helpful in the suffixing of **full**, as **gleefully** and **hopefully**. But observe **blue** and **bluely, foul** and **foully, whole** and **wholly**. Your only safe guide is the dictionary, in the introduction of which spelling rules are usually explained.

Words bearing **like** as suffix are, as a rule, adjectives, and **like** forms solid compounds unless the root ends with **l** or **ll**; thus, **childlike** and **manlike**, but **girl-like** and **shell-like**. But do not add **like** loosely to an expression in modification of the whole or as the equivalent of **somewhat or to a degree**, or some other word or phrase. Use **He is musical in a way** and **She was somewhat angry**, not **He is musical like** and **She was angry like**. Even such expressions as **It is conical like** and **She is gnomish like** cannot be justified, though they are sometimes used. **Conical** is an adjective meaning like a cone, and **gnomish** is an adjective meaning like a gnome; thus, **like** is superfluous because repetitive. Say **It is like a cone** or **conelike** and **She is like a gnome** or **gnomelike**, preferably the former in each example.

Like has been called one of the most versatile words in the language, from the point of view of grammatical use. It is a noun in **Like begets like**; it may be regarded as a pronoun in **I never saw the like;** it is an adjective in **Like environment begets like habit;** it is a verb in **I like him;** it is an adverb in the colloquial **They played like mad;** it is a preposition in **He looks like her;** it is a conjunction in the colloquial **He will do it as like** (preferably **likely**) **as not** and in **He took to water like a duck** (page 209); it is an interjection in the matching game in which **"Like!"** is called rapidly by the players.

The **s** in the adverbs **awares** and **needs** is an old suffix, and it is still heard if not written in **once** and **thrice** and **twice.** The **om** is similarly a suffix in **seldom** and **whilom.** **Abaft, abed, abeam, aboard, along, before, beyond** illustrate adverb formation by means of prefix; **inwardly, repeatedly, untowardly,** by means of both prefix and suffix; **likewise, meanwhile, straightaway, thereto,** by means of root combinations.

There are, again, many words that are wrenched out of their ordinary or normal functioning as other parts of speech to serve as adverbs; thus, in **I went home,** the noun **home** may be construed as an adverb of direction modifying **went** or as object of the understood preposition **to** or **toward;** in **I don't care a cent,** a **cent** may be construed as phrasal adverbs of manner modifying **care.** Though some authorities use these words as direct objects, some as objects of **for** or **to the extent of** understood, they nevertheless indicate manner or method strictly and are thus adverbial in nature. In **Beauty is only skin deep,** the noun **skin** may be construed as an adverb of degree modifying **deep;** in **Bang went the door** and **Whizz went the arrow, Bang** and **Whizz** are adverbs of manner modifying their respective verbs; in **I am somewhat sleepy,** somewhat is an adverb of degree modifying **sleepy;** in **I am none the worse for your carelessness, none** is an adverb of degree modifying the article **the** which in turn modifies the predicate adjective **worse.**

Some words, generally regarded as pure adverbs, are frequently used as adjuncts of nouns and pronouns, as **above, altogether, below, chiefly, deep, early, entirely, especially, even, hard, hardly, likewise, long, loud, merely, mostly, near, never, not, only, particularly, partly, pretty, quick, really, scarcely, simply, solely, then, too, well;** some of these are the same whether used as adjectives or as adverbs; some have both adjective and adverb forms that are used interchangeably, namely, **deep** and **deeply, near** and **nearly, quick** and **quickly.**

But care must be exercised not to make mistakes in this confusing arrangement of the language. You cannot, for instance, say **a softly answer** and **He spoke soft** for **a soft answer** and **He spoke softly**; but you may say **a deep drink** and **I shall drink deep**, and **a long journey** and **I waited long**, and **an early hour** and **He came early**.

There may be a difference in meaning, too, between one form of adverb and another. If you say **hard earned** you mean laboriously earned; if you say **hardly earned** you mean scarcely or barely earned. If you say **Hardly a man is now alive**, you mean few men; **hardly** is an adjective modifying **man**, not an adverb modifying **a**. In **Not enjoyment and not sorrow is our destined end or way**, **not** in each instance is an adjective adjunct modifying **enjoyment** and **sorrow** respectively. In such colloquialisms as **never a one, never the day, never a word, not a bit, not a cent**, the initial word is without adverbial nature and is, again, an adjective adjunct modifying the following noun or pronoun. The use of **then** as an adjective, as in **The then president ruled otherwise**, is by some authorities regarded as an impropriety; but it is nevertheless so used by the best speakers and writers, chiefly because it has no substitute that is not longer and more or less bungling— **the president at the time**.

A **simple adverb** is one consisting of a single word, as **frankly, here, now, when**.

A **compound** or **derived adverb** is one made up of two or more words in a solid compound, as **elsewhere, herein, hereto, herewith, notwithstanding, thereupon, wherever, wheresoever**. Writers should be cautioned against using most adverbs of this type in all except the most formal writing; they are generally considered very stilted.

A **phrasal adverb** is a group of two or more words idiomatically used as a unit adverb, as **arm in arm, between times, here and there, from here, from where, from there, for long, at once, on high, for a while, in there, in the meantime, in the meanwhile**. Note that in such unit adverbial phrases the adverb is frequently used substantively as object of a preposition. And adverbs, like other parts of speech, are used as nouns in other ways, as **a firm no, a hesitating yes, Onward is the word, everlasting nay, eternal yea**. **Time** and **meantime** are preferable

in substantive uses to **while** and **meanwhile.** Use **He stayed for
a time** rather than **for a while,** and **Meanwhile** or **In the
meantime he ate his luncheon** rather than **In the meanwhile.**
But **betimes,** meaning early or in good time, is a solid but
archaic adverb, as **He came betimes;** and **between times** (two
words) is, again, preferable to **between while** or **between
whiles.**

An **adverb of affirmation,** as the name implies, is one that
indicates assent or approval, as **absolutely, amen, certainly,
doubtless, indeed, indubitably, quite, really, surely, truly, un-
doubtedly, verily, yes,** and such expressions as **of a truth, yes
indeed, so be it, as you say, by all means,** and (slang) **I'll say,
You said it, Take it from me.** Inasmuch as such adverbial
forms modify or influence whole expressions rather than single
words, they are sometimes called **independent** or **absolute** or
exclamatory adverbs. In **Certainly he is right** and **Verily I say
unto you, Certainly** and **Verily** are affirmative adverbs; they
are, as a matter of fact, little more than introductory par-
ticles. In **Away, villain** and **Forward, men,** **Away** and **Forward**
are exclamatory adverbs. In **Frankly, I don't know** and **Really,
you are too subtle for me, Frankly** and **Really** are absolute or
independent adverbs. **Also, likewise, nevertheless, probably,
therefore** may or may not be used as affirmative adverbs, may
or may not be used independently. Such affirmative adverbs as
yes, certainly, quite, surely, and such negative adverbs as **no,
never, not at all** are sometimes called responsives (page 174).

An **adverb of cause or reason** is one that indicates the
answer to such questions as why, on what account, for what
purpose. The principal adverbs under this classification are
**because, consequently, hence, then, thence, therefore, thus,
wherefore.** Most adverbs of cause are used to establish conjunctive relationships (page 201); some are used as adverbs
of place or direction. **Hence,** for instance, in **He has gone
hence** is an adverb of direction; in **It is raining; hence, I shall
remain at home,** it is an adverb of reason.

Do not use the words **reason** and **because** in the same related sequence, for they have the same meaning and significance. To say **The reason is because** is very much the same
as saying **The reason is reason** or **Because is because.** Say **The
reason for his illness is exposure,** not **The reason for his illness
is because he was exposed;** say **The reason for his absence is**

that he is out of town, not The reason for his absence is because he is out of town; say The reason for his dismissal is inefficiency, not Because he was inefficient is the reason why he was dismissed. Because (page 208) may be followed by of, never by why; reason may be followed by for and by why though the latter—reason why—is idiomatic rather than entirely logical.

An **adverb of degree** indicates greater or less intensity of action or quality of action, that is, it answers the question how much, how little, is it more or is it less, in what degree. The principal adverbs of degree are **all, almost, altogether, as, barely, besides, but** (only), **chiefly, clear, completely, enough, entirely, equally, even, ever so, exceedingly, excessively, extravagantly, extremely, far, full, fully, generally, greatly, hardly, how, however, howsoever, immeasurably, inconceivably, infinitely, intolerably, little, mainly, merely, much, more, most, nearly, needs, no, none, only, partially, partly, perfectly, principally, quite, rather, really, scarcely, so, some, stark, sure, surely, sufficiently, the, too, very, wholly.** Some of these are used also as adverbs of manner (see below); they are adverbs of degree when used in accordance with the definition above. Some, such as **all, altogether, entirely,** are called **completing adverbs;** some, such as **little, mainly, much,** are called **partitive adverbs;** some, such as **barely, no, only,** are called **subtractive adverbs. Any** as an adverb of degree is a questionable usage, as in I wasn't hurt any. In this use it means at all or to any degree.

As (pages 201 and 206) is an adverb of degree in He is as awkward as any one can possibly be.

Even, as adverb of degree, is chiefly an intensifying particle; it functions also as an adjective meaning level, and as a verb meaning to make level or regular.

Ever so should be kept distinct from **never so** as an intensifying adverb of degree, as I am ever so cold and Be it ever so humble. But note that in time statements **never so** is correct, as I was never so cold and My spirit was never so humble as it is now (see below).

While the superlative **most** is used as an adverb in the formation of the third degree of comparison, it is, nevertheless, an adjective in general usage. It should not be used outside its superlative function for the adverb **almost** to modify adjectives and adverbs. And it should not be used to modify verbs directly. **This pail is most full** and **I am most finished** are incorrect; use, rather, **This pail is almost full** and **I am almost finished**. If, however, the former is used comparatively, that is, if the meaning is that this pail compared with others is more nearly filled than the others, then **most full** would not be wrong though **fullest** would be preferable. But if **pail** is considered as the only one under consideration, **full** must be modified by the adverb **almost.**

Near is a verb, a preposition, an adjective, and an adverb (of place principally); **nearly** is an adverb of degree. The latter means almost, narrowly, at no great distance, within a little; the former, as adverb, means close or close to. Use them only with these meanings, as **I am nearly done, I was nearly caught, He is nearly there, We have nearly moved him.** But use **I came near** (close to) **falling,** not **I came nearly falling;** use **He drove near,** not **He drove nearly;** use **We can nearly see the house,** not **We can near see the house.** Do not use the expression **nowhere near** or **nowhere like** for **not nearly;** nowhere is an adverb of place, not degree. **Anywhere near** and **somewhere near,** and **anywhere like** and **somewhere like** are similarly incorrect.

Needs, as an adverb of degree, means necessarily, as **He needs must go.** It is a noun, of course, in **His needs are few,** and a verb in **He needs only a little.**

No, as an adjective, is equivalent to **none;** as an adverb of degree (and of negation) it means **not,** that is, no degree. As the latter, it is used before comparatives, as **no more, no less** and **no earlier, no later.** In direct modification of verbs, **no** is never used but **not is.** It is thus wrong to say **whether or no** unless the implied or understood part after **no** includes a noun for it to modify, as in **whether he is an actor or no** (actor). But in **whether he is going or not,** the verb **going** is understood after the expression **whether or not; no** would, therefore, be wrong in place of **not,** for **no** as an adjective cannot modify a verb and as an adverb it usually precedes a comparative.

None has been explained as an adjective (page 87) and as a pronoun (page 55). It is used as an adverb of degree in such expression as **He is none the worse for the experience.** Used in direct modification of a verb, **none,** like **nothing,** is now archaic, as **He hath none requited us.**

Plenty is not an adverb; it is preferably used as a noun; it may be used as an adjective. Do not use it as an adverb of degree instead of **very. He is plenty angry** is substandard usage (page 84).

Rather, as adverb of degree, is not preceded by **more** or **most.** Like the adjective **preferable,** it is not compared. Do not use **kind of** or **sort of** for **rather,** as in the substandard **I am kind of tired** and **He is sort of angry** for **rather tired** and **rather angry** respectively.

Real is an adjective and a noun; **really** is an adverb of degree and, as pointed out above, sometimes an adjective. Do not confuse the two. **Real gold, real man, real friendship** are correct; **real fine, real clear, real good** are incorrect. **Really** or **very** should be used in the last three examples. In the expression **Is it really you, really** is used as an adjective with the significance of an intensifying reflexive pronoun—**Is it you yourself**—or of the adjective phrase **in reality.** In **The real is all that interests me, real** is an abstract noun.

Older grammars customarily stated that the adverbs of degree **so, too, very** are preferably used to modify adjectives and adverbs, not verbs directly. The authority of usage has modified this, so that **I was so surprised** and **I was too hurt** and **I was very amused** are quite as acceptable as **I was so happily surprised** and **I was too seriously hurt** and **I was very much amused.**

Some should be used sparingly, if at all, to modify a numeral adjective or a verb directly. Use **About thirty were present,** not **Some thirty were present.** Use **She wept a little** or **She wept tragically,** not **She wept some.**

That and **this** should not be used for **so** as adverbs of degree. Though **that much** and **this high, that slow** and **this quick,** and other expressions like them, are commonly heard in colloquial usage, they are not grammatically correct. And even the most radical moderns would not think of using the plural forms of **that** and **this** to modify adverbs—those much and these high (page 102).

The use of **barely, hardly, merely, only, scarcely, but** meaning **only,** and other partitives, in the same construction with a negative, such as **no** or **not,** constitutes the double negative error (page 240), for these adverbs indicate negation; thus, **I haven't scarcely accomplished anything** and **He hasn't only (or but) one** are substandard. The correction of such expressions is usually made by omitting the negative, and retaining the partitive adverb, as **I have accomplished scarcely anything** and **He has only (or but) one.** But negatives and such partitives as these may be used in the same sentence provided they do not clash in modification, that is, provided each modifies a different term, as **I need hardly tell you that you barely escaped** and **I only know that he has hardly a penny to his name,** just as pure negatives may be.

Like other modifiers, adverbs should be placed as closely as possible to the words they modify. Otherwise misunderstanding is certain to result. Among **Having nearly lost a pint of blood, John fainted** and **Having lost nearly a pint of blood, John fainted** and **Having lost a pint of blood, John nearly fainted,** it is evident that there is a difference of meaning caused by placement of the word **nearly,** usually an adverb of degree. The first means that he did not lose a pint of blood but almost did, and fear or shock caused him to faint; the second means that he fainted because he lost almost a pint of blood; the third means that, having lost a full pint of blood, he almost fainted.

Actually, almost, barely, hardly, merely, nearly, only, quite, really, scarcely are the words (usually adverbs) that probably cause ambiguity or vagueness most frequently as a result of misplacement. Note the difference between **I actually was there** and **I was actually there,** between **She merely whispered a word to me** and **She whispered merely a word to me,** between **I really want you to play** and **I want you really to play;** and among **Only John asked me to go with him, John only asked me to go with him, John asked only me to go with him, John asked me only to go with him, John asked me to go only with him, John asked me to go with him only.** In at least two of the last group, **only** is necessarily ambiguous; that is, it may modify the word before it or the word after it, and there is no correction possible except by way of rephrasing or rewording. For instance, in **John only asked me to go with him**, **only** may be an adjective modifying **John** or an adverb modifying **asked**. A term that thus "squints at" or "flirts with" two possible bases of modification, forms what is called in grammar a squinting construction. Inasmuch as it is invariably ambiguous, it is, of course, to be avoided. This construction occurs also with phrases and clauses (page 245) as well as with single words, usually adverbs, as **The singer whom the audience applauded enthusiastically took his curtain calls** and **Reading in many fields improves our outlook** and **Certain boys and girls I know would enjoy the game.**

It has already been pointed out (page 92) that **the** is an adverb of degree in such comparative phrases as **the more the merrier** and **the higher the clearer.** Similarly, in the colloquial expression **easy come, easy go, easy,** customarily an adjective, may be regarded as an adverb of degree.

An **adverb of direction** indicates direction toward or from, to which place or from which place. It is sometimes included under the classification of adverb of place (page 175). The adverbs **above, back, backwards, below, down, downwards, forth, forwards, hence, hither, hitherwards, in, inwards, on, onwards, out, outwards, thence, thither, thitherwards, up, upwards, whence, whither, yonder** are the principal adverbs of direction. Such colloquial adverb phrases as **up there, down there, in here, back and forth, to and fro, in and out, up and down, inside out** are directive adverbial phrases. But do not use **that there** and **this here** as adverbial phrases of direction, for **this, that, these, those** are demonstrative adjectives or pronouns and they may not modify adverbs (page 102).

The suffix **wards** always denotes adverb form; the suffix **ward,** either adjective or adverb; thus, **an upward trend** and **He looked upwards** or **upward.** The adjective may either precede or follow the noun, as **a forward look** or **a look forward,** not **a forwards look,** preferably not **a look forwards.** Euphony is the only deciding factor as to the use of the adverb ending with **ward** or **wards.**

If you feel compelled to use the obsolescent forms **hence, thence, whence,** do not use **from** before them, for it is contained in them, **hence** meaning from here, **thence** from there,

whence from where. **He went from Paris to Lyons and thence to Marseilles** is correct, rather than **He went from Paris to Lyons and from thence to Marseilles.**

An **adverb of doubt** indicates hesitation or indecision or vacillation, as **haply, however, maybe, nevertheless, notwithstanding, peradventure, perchance, perhaps, possibly, probably,** and the adverbial unit phrases **as yet, better or worse, whether or no, yes and no.** The adverbs **well** and **why,** used at the beginning of an expression to indicate indecision or doubt, belong in this classification of adverbs. They are also sometimes called independent or introductory adverbs. Adverbs of doubt are sometimes called **alternative adverbs.**

An **adverb of manner** indicates manner of action or state or quality, the manner of stating it, and thus the answer to the question how or in what way or by what method. The numerous adverbs formed by adding **ly** to adjectives belong under this heading, as **beautifully, foolishly, justly, quickly, rapidly,** as do also, as a rule, such words as **across, anyway, apart, asunder, else** (meaning in a different manner), **generally, how, however, howsoever, like, likewise, namely, necessarily, otherwise, particularly, so, somehow, thus, together, well,** and such phrases as **arm in arm, hand in hand, face to face, head over heels, one by one.** This is by far the most comprehensive classification of adverbs, but adverbs of manner offer probably least difficulty in usage and thus least temptation to error.

How is sometimes wrongly used for **that, in which,** or **by which,** and so on, as in such an incorrect expression as **I know of no rule how it may be done** which should, of course, read **I know of no rule by which** or **under which it may be done.**

Well is likewise troublesome. In **He did it well,** for instance, **well** is an adverb of manner modifying **did.** In **She is not a well woman, well** is an adjective modifying **woman. Good** and **well** are frequently confused. The former is an adjective principally; the latter, an adverb principally; thus, you say **He plays well** and **His playing is good, He recited well** and **His recitation was good.** But you also say **All's well** and **That is well and good** in both of which **well** is a predicate adjective. The only guidance for the avoidance of such errors as **He played good** and **His recitation was well** is that pointed out on page 83: Decide whether the word is used predicatively—to describe or explain the subject—or adverbially—to modify action expressed by a verb; if the former, use **good**; if the latter, **well.**

The adverb and the adverbial phrase may be used after an intransitive verb as adverb complement, as **The book is here** and **The paper is there** and **Every boy is in his place** (page 175). But these are special constructions, so named because grammarians have not known how otherwise to construe them. As a rule, adverbs do not stand after copulative verbs as complements. It has been explained on page 83 that in **She looks bad, bad** is predicate adjective; that in **She looks badly, badly** is an adverb modifying **looks,** the sentence meaning probably that in looking for something that is lost she looks for it unthoroughly. Distinction between the two constructions must be clearly made if you are to avoid one of the most substandard usages in the language.

Note **He is sure to come** in which **sure** is predicate adjective, and **He will surely come** in which **surely** is an adverb of degree modifying **will come. Sure** is primarily an adjective; though like **quick,** it may be an adverb. But it is used in a slang or illiterate way when it is made to do service for the pure adverb **surely.** The correct answer to such questions as **Will you do it** and **Are you going** is **surely,** not **sure,** for the answer is an adverb pertaining to **will do** and **are going.** Reserve **sure** for adjective uses, as **I am sure, He is sure of himself** and **He is the surest person I know.**

An **adverb of negation** indicates denial, as **nay, no, not, nowise, never.** The last, though usually classed as an adverb of time, is, however, used as pure negative in such expressions as **He was never the lad to say no** and **Never breathe it to a soul,** in which **never** is really an emphatic **not** though it may literally denote an element of time. Like **yes, no** may imply or stand for a complete statement, as **Are you going? No,** in which **No** stands for **I am not,** and **Yes** would stand for **I am.** Neither **yes** nor **no** is used in direct relation with a verb, therefore, but rather as substitute for a complete statement. You do not say **I will yes go** and **I will no go** but **I will go** and **I will not go.**

It has been seen above that both of these adverbs may be used in alternative phrases, as **whether or no** and **yes or (and) no.** Standing at the beginning of a statement, **yes** and **no** are usually unattached as far as modification is concerned, and are thus independent or absolute or introductory adverbs. They are sometimes called **responsives** (page 166), and this defines their chief use. The phrases **not at all** and **in vain** and **by no means** are classifiable here as negative adverb phrases. It has been pointed out on pages 170 and 240 that two negatives used in the same construction constitute a double negative, and, considered from a strictly grammatical viewpoint, supposedly cancel each other out, the result being an unintended affirmative. Semantically, of course, this conclusion is absurd. Both the speaker and the auditor of **I haven't done nothing** know perfectly well that the speaker means **I have done nothing,** just as **Frank won't never do it** implies Frank **will never do it.** That the so-called double negative should not be used in English is clear; the objection to it, however, lies in the fact that it is redundant. Note, however, that two negatives used in consecutive constructions may be used to cancel negation and make a stronger affirmation; thus, **There was no student who was not in his seat** is an emphatic way of saying **Every student was in his seat** (page 170). And two negatives may even be used in the same construction for the sake of intensifying or distinguishing an expression, as **He is not unkindly** for the colorless **He is kindly,** and **Not only did he not come but he sent no regrets** for **He neither came nor sent regrets.** This use of the double negative is akin to the figure of speech called **litotes** or **miosis (meiosis)** which is deliberate understatement for the sake of the emphasis of restraint or for the sake of mollifying a harsh positive. Macaulay's **litotes** in his essay on Milton is still the perfect example: "The Puritan has been rescued by no common deliverer from the grasp of no common foe."

As previously explained (page 168) the negative adjective **no** must not be used for the negative adverb **not** in relation to a verb, especially a participle. **Will you play or not (play)** is correct. **Will you play or no (play)** is incorrect. The final negatives are really unnecessary in such yes-and-no constructions as these. The use of **no** in direct modification of a verb is one of the most persistent errors made by a child beginning to talk and by a foreigner taking up the study of English, as **I no understand** and **I no can do.**

An **adverb of number** indicates order or position in place of
time; it is formed very often by the addition of **ly** to ordinals,
as **secondly, thirdly, tenthly,** and it is thus sometimes called a
numeral adverb. Such adverbs are rapidly becoming archaic,
for while both ordinals and cardinals are nouns and adjectives,
they may also be used adverbially. In **He stood fifteenth in
line, fifteenth** is not an adverb but a predicate noun or adjective—**He stood fifteenth man in line.** You would not, however,
say **He ran fifteenthly** but **He ran fifteenth** in which **fifteenth**
is properly construed as adverbial. Moreover, **ly** does not
blend with some ordinals, as, for instance, **seventhly** and
eleventhly and **fifteenthly.** Euphony is made the deciding factor between adjective and adverb in such instances. Note that
firstly is never used, **first** being both adjective and adverb.

An **adverb of place** or **location** indicates position in or at
which, and answers the question where, or in (or at) what
place. These are the most commonly used adverbs of place:
about, anywhere, around, before, behind, elsewhere, first (see
above), **everywhere, foremost, here, hereabout, hereat, hereto,
inside, nowhere, near, on, outside, secondly** (and so on),
**somewhere, there, thereabout, thereat, thereto, therewith, top-
most, upon, where, whereabouts, whereat, wherever, wheresoever, whereto, within, without.** Such locative adverb phrases
as **in back, in front, here and there, in there, in here, at rest**
likewise belong in this category.

The distinction between adverbs of direction and adverbs of
place is not important (see above); they are frequently
grouped together. But the former, as a rule, denote some
degree of motion; the latter, fixed position. **Hither, thither,
whither** are for this reason regarded by some authorities more
correctly used with verbs of motion, and **here, there, where**
with verbs of state or condition. But this rule is as often
violated as observed, even by the best speakers and writers.
While **from** is sometimes required after **where,** as in **Where
does he come from,** at rarely is. Do not say **Where is he at**
for **Where is he; at** is repetitive and superfluous (page 195).
But with **from, where** takes on substantive quality, standing
for **what place.**

Do not add **s** to **anyway, anywhere, everywhere, nowhere,
somewhere; anyways, anywheres,** and so on, are illiterate

forms. Do not write **any place, every place, no place, some place** as single words, and do not use them as substitutes, respectively, for **anywhere, everywhere, nowhere, somewhere. Any** modifies **place; in any place** is equivalent to **anywhere.** Use **I cannot find my slippers anywhere** or **in any place** (preferably the former), not **I cannot find my slippers anyplace** or **anywheres.** This instruction applies, of course, to the other forms above mentioned.

Anywise, endwise, nowise, somewise are preferred by some authorities to **anyway, endway, noway, someway.** None of these four forms should be spelled and pronounced with final **s,** though in provincial and colloquial usage this error is frequently made. The **how** forms—**anyhow, nohow, everyhow, somehow**—especially the second and the third, are not recommended though they are frequently heard and sometimes seen. Adverbs ending with **way** or **ways** are usually regarded as adverbs of place; with **wise,** as adverbs of manner. But the two suffixes are used more or less interchangeably (see **ward**).

Do not use **where** loosely for its more precise phrase equivalent, as **This is a situation where expenditure pays** or **He read a paper where he made the problem clear.** In neither of these statements is place as represented by **where** representative of the meaning. They should be **This is a situation in which expenditure pays** and **He read a paper in which** or **by which** or **through which he made the problem clear.** Do not use **where** superfluously, as **I see by the paper where they have had a fire in Bridgeport** and **I read by the timetable where there is a train at nine.** These are awkward and illiterate provincialisms for **The paper reports that there has been a fire in Bridgeport** and **There is a nine o'clock train listed in the timetable. Where** is used wrongly again as the initial word in a definition unless, of course, the definition calls for pointing out place or location. It is colloquial to say **A railway junction is where lines meet or cross** but it is preferable to say **A railway junction is a place where lines meet or cross,** for here **place** is definitely required by the definition and **where,** meaning **at which,** is an adverb of place. But it is incorrect to say **A quandary is where you are in doubt or perplexity,** for this gives to **quandary** a place value whereas it is a state or condition of mind. There is, in other words, nothing of "whereness" in **quandary;** it means, rather, mental doubt or perplexity.

There, frequently used as an adverb of place, is quite as frequently used as an expletive or introductory adverb without any relation whatever to other words in an expression, as **There is a tide in the affairs of men.** In its use as an introductory word, **there** is similar to **it** (page 51) in the same capacity. But unlike **it** similarly placed, **there** is not taken as subject of the verb that follows. On the contrary, the subject of a sentence introduced by **there** tends to follow the verb, and confusion of number thus sometimes results. **There** sounds like a singular, but it, of course, has no number. Say **There are a lady and a gentleman in the room,** not **There is a lady and a gentleman in the room.** While this introductory adverb is regarded as a weak beginning, it has the virtue of postponing to the latter part of a statement the more important elements, and thus builds for periodic form (page 256) or emphatic placement of the chief idea. But as between such colloquial expressions as **There is no one going** and **No one is going,** the latter (and shorter) is considered the better. **There** should be used sparingly, if at all, as the first word in a formal essay or story or news item or other piece of writing.

About should be used to mean approximately or near, and **around** to mean on all sides, here and there, in circumference; thus, **about three o'clock** is preferable to **around three o'clock** as is **around the block** to **about the block. I have about a dollar in my pocket** and **I am about done** and **Please pass them around** are correct; **I have around a dollar in my pocket** and **Please pass them about** are, strictly speaking, incorrect. In the sense of **at random,** these two adverbs are used interchangeably, as **Let's walk around** or **about.** Do not correlate **or** with **about** or **around.** In the following incorrect sentence, for instance, **about** means approximately, and **or** repeats the idea: **I am about (around) six or seven dollars in debt.** Say, rather, **I am about seven dollars in debt** or **I am six or seven dollars in debt** (page 194).

In a usage now obsolescent, if not archaic, adverbs of direction and place were sometimes considered to stand for verbs, the verbs themselves being omitted, as **Let's away** and **I'll in** and **I'll out.** But in these usages, which were sometimes poetical and sometimes substandard, the verb must be clearly and easily understood, as **Let us go away, I will go in, I will go out.** The adverb should not be used substantively in such expressions; **I want in** is a substandard short cut for **I want to come** or **get in.**

An **adverb of time** indicates date, duration, repetition, frequency, and answers the questions when, at what time, how long, how soon, how often, at what intervals, and the like. Some adverbs are used of present time, as **immediately, instantly, now, nowadays, presently, today, tonight, yet;** some are used of past time, as **ago, already, anciently, erstwhile, heretofore, hitherto, lately, recently, since, yesterday;** some are used of future time, as **hereafter, henceforth, soon, to-morrow,** and the adverb phrases **at length, by and by, for evermore;** some are used of time as **during** or repeated or continuous, as **again, always, continually, continuously, daily, eternally, ever, forever, frequently, monthly, never, occasionally, often, once, perpetually, quarterly, rarely, seldom, sometimes, twice, thrice, weekly, while, yearly,** and the adverb phrases **at times, now and then, off and on.** Some adverbs of time do all or none of these things, that is, they show relationships of time as between or among periods or events, as **after, before, early, late, meanwhile, meantime, seasonably, then, till, until, when, while,** and the adverb phrases **after all, at last, at length, in general, in particular, in short, since then, till now.**

Mistakes are sometimes made in the use of **while** and **when.** Remember that **while** indicates duration, that **when** indicates a fixed or stated period of time. If you are in doubt as to whether you should use **when** or **while** in a sentence, test the construction by substituting **during** or a **during**-phrase. If it works, use **while;** thus, in **While I am here I shall do some work** and **While I was doing my work I fell asleep, while** means **during the time,** but in **When I saw the right turn I knew I was near your house** and **When I have finished my work I shall play tennis with you, when** means **at the time at which** or **at the certain fixed time.**

Again, be careful in regard to the use of **when** in definitions (see **where** above). Unless the definition itself actually pertains to time **when** should not be used. To write **Cheating is when you deceive or defraud or trick or swindle** is incorrect because it identifies **cheating** with "whenness" or time, and the definition of cheating has nothing to do with time. **Cheating is deceiving or defrauding or tricking or swindling** is the correct form of the definition. But in **Midnight is when you**

go, when is permissible to initiate the definition for the reason that **midnight** is a time or a "when." But **Midnight is the hour at which you go** is preferred usage.

Note that **ever,** as an adverb of time, means at all times, always, at any time; and that **never** means the opposite—not ever, at no time, not in any degree or manner or state. Say, therefore, **I seldom if ever (at any time) go there** and **I seldom or never (at no time) go there,** not **seldom or ever** or **seldom if never.** But these are intensive forms, and were once regarded as affected. It is better to say **I very seldom go there. Rarely** used in the sense of **seldom** follows the same instruction. Do not misplace **ever** and **never** in such expressions as **I don't ever wish to see him again** and **I never thought I should get to Boston.** In the first **ever** modifies **again,** and in the second **never** modifies **should get;** the readings should be **I don't wish to see him ever again** and **I thought I should never get to Boston.** It is, of course, possible, but not probable, for the one to modify **wish** and the other to modify **thought.** The point is to place the adverbs correctly.

Ever or **ever so,** as an adverb of degree, is explained on page 167. Say **Be it ever so humble there is no place like home,** not **never so humble,** for the meaning is that of degree, not that of time. **Never so** is used provincially as a clipped form with any adjective or adverb understood after it, as **never so well, never so beautiful;** thus, in answer to **Is John well,** the correct answer may be **never so,** but this usage is not general. Do not use **never** as an abstract negative for **not,** as **I never did it** for **I did not do it.** But in certain context, of course, the former in each case may be correct, as **I never did a thing like that** and **I never remember where my glasses are.** Do not use **ever** superfluously, as in **Before I ever do a thing like that I must be advised** and **Where ever have you been.** In both of these **ever** is unnecessary except perhaps for intensifying meaning.

It has been observed by this time that here as elsewhere in connection with the parts of speech, it is use or function that decides classification. The above classifications are variable, as are some of the words under each. If the adverbs of place —**whence, where, whither**—are used in questions, they may correctly be called **interrogative adverbs,** as may also the adverb of time **when,** the adverb of manner **how,** the adverb of cause why, and so forth. If such adverbs as **hence, here, hither, then, thence, thither, thus** are made to point out definitely, they are classed by some authorities as **demonstrative adverbs,** correlative to **this, these, that, those.** If such adverbs as **after, also, as, because, before, besides, hence, how, however, since, so, therefore, till, until, whence, when, whenever, where, wherever, while, whither, why** are used to express degree, manner, place, reason, time, and the like, and at the same time to establish connection between a principal statement or clause and a subordinate one, they are called **conjunctive adverbs** or **relative adverbs** (page 200). In **He stayed till I came,** the conjunctive adverb **till** indicates time in relation to **came,** and is thus an adverb modifying **came.** But it also relates to the preceding clause **He stayed,** establishing relationship and connection between **stayed** and **came,** and modifying **stayed** also. It implies, in other words, a logical connection between the two statements, and in addition sets up a time relationship.

Perhaps the two most commonly confused adverbs, as well as the most frequently used ones, are **when** and **where.** Note that they are simple modifiers in **When did he come** and **Where did he go.** But used as conjunctions (page 201) they may be either adjective or adverb in function. If you say **This is the day when the battle was fought,** the relative adverb **when** is equivalent to **on which** and the clause following has adjective quality modifying **day;** you might say **This is the anniversary day of the battle.** Similarly if you say **This is the field where the athletes were admitted,** the relative adverb **where** is equivalent to **to which,** and the clause following has adjective quality modifying **field.** But you cannot substitute adjective phrases for **when** and **where** in **I laughed when he fell** and **He has excellent light where he studies,** for in the first **when** definitely denotes time in relation to both verbs, and in the second **where** definitely denotes place. Even if you resolve **when** into **at the time at which** and **where** into **at the place at which,** the phrasal modification thus set up is said grammatically to belong to the verb. Note that in adjective uses the dependent clause cannot well stand before the main or principal clause, but that in the adverbial uses the dependent clause may stand either before or after the main or principal clause; thus, you may say **When he fell I laughed,** and **Where he studies he has excellent light,** but you may not say **When the battle was fought this is the day** and **Where the athletes were admitted this is the field** (page 229).

It is explained elsewhere (page 191) that certain verbs are followed by adverbs and prepositions that idiomatically lose their adverbial or prepositional nature and become embedded in the meaning of the verbs, as **to turn on, to stand by, to do without, to give up, to hold out, to lay up, to try out.** When such particle after the verb is an adverb it is called a **verbal adverb;** when it is a preposition, it is called a **verbal preposition.** Such word may not be merged with a following phrase that begins with the same word; it is too much a part of the preceding verb to be spared. **I was laughed at at school today** and **I shall give in in your interests** are, therefore, correct, though they may be awkward and cannot be recommended for anything but colloquial use. But do not confuse such verbal adverbs with adverbs that are used repetitiously and thus superfluously after verbs, as **refer back, repeat again, subjugate under, start out, dive in, do over again, lose out, divide up, run just about approximately a mile, come back still yet again.** Such expressions as these are wordy and bungling.

COMPARISON

Adverbs are compared, as adjectives are, to indicate different degrees of limiting or qualifying. But fewer adverbs are capable of comparison, and more adverbs are compared by means of **more** and **most, less** and **least** than by adding the **er** and **est** suffixes. Adverbs undergo no other modification or inflection, and thus have no declension. Note these regular comparisons:

Positive	*Comparative*	*Superlative*
deep	deeper	deepest
early	earlier	earliest
fast	faster	fastest
hard	harder	hardest
long	longer	longest
often	oftener	oftenest
quick	quicker	quickest
soon	sooner	soonest

Practically all of these, as well as those below, may be used as both adjectives and adverbs. Adverbs of quality—**lovely, wisely, wrongly**—are compared by means of **more** and **most** or **less** and **least.** The exact positive form of **manly** as an adverb, it has been pointed out (page 163), would be **manlily;**

the comparative would thus be **manlilier**, and the superlative **manliliest**. These forms are impracticable for daily use, so **more manly** and **most manly** are used. But as adjectives, **friendly, kindly, likely,** and **manly,** and so on, may be compared regularly, as **friendlier, friendliest; kindlier, kindliest; likelier, likeliest; manlier, manliest.** For the sake of euphony, the adverb **just** is preferably compared **more just** and **most just** rather than **juster and justest.** While the adjectives **shy** and **sly** must be compared **shyer and shyest** or **shier and shiest, slyer and slyest** or **slier and sliest,** the adverbs **shyly** and **slyly** are preferably compared by means of **more** and **less, most** and **least.** But **shylier** and **shyliest, slylier** and **slyliest** are sometimes used and they occur in literature.

The irregular adverb comparisons follow the irregular adjective comparisons for the most part; thus,

Positive	Comparative	Superlative
badly or ill	worse	worst
far	farther	farthest (distance)
forth	further	furthest (progress)
late	later	latest or last
little	less	least
much	more	most
near	nearer	nearest or next
nearly	more nearly	most nearly
well	better	best

Such adverbs as **again, before, how, now, only, quite, sometimes, too,** very do not admit of comparison except by some special form; thus, **again and again** is an intensified form of **again,** just now of **now, so very** and **too very** of **very** (as an adjective **very, verier, veriest**), **only sometimes** of **sometimes,** and so on. The facetious **only, onlier, onliest** is not recommended for anything but humor, and questionably for that at this late date.

Certain other adverbs, like certain adjectives, do not admit freely of comparison, as **completely, deadly, horizontally, immortally, infinitely, perfectly, perpendicularly, secondly** (and so forth), **squarely, totally, uniquely, universally.** These are subject to the modifications explained on page 98.

Adverbs, like adjectives, ought to be used with restraint. Comparatives and superlatives should not be used exaggeratedly for the purpose of intensifying expression, as, for instance, **just too stupendously attractive** and **really marvelously and intriguingly clever.** The use of **much, so, too, very** to emphasize degree in the use of adjective and adverb phrases is equally objectionable. **You've taken much too much trouble; It is so, so dear of you; It is all too, too dreadfully sad; He was very, very surprisingly rude to her,** and other similarly exaggerated expressions, have been called by at least one authority the "debutante delights" of grammar. **Awfully, gorgeously, grandly, terribly, marvelously, wonderfully** are the most common offenders in such extravagant usage. The first is generally accepted as British colloquialism for **very,** but **thanks awfully** eludes recommendation—yet—in the United States.

It will be noted that many adverbs and adjectives are alike in form, and that it is, again, use in an expression that decides what part of speech such words are. In a **little used car, little** is an adverb; in a **little man, little** is an adjective.

It is incorrect to use double comparatives and double superlatives of adverbs, as **more sooner** and **most slowest,** though such double forms were once allowable and are frequent in literature up to the beginning of the nineteenth century.

While many adverbs are formed from adjectives by the addition of **ly,** this added syllable must not be misunderstood as an increase in degree of quality or limitation. The suffix is not added to such adverbs as **fast** and **much** and **thus,** for instance, though **fastly, muchly, thusly** are sometimes used by illiterate persons with the mistaken idea that they are intensified forms—and by over-optimistic humorists. **Ill** is both adjective and adverb; the form **illy,** though sometimes seen and heard, is now archaic. **First-rate, second-rate, third-rate,** and so on, are the same both as adjectives and as adverbs; they do not take **ly** and they are preferably never compared.

Chapter Six

PREPOSITION

DEFINITION AND CLASSIFICATION

A preposition is a word or a term that shows relationship between a word that follows it, called its object, and a word before it to which it pertains or relates. The preceding word is known as the antecedent, and the following word is known as the subsequent; thus, in **The story of the game has been written by the manager, of** and **by** are prepositions, the former having **story** as the antecedent and **game** as subsequent, the latter having **has been written** as antecedent and **manager** as subsequent. **Of the game** and **by the manager** are called prepositional phrases.

The antecedent term may be any part of speech, or a phrase. A prepositional phrase may be used independently or elliptically (page 189), and thus have no antecedent, as **In the last analysis, we are obliged to admit defeat,** in which **In the last analysis** is an independent prepositional phrase. The object or subsequent term is usually a noun or a pronoun; but it may be an adjective, as **from bad to worse;** an adverb, as **from below to above;** a phrase, as **Duty resides in doing the right;** a clause, as **There is much in what you say.** And conjunctions and interjections may be subsequent terms, used out of their natural functioning, as **from and to but** and from your ha-ha's to your tut-tut's. In the infinitive—to see, to live, to run— the preposition **to** is called the introductory or sign preposition, the subsequent term always being a verb. But this verb is not to be called the object of **to;** the infinitive made up of the preposition and the verb is a unit form the members of which are to be regarded as inseparable (page 246).

Both antecedent and subsequent terms are usually expressed, but either may be understood. In **Here is the boat we came in,** the object of **in** is understood, as **Here is the boat in which we came** or **Here is the boat which we came in.** In **All must do the work, from highest to lowest,** the antecedent term is understood, as **All must do the work, counting** (or **including everybody) from highest to lowest.**

The antecedent term is sometimes hidden, especially in a sentence that begins with a prepositional phrase; thus, in **By what route he intends to go we do not know,** the antecedent term of the phrase **By what route is go,** though the relationship may not be quite clear on first reading. By turning the expression around—no matter how awkward it may thus sound—the true relationship is easily established, as **He intends to go by what route we do not know.**

The preposition **for** used, as it often is, before the subject of an infinitive, has no antecedent term, as **For him to go so soon is ridiculous.** This has become idiomatic form in English usage. It is possible, of course, to understand it and to regard the whole introductory subject phrase as appositive, but this makes for unnecessary trouble. Exactly the same constructional situation arises in connection with the infinitive phrase used as subject, as **To educate one's self to hard work is a saving grace in living.**

A **simple preposition** consists of a single monosyllabic word, as **a (a-going), as, at, by, down, for, from, in, like, mid, of, off, on, per, plus, round, sans, save, since, spite, through, till, to, toward, up, with.**

A **compound** or **derived preposition** consists of two or more syllables and is usually made up of two or more words or is formed by prefixing and suffixing, as **aboard, about, above, across, after, against, aloft, along, alongside, aloof, amid, among, anent, around, aslant, aslope, astride, before, behind, below, beneath, beside, between, beyond, despite, except, inside, into, minus, onto, opposite, outside, over, through, throughout, under, underneath, until, unto, upon, versus, via, within, without.**

A **participial preposition** is a participial form used with the force of a preposition rather than with the force of an adjective, gerund, or verbal noun, as **barring, concerning, considering, during, excepting, notwithstanding, past, pending, providing, regarding, respecting, saving, touching.** It will be observed that a few of these—**during, notwithstanding, regarding**—are now used almost exclusively as prepositions; that others—**providing, touching**—are more commonly participles than prepositions.

A **phrasal preposition** is a group of two or more words that may be used as a unit preposition and is at the same time capable of being resolved into its constituent parts, as **according to, as to, because of, by means of, for the sake of, in consequence of, in reference to, in regard to, in respect to, in spite of, instead of, in any event, in accordance with, in reply to, in that, on account of, on the part of, out of, out of respect for, owing to, with a view to, with reference to, with regard to, with respect to, in addition to, along with, together with, as well as** (page 202). Note that the phrasal prepositions **because of, on account of, owing to** are used in adverbial relationships only, not in adjective relationships; that the participial prepositional combinations—**regarded as, caused by, related to,** and so on—are used in adjective relationships only. To the latter group some authorities add **due to** as a phrasal preposition. But **due** is preferably regarded as an adjective modified by a following phrase introduced usually by **to** (page 187). Again, some authorities prefer to call **in regard to (this)** two separate prepositional phrases, **in regard** being one and **to this** another, **regard** being antecedent to **to.** But the expression is probably better considered to be a unit or single prepositional form.

If a phrasal preposition is used to indicate more than one relationship between antecedent and subsequent terms, it is called a **complex preposition;** thus, if you say **I was in among the first,** you mean more than **in** and more than **among;** if you say **I could not get out from under the bridge,** you indicate a complex relationship between antecedent and subsequent terms—you do not mean merely **out** or **from** or **under** but the three ideas combined in a complex idea (though **out** may be considered an adverb modifying the phrase **from under the bridge**). Other similarly used prepositional phrases are **as of, over against, from among, from out, from between.**

Adjective and adverbial phrases, like adjectives and adverbs themselves, should be placed as closely as possible to the words they modify. Otherwise confusion and absurdity may easily result. Note **Is there a person with one arm by the name of Harrison in the room** and **A boy to open oysters with a reference is wanted by a woman on Lombard Street with a large restaurant,** in which misplacement of prepositional phrases makes awkward and absurd meanings. Not only are prepositional phrases sometimes misplaced with such confusing results as these, but they are sometimes left hanging or suspended or dangling, as participles are (page 144), either with nothing to modify or with a direction of modification that is ridiculous. In **On their arrival the doors were opened wide,** the phrase **On their arrival** seems to pertain to **doors.** But this gives absurd meaning. The phrase really pertains to something or somebody implied but not mentioned in the sentence. The meaning is probably **The doors were opened wide when they** (the guests) arrived or **On their arrival they found the doors opened wide to receive them.** Note again **Due to illness school is closed today.** Due may be an adjective, as **Those bills are due;** it may be an adverb, as **They went due west;** it may be a noun, as **Give every devil his due.** But it is neither a preposition nor a conjunction, and should not be used for **because of, on account of, owing to, or inasmuch as.** The opening phrase in the above sentence should therefore read **Owing to illness** or **Because of illness** or **On account of illness.** But this change does not make the expression entirely satisfactory, for the phrase still seems to pertain to **school,** and this conveys a somewhat absurd meaning. Say **Because of the teacher's illness school is closed today** or **Inasmuch as the teacher is ill, school is closed today.**

It is by this time clear that many of the words above listed as prepositions of different kinds are sometimes used as adjectives or as adverbs. The meanings and uses of prepositions, as of adjectives and adverbs, are so varied, not to say tricky, that your only safe guide in any cases of doubt is the dictionary. Most prepositions are usable in two or more relationships and meanings, for the preposition is the most idiom-ridden part of speech in English grammar. It is also the part of speech that places probably the greatest demands upon speakers and writers for conveying niceties of relationships. Used without antecedent and subsequent terms, the word that may very often be mistaken for a preposition will be found actually to be an adjective or an adverb or an inherent part of a verb phrase.

With the exception of its use in verb phrases, such as **laugh at** and **stand by** and **drive in,** in which it is a component part of the verb (page 181), the preposition most often introduces a phrase having the property of an adjective or of an adverb. If this phrase modifies a noun or a pronoun, it is called an **adjective phrase,** and such phrase may either describe or limit, as, respectively, **a woman of great charm** and **a period of six years.** If it modifies a verb, an adjective, or an adverb, it is called an **adverb** or **adverbial phrase,** and as such it may be used to express various relationships, namely:

Accompaniment	She came with Mary.
Agency	The speech was made by Brown.
Appeal	Work with all your might.
Cause	She left because of illness.
Condition	He is in sorry straits.
Degree	We arrived earlier by two hours.
Destination	They are going to China.
Direction	They motored toward the ocean.
Instrument	They held him by the arms.
Manner	They make the clothes by machine.
Measure	Buy it by the pound.
Purpose	She worked in behalf of the refugee.
Situation (Place)	Their home is by the sea.
Source	She came from the Far East.
Time	They leave at nine o'clock.

SPECIAL USES

A prepositional phrase may be used as subject, as **For her to appear would be altogether disgraceful;** as object, as **She exclaimed: "Not on your life!";** as objective complement, as **They bored the rifles all of the same caliber;** as attribute complement, as **He seemed in a sad condition;** as appositive, as **The city of Harrisburg is located on the Susquehanna River;** as object of a preposition, as **He kept shouting from beyond the breakwater.**

In normal order, the object of a preposition (the subsequent term) follows the preposition. But the relative pronoun **that** used as object usually precedes its preposition, as **This is the one that I have been looking for** rather than **This is the one for that I have been looking.** The pronouns **which** and **whom** frequently precede their prepositions, but by no means always, as **He is the man whom I must confer with** and **Whom do you take me for** and **Which shall I decide upon** for **He is the man with whom I must confer** and **For whom do you take me** and **Upon which shall I decide.** For the sake of coherence it is usually better to keep preposition and object together if this can be done without violating or straining idiom; and idiom would be strained in at least the last two of the above examples.

The prepositional phrase with **of** is discussed under possessive pronouns (page 68). But **of**-phrases are not always possessive. In **this book of mine**, the phrase of mine is possessive. But in **the name of Harrison** the phrase is appositive, as it is also in **the city of London** and **the award of merit**. And it has been pointed out above that it may be descriptive, as **a thing of beauty** and **a tower of perfect symmetry**, and also limiting, as **a child of ten** and **a loft of twenty floors**. The preposition **of** is the one most frequently used in complex subsequent terms, such as phrases and clauses, as **I am sure of his coming early and alone** and **I have no idea of what you can possibly mean**.

Both adjective and adverbial prepositional phrases may be used to modify adjuncts of nouns. If you say **Brooklyn, the city of many churches, is a part of Greater New York**, the adjective phrase **of many churches** modifies **city** which is in apposition with **Brooklyn**. If you say **The athlete, keen for the contest, stood tense and ready**, the adverbial phrase **for the contest** modifies the adjective **keen** which modifies **athlete**.

It has been seen on pages 79 and 162 that economy of expression is effected by reducing phrases to single adjectives and adverbs. It is sometimes desirable, on the other hand, to expand adjectives and adverbs into corresponding phrases. This may make for force and clarity as well as for rhythm in sentence structure. **I should like to take it now** is weak and mild compared to **I should like to take it at this very moment**. Note, again, the difference between **The bell must be rung at two o'clock** and **The bell must be rung on the stroke of two**, between **He came then** and **He came on the dot**, between **Please sign here** and **Please sign on the dotted line**.

Such prepositional phrases as **in the last analysis, in the long run, in the main, for example, for instance, in truth, in a word, in any case** are called elliptical phrases (page 184), for the reason that they are usually thrown into expression in a detached or independent manner, as **This, for example, may be used at any time** and **In any event, let me know how it is**. Do not confuse this detached use of prepositional phrases with the participial independent, as **all things considered** and **such being the case.** On not too frequent occasions the independent use of a prepositional phrase is exclamatory or interjectional, as **O, for some food.** This, of course, means **I want some food,** but as expressed it is an exclamatory or interjectional prepositional phrase.

In many foreign languages the noun following a preposition must be inflected to conform with prepositional influence; that is, a noun following a preposition must be inflected for case. In English the construction is simpler; no inflection is necessary inasmuch as the nominative and objective cases of nouns are the same. But care must be exercised in using inflected pronouns as objects when they precede or do not immediately follow their prepositions. **Between you and I,** for instance, is wrong; it should be **between you and me. It was intended for you and I** is likewise wrong; it should be **It was intended for you and me.** Again, **He is different from you and I** should read **He is different from you and me.** And **Who did you give it to** should read **Whom did you give it to.** The last is probably the most commonly heard error in this classification, though all are frequently heard. The best corrective, perhaps, is that of turning the interrogative form into the declarative, no matter how awkward the result may be, as **You did give it to whom.** In the preceding examples, error may usually be detected by omitting the first object and the conjunction in the compound phrase; thus, in **This was provided for you and he,** the reading would become **This was provided for he,** and this appears and sounds ridiculous.

A prepositional phrase that modifies all members of a compound construction is as a rule expressed after the last member of the compound, as **The time and place and purpose of the conference must now be clear to all.** But each member of such compound construction may require individual modification, as **The purpose of the conference and the speaker of the day will be announced.** Sometimes one or more members of such compound term may be submerged in a prepositional phrase; thus, **The man and his wife have arrived** may be expressed **The man with his wife has arrived.** Note the change in the number of the predicate. **Wife,** in the second example, while subject in idea is not subject grammatically but is, rather, object of the preposition **with.**

It follows from the foregoing example that a singular subject followed by a prepositional phrase with a plural object, must have a singular predicate. The ear sometimes "tunes in" the predicate with the number of the noun nearer or nearest to the predicate. This sort of error is called the error of proximity (page 207); thus, you must say **The man with his daughters has arrived**, not **have arrived; Every one of the fellows is present**, not **are present; Not one of all those flowers has remained fresh**, not **have remained fresh**. It is sound alone in these examples that inclines a speaker or a writer to pluralize predicates; and while the subjects actually are plural in idea they are not so grammatically. The subsequent term in a prepositional phrase is necessarily in the objective case and it cannot therefore be regarded as subject. If doubt exists as to number of the predicate in such usage, read the sentence without the phrase following the essential subject, and correct number agreement will probably be supplied by ear. It is the prepositional phrase of accompaniment following a singular subject, that most easily tempts to this kind of error. Say **John in addition to Harry and Bill** *is* **going** and **The officer along with the eight privates** *has* **gone to investigate**. Conversely, say **The girls along with Mary** *are* **going to the party** and **Eight privates together with an officer** *have* **gone to investigate**, for like most good rules this one works both ways.

Agreement in number between subject and predicate may again be mistaken in a sentence beginning with a prepositional phrase and having its subject after the predicate, as **To the victor belong the spoils**, that is, **The spoils belong to the victor**. But the singular **victor** immediately preceding the predicate **belong** may tempt one to say **belongs**.

It has been pointed out on page 181 that there are many prepositions and adverbs that are inseparable from verbs, are, indeed, a component part of verb phrases. **To laugh at** is probably the most frequently used combination of this kind, but **to look into, to look at, to go through with, to tune in, to give in, to make up for, to stand up for, to put up with, to track down, to stand for, to break into** are likewise in common use. The word following the verb in such phrases as these may in and of itself be either a preposition or an adverb—**verbal preposition** or **verbal adverb**. The context must decide in all such expressions just which quality of functioning predominates, and the part of speech thus decided upon. In **He will get over,** over is an adverb modifying **will get.** In **He will get over the bridge, over the bridge** is a prepositional phrase modifying **will get.** In **He will get over the disappointment, will get over** is preferably regarded as predicate and **disappointment** as object; the sentence really says **He will survive or outlive the disappointment.** In this last example the word **over** is so closely imbedded in the meaning of the verb that it would be absurd to say that **over the disappointment** is an adverbial phrase of manner modifying **will get.**

This use of the preposition (or adverb) as part of a verb very often makes a verb transitive (page 106), as in the last example above, and as again in **The robbers broke into the bank.** Needless to say, awkward repetition of the preposition in such constructions as these is to be avoided; for instance, **He yields in every way** is better than **He gives in in every way,** and **This is the platform on which I stand on this occasion** is better than **This is the platform I stand on on this occasion** (page 258).

Do not use prepositions as verbs, however, to the exclusion of verbs themselves. It may be colloquial (though it is probably not even good provincialism) to say **I'll at him** and **Toward him now** and **Under your opponent** and **We're through it.** Even **Have at 'm** was regarded as slang in the days when knighthood was in flower, and **Run him through** was technical, if nothing worse, when missionaries of chivalry were abroad.

The so-called suspended prepositional construction, though much used by speakers and writers, is to be avoided, at least until you are quite sure that you can handle it correctly. **I am interested in and curious about Harry** is somewhat wordy and awkward but nevertheless correct. Idiom requires **in** after **interested** and **about** after **curious.** But it is very easy to forget the first of these prepositions, and to say incorrectly **I am interested and curious about Harry. I am interested in Harry and curious about him** is better form, just as **government of the people, by the people, and for the people** is better form than the suspended **government of, for, and by the people.** The lurking temptation to omit one preposition—or more than one—in this kind of suspended construction is frequently yielded to by even the best speakers and writers, and the result may be ridiculous. The young valedictorian who de-

claimed **I have always been eager but fearful of commencement** should have omitted **but fearful** during rehearsals of his
speech and he would probably have corrected the absurd and
erroneous **eager of commencement** just as result of hearing the
terrible phrase.

Do not omit prepositions. Say **The room is eight feet in
diameter,** not **The room is eight feet diameter.**

But do not use prepositions superfluously. Use **Follow him,**
not **Follow on after him.** Use **about one o'clock** or **at one
o'clock,** not **at about one o'clock.** Use **He wishes to go,** not
He wishes for to go. Behind is, as a rule, preferable to **in back
of; within** to **inside of; without** to **outside of; off** to **off of;
alongside** to **alongside of,** and so on.

A preposition may correctly be used as the last word in a
sentence. Indeed, it very often should be, sometimes must be.
Whom did you give it to and **We were all told to stand by** are
not improvable. But a preposition should not be loosely or
awkwardly or incoherently placed at the end of a sentence, as
He is the man whom I was stood up for by for **He is the man
who stood up for me** or **He is the man by whom I was sup-
ported.** The following prepositional colloquy is now a classic:

SICK CHILD: I want to be read to.
MOTHER: What book do you want to be read to out of?
SICK CHILD: *Robinson Crusoe.*
(Mother goes out and returns with *The Swiss Family
   Robinson*)
SICK CHILD: What did you bring me that book to be read
   to out of in for?

Comparisons made by means of **like** as a preposition may
come out absurdly either because of the omission of a separative **that (those)** after it or because of failure to use a possessive case following it. **He has a nose like that of a horse** is
correct, as is also **He has a nose like a horse's.** But **He has a
nose like a horse** is not at all the expression of what is intended. The comparison is obviously between two noses, not
between a nose and a horse.

The preposition has been mentioned on page 187 as the
most idiom-ridden part of speech. This means that many

idioms in the language—probably the majority of our every-day idioms—are concerned with prepositions, and that fine distinctions are very often necessary in their use. Of all the various kinds of slips of speech, none is more likely to con-demn a speaker or a writer than his failure to fit the right preposition to a verb or an adjective, such as **accompany by** (a person) and **accompany with** (an inanimate thing), **ac-cused of** (a wrong) and **accused by** (a person), **in accordance to** (law) and **in accordance with** (a person or a group), **agree to** or **about** (a course of action) and **agree with** (a person), **convenient to** (a person or a place) and **convenient for** (a use or purpose), **correspond to** (objects) and **correspond with** (persons), **differ from** (a person or thing) and **differ from** or **with** or **about** (an idea or opinion), **part from** (a person) and **part with** (a thing), **taste of** (food) and **taste for** (art), **wait for** (person or event) and **wait at** (a place) and **wait on** (a customer), and so forth. These are but comparatively few of the prepositional idioms in daily use—in daily misuse! The dictionary will set you right regarding them and a host of others if you will take the time to consult it.[1]

About and **around** are sometimes called prepositional ad-verbs or adverbial prepositions (page 177). They should not be used interchangeably in regard to space and time, but un-fortunately they are. **About** means approximately, in the neighborhood of, concerned with, on the point of, as **He is about twelve, Be about your work, Wist ye not that I must be about my Father's business** (Luke 2:49), **We were about to go. Around** means on all sides, from various sides, encircling, circling among, as **We raced around the reservoir, She tied it around her waist, Let's look around the house.** Do not use **around three yards** or **around an hour** or **around five dollars,** for **about** in each case. Do not use **around** and **about** together, as **around about ten dollars.** Avoid using **just** to modify **about** and **around; just about right** and **just around the corner** mean, respectively, precisely approximately right and exactly or closely encompassing the corner! Both expression are, how-ever, colloquial.

Among and **amongst** are preferably used to denote being surrounded by more than two individual units or beings. They are followed by plural or collective nouns, as **Among my friends you stand first** and **She is among the missing.** Do not say **John and Bill did this among them** (see **between**), but **John, Bill, and Harry did this among them** is correct. **Amongst** is now archaic except in biblical and poetic uses.

As is listed on page 185 above as a preposition, but its use as such is strictly limited, and some authorities rule that it should never be so used. In the sentence **We selected her as leader, as** is preferably regarded as an introductory word or conjunction to the objective complement **leader.** Similarly, in **He appeared as Hamlet, as** is preferably regarded as introductory to the predicate noun **Hamlet.** But in **He took a job as clerk, as** may be regarded as a preposition with **clerk** as object and **job** as antecedent, **as clerk** being equivalent to the adjective **clerical.** And in **He comes early as a rule, as** is again a preposition with **rule** as object and **comes** as antecedent, **as a rule** being equivalent to the adverb **usually.** Do not use **as per** as a phrasal preposition in place of **according to.** Say **Your goods were shipped according to orders,** not **as per orders.**

At is a preposition of position or place. **Where** is an adverb of position or place. Do not, therefore, use the two words together, as in **Where (Wherever) is he at,** for **at** is superfluous since it repeats **where. By** means by the side of, at hand, near. Do not use it for **at** in the sense of place, as in **I am by my uncle's** for **I am at my uncle's.** It is preferable to express **at** in **He is at home. He is home** appears, however, to be acceptable colloquialism in much present-day speaking and writing (page 199).

Beside is almost always a preposition meaning near by, by the side of, on the side of, at the side of, and, in figurative use, compared with, as in **He sat beside me** and **Place this beside that** and **This is great beside the others.** The idiomatic **beside himself with grief** means mentally disturbed or out of one's wits, that is, another (or double) person by the side of himself.

Besides is almost always an adverb meaning in addition, over and above, moreover, other than. But it is sometimes used as a preposition with the same meanings. These are correct: **There are, besides, five others in the room** and **There are five others besides me.** Note that if **beside** were used in the latter, the meaning would be ambiguous—in addition to or by the side of.

Between and **betwixt** are preferably used of two units or individuals or groups. Say **John and Bill did this between them** and **Between the newspapers and the magazines I have too much to read** and **Between Tom and Dick and Harry on the one side, and Belle and Jane and Clara on the other I find myself between the devils and the deep blue shes**. **Betwixt** is now archaic except in biblical and poetic uses, and in the colloquialism **betwixt and between**.

But, meaning except, is a preposition. It has been seen on page 167 as an adverb meaning **only,** on page 200 as a coordinate adversative conjunction, and on page 71 as a relative pronoun. It is correctly used as a preposition in **Everybody went but me,** that is, **Everybody went except me** (see below). Note carefully the use of **but** in such expressions as **all but** and **everything but** and **anything but,** meaning **all except** and **everything except** and **anything except**; thus, **all but done** means almost done, and **everything but done** and **anything but done** mean not nearly done. Do not confuse these uses with **but,** the adverb meaning **only,** as in **I can but help him** (I can only help him, that is, the least I can do is to help him), and with **but** meaning **except** again, as in **I cannot but help him** (I cannot do anything except help him).

Except is a preposition and a verb, not a conjunction. Do not use it for **unless** in such expression as **We shall not fight unless you do.** It is correctly used in **Everybody is going except me. Except** is sometimes wrongly used for **but.** Say **I should have gone but I was ill,** not **I should have gone except I was ill.** The latter is a solecism. The participial preposition **excepting** is used preferably only with **not** as a modifier, as **This means everybody in the class, not excepting you,** in which it retains much of its verb nature, and in which the final phrase is added for emphasis. But note that **not** is not used with **except** when a different meaning is desired, as **This means everybody in the class except you.**

For is much more generally used as a preposition than as a conjunction. It is a conjunction when it is used in the sense of because, as **I am remaining at home for I want to finish my**

work. But **for** is regarded as less immediate than **because,** and the matter that it introduces is relatively independent and is usually added as explanation or proof. It may thus be used sometimes at the beginning of a new sentence that elaborates the meaning of a preceding one. The term **for as much** or **forasmuch** is both a phrasal conjunction and a phrasal preposition meaning *since, seeing that, in consideration that,* and is in many constructions used interchangeably with **for.**

From, not than, is used after **differ, different, differently.** Other prepositions sometimes used after these words are **about, on, in, in that, with.** The noun **difference** is usually followed by **between** or **among** when it is phrased with a preposition at all. The following are correct: **I differ with you, We differ in our points of view, My opinion is different from yours, We differ in that you view it in one way and I in another, We differ only on or about matters of no importance.** Do not say **This is different than that.** You may say **There is a difference between this and that** and **This is different from that** (not **different to).** You **differ with** a person when you disagree with him, and you react **differently from** him (not **to** him). Do not say **sick from a fever** or **sick of a fever** (though this is biblical) but **sick with a fever.**

In denotes situation or position without change as from one kind of location to another. **Into** denotes change of situation or position as from one kind of location to another. **To walk in the park** means to walk within a place called a park —to be already in the park when walking begins and to remain there after walking is done. **To walk into the park** means to walk from some place outside the park and thus enter the park.

Although **notwithstanding,** used before a nominative, may be a conjunction, as **John traveled by air notwithstanding the weather was unfavorable,** it is preferably confined to prepositional uses whenever possible, as **John traveled by air notwithstanding unfavorable weather.** This word is by some authorities regarded as high-sounding and affected, but it nevertheless has some practical everyday uses. Its transposition in the now hackneyed expression **Your opinion to the contrary notwithstanding, I cannot believe it** must not be permitted to confuse construction. Its object is **opinion**—**Notwithstanding your opinion to the contrary, I cannot believe it. Notwithstanding**

that means **although,** as **Notwithstanding that he is ill, he is determined to go.**

Of must not be used for **have.** Use **I must have known,** not **I must of known.** Do not use **of** superfluously after **had,** as if **I had of known** for **if I had known.** Do not use **of** or **from** (or both) after **off.** Use **Keep off the grass,** not **Keep off of (from) the grass.** The noun **type,** meaning style or kind, should as a rule be followed immediately by **of.** Do not use **new type bat** or **new type of a bat** but **new type of bat,** thus making **type** a noun modified by the phrase **of bat.** You would not say **what kind bat** or **what sort bat. Style** and **manner** follow the same instruction (page 88).

On expresses more than one notion. Do not confuse its different uses. In **The book is on the table** it denotes position. In **He talked on insects** it means about. In **He came on receiving my telegram** it means as soon as or as result of. It has still other meanings and uses, and requires nice adjustment to the sense of expression. Do not use it in the sense of **from** or **of.** It is correct to say **He took it from me** and **We have a special sale of household goods;** it is incorrect to use **on** for **from** in the one and for **of** in the other.

On account of and **because of** are phrasal prepositions. Do not use either in the sense of **because** alone. Use **He went home because of** or **on account of illness** and **He went home because he was ill.** Do not use **He went home because of** or **on account of he was ill** (pages 166 and 208).

Onto should not be used in the sense of place upon. Either **on** or **upon** is preferable in such meaning. A few authorities used to regard **onto** as great a vulgarism as **ain't.** But after verbs of motion **onto (on** plus **to)** may be necessary for clarity, and may thus be analogous to **in** and **to** and **into.** In **They stepped on the ice** the meaning may be that they were already on the ice and were stepping on it; in **They stepped onto the ice** the meaning is that they changed from one kind of surface to another. The former is, however, commonly used with both meanings.

Referring to is a much abused phrasal-participial preposition, especially in business expression. **In reference to** or **with reference to** is preferable. But both the participial and the prepositional form tempt to the commission of the dangling error (page 144); thus, **Referring to that question it may be emphatically denied** and **In (or With) reference to that question it may be emphatically denied** are loose and incoherent as result of dangling introductory phrases; in **Referring to that question I emphatically deny its implications** and **In (or With) reference to that question I emphatically deny its implications** both introductory phrases are tied to definite modification.

To is usually understood rather than expressed before **home**. Say **I am going home**, not **I am going to home**. Do not confuse the preposition **to** with the adverb **too** (also, very, likewise) and the adjective **two** (2).

Without, as an adverb, means outside; as a preposition, on or at the outside. It is not a conjunction and must not be used for **unless**. Use **I will not go unless you do**, not **I will not go without you do**, not **I will not go except you do** (see **except**). But it is correct to use **I will not go without you.**

Chapter Seven

CONJUNCTION

DEFINITION AND CLASSIFICATION

A conjunction is a word or a term that "conjoins" or connects words, phrases, clauses, or sentences, and at the same time establishes relationship between or among the elements thus connected. But a conjunction does not influence case as a preposition does.

There are two general classifications of conjunctions, namely, **co-ordinate** and **subordinate.** Co-ordinate conjunctions, as the term implies, connect elements of equal rank—words, phrases, clauses. Subordinate conjunctions connect dependent or minor elements to independent or major ones. The former connect the clauses of a compound sentence; the latter connect dependent clauses with independent clauses in complex sentences. Adjective clauses are connected with independent clauses by means of relative pronouns (page 71) which are called **conjunctive relatives** or **relative conjunctions.** Adverbial clauses are connected with independent clauses by means of adverbs called **relative** or **conjunctive adverbs** or **adverbial conjunctions.** Noun clauses are sometimes introduced before or after independent clauses by **introductory words** or **introductory conjunctions** (see below).

Co-ordinate conjunctions are classified as follows: *additive* or *copulative*—also, and, besides, both, likewise, moreover, then; *adversative* or *contrasting*—but, however, nevertheless, notwithstanding, still, yet; *disjunctive* or *separative* —but, either, else, or, neither, nor, other, otherwise; *final* or *illative*—consequently, for, hence, so, thus, therefore, as a consequence, as a result, in fine, so that, so then.

The names and the illustrative terms define the character and the office in each case; namely, additive conjunctions add, adversative conjunctions oppose or contrast, disjunctive conjunctions separate or denote choice, final or illative conjunctions conclude or infer.

Subordinate conjunctions are classified as follows: *cause* or *reason*—as, because, for, hence, inasmuch, since, whereas, wherefore; *comparison* or *degree*—as, else, other, otherwise, rather, than, as much as, as well as; *concession*—although, provided, nevertheless, save, though, though—yet; *condition* —if, provided, since, unless; *manner*—as, how; *place*—after, before, whence, where, whereat, wherever; *purpose* or *result* —lest, that, so that, in order that; *time*—as, before, ere, since, still, till, until, when, whenever, while; *introductory to noun clauses*—as, how, that, what, whether; *introductory to adjective clauses (relative conjunctions)*—as, but, same, such, that, which, who (and the ever compounds).

These, again, speak for themselves by both name and illustration. Others may be added to most of these lists. Note that one conjunction may quite properly be classified under two or more headings. **After,** for instance, is used of both place and time; as may stand for cause, comparison, manner, time, and may belong to adjective clauses and to noun clauses. All but those in the last two classifications are called adverbial conjunctions or conjunctive adverbs.

Correlative or **corresponsive conjunctions** are conjunctions that are used in pairs so that one complements the other or corresponds to it. Some correlatives are co-ordinate; some are subordinate. The pairs or "teams" of such conjunctions are as follows: **both—and** (Both boys and girls are going); **either— or** (Either boys or girls will go); **neither—nor** (Neither boys nor girls will go); **whether—or** (Whether boys or girls are going has not been decided); **not only—but also** (Not only boys but girls also are going); **as—as** (We all try to be as clever as John is); **as—so** (As two is to four, so six is to twelve); **if—then** (If you fail ignominiously, then you must try again); **such—as** (Such as we saw we liked); **such—that** (His speech is such that no one will listen to him); **so—as** (His behavior was so bad as to make us all ashamed); **so— that** (She was so burned that she could not recover); **though (although)—yet** (Though you hate me, yet I will do you this good turn); **whereas—therefore** (Whereas we have been defeated, we shall therefore work harder than ever for ultimate success).

Note in the above illustrative sentences that **as—as** and **as—so** express proportions, the former by adjective or ad-

verb, the latter by verb; that **if—then, such—that, so—as,**
and **so—that** express consequence; that **though—yet** and sometimes **if—then** express condition; that **whereas—therefore** express result.

Conjunctions, especially correlative conjunctions, are sometimes misplaced. Care must be taken to make each member
of the pair stand as closely as possible to the words or other
elements that they connect. In **Either I must write to him or
telephone to him** the correlative terms are **write** and **telephone,**
and their correlative connectives must respectively precede
them, as **I must either write to him or telephone to him.** Note
similar misplacement in **Both a man wealthy and respected is
required in this work** for **A man both wealthy and respected
is required in this work,** and in **Not only is he ill but also
penniless** for **He is not only ill but also penniless.**

Conjunctions are also classified, as other parts of speech
are, according to their makeup. **Simple** conjunctions are those
of a single word, as **and, but, so, though. Compound** or derived conjunctions are made up of two or more words that
stand as one, as **however, indeed, nevertheless, notwithstanding.** Phrasal conjunctions consist of two or more words used
together as units, as **on the one hand, on the other hand, in
the first place, on the contrary, and so forth, in conclusion,
for as much, as if, as though, for instance, but that, even if, in
case that, in order that, provided that, as well as.** A few of
these are used occasionally as phrasal prepositions. The last—
as well as—is listed on page 186 as a phrasal preposition, and
this listing is sanctioned by some authorities; others contend
that it may be used conjunctively only. In the sentence **John
as well as the other boys is going to the game,** it is simple to
construe **as well as** as a preposition with **boys** as object than to
construe it as a conjunction and thus require the understanding of a predicate for **boys (are).** And the prepositional construction probably makes the sentence more easily understood.

Niceties of transition between one part of an expression
and another, or between two expressions, depend in large
measure upon the careful selection and adjustment of conjunctions. Do not use an additive conjunction, for instance, where
an adversative one is required, or vice versa, as **I am ill** *and*
I am going to school for **I am ill** *but* **I am going to school,** or

He fell *but* he was hurt for He fell *and* he was hurt, or He drove recklessly *and* he had no accidents for He drove recklessly *but* he had no accidents. Do not use a conjunction of condition where a conjunction of concession is required, as I will do it *if* it kills me for I will do it *though* it kills me.

Select, from the three lists of classified conjunctions above, those that properly convey the shades of relationships you wish to express. It has been said that proportionately as one thinks clearly and speaks in simple straightforward language, he will be clear and direct without calling to his assistance such "propping-up" words as however, nevertheless, therefore, notwithstanding. This may be a part-truth. But it is certain that such transitional words as these not only make easy and graceful changes possible in expression but also shade and emphasize such turns of meaning as make it challenging and interesting. It may be sufficient to say Bill is sick. He is not going to school today. It is certainly elementary. But Because Bill is sick he is not going to school today and Though Bill is sick he is nevertheless going to school today evince subtle distinctions of word relationships through the use of conjunctions.

Singular nouns and pronouns connected by and in a compound subject require a plural predicate, for the predicate must agree with them jointly; thus, Rain and snow have fallen heavily today. This rule does not hold in firm names that themselves denote a single organization as in Johnson and Johnson *has* placed a new paste on the market and Rogers and Peet *has* opened a new branch (page 160). And it does not hold in case nouns so connected are so closely related as to be regarded as one, as in My bed and board is paid for and My bread and butter tastes good and Wind and storm has wrought havoc, though there is much good usage to justify plural predication with these and similar subjects.

If three or more nouns or pronouns are connected by the same conjunction, that conjunction is usually omitted (though of course understood) except between the last two, as Men, women, boys, and girls are always welcome. The comma is preferably used even before the conjunction, as here, in such expressions. If all conjunctions are expressed—men and women and boys and girls—stateliness and emphasis may result by thus slackening the pace; on the other hand, a stilted and artificial effect may be produced. If all conjunctions are omitted—**men, women, boys, girls**—a dynamic or rushing or pressing effect may result; on the other hand, there may be an impression of confusion and hurry. The former construction is known as **polysyndeton;** the latter, as **asyndeton.**

If nouns and pronouns in a compound subject are not connected by **and** but by some other conjunction, the predicate is singular provided all subjects are singular, and plural if any one is plural (page 156); thus, **Either Bill or John is going, Neither boys nor girls are going, Three boys but only one girl are going.**

SPECIAL USES

Do not omit conjunctions, especially in making comparisons. In **He plays as well if not better than she,** final **as** of the phrasal conjunction **as well as** is omitted, and the sentence is incorrect. It should read **He plays as well as if not better than she** or **He plays as well as she if not better.** In **This is softer in texture and just as thin as that,** the comparative **softer** is left hanging without the necessary **than** to complete the comparison. It should read **This is softer than that in texture and just as thin** or **This is just as thin as that and is softer in texture.** Note that the completion of the comparison may be understood at the end of the sentence, and the latter reading in each example is recommended by most authorities.

Do not use conjunctions superfluously. Such correlatives as **both—and** and **not only—but also** sometimes yield important emphasis, but the two are by no means always necessary. In **He is up and doing** and **It is rainy and damp,** for instance, there could be no point in using **both—and,** for the second member of each compound phrase is expected and is, indeed, a part of the first. But in **He is not only determined but also stubborn,** the correlatives bring to bear an emphasis that characterizes him much more strongly than **He is determined and stubborn** does. In **Her charms are regarded as irresistible, as is superfluous.** The abbreviation **etc.** stands for **and so forth;** do not, therefore, write **and etc.** for **and** is superfluous. In **John is either going swimming or else motoring, else** is superfluous, for **either—or** makes the alternative quite clear. **And** and **so** are frequently thrown into expressions unnecessarily, as **He came early and so we accomplished a great deal.** The relationship between clauses here is made logical by the use of a single subordinate conjunction, as **Because he came early, we accomplished a great deal.**

And means plus, as a rule, and its use therefore presupposes a similar preceding term (or more than one) in an expression to which a following one is added. You must say **The boy who won the prize and who is going to Europe is coming to dinner,** for here **and** connects the two co-ordinate relative clauses **who won the prize** and **who is going to Europe;** a preceding **who** is added by **and** to a following **who.** But in **The prize-winning boy** (or **The prize winner**) **and who is going to Europe is coming to dinner,** the co-ordinate conjunction **and** has no similar term before it that it may logically add to **who** following it. The rule is sometimes put in the following imperative form: Do not use **and who, and which, and that** in a sentence unless there is a preceding co-ordinate **who, which, that** (or more than one) to establish additive or adversative connection. The rule applies also to other additives as well as to adversatives—especially **but,** for "subtraction" must also be kept co-ordinate.

The verbs **come, go, try** are often wrongly followed by **and** when they have after them the infinitive used substantively or adverbially. **Come and see** and **go and look** and **try and do** are colloquial but they are in most usage incorrect. They should read **come (to) see** and **go (to) look** and **try to do** (after **go** and **come** the infinitive is frequently elliptical). Such connection by means of **and** is correct only in those comparatively rare instances in which the two verbs have co-ordinate or equal relationship. **Come and get** is strictly correct, for instance, only provided the coming and getting are equally important. Otherwise, **to get** is an infinitive used as a phrase of purpose modifying **come**—**You come to get.** Similarly, **to look** is used adverbially to modify **go; to do** is used as object of **try.** This error is made after other verbs, but after these principally.

The pairing of correlatives as set down above must be respected. Use **or** after **either,** and **nor** after **neither.** Do not say **I have neither an apple or a pear. Or** and **either** are always correlative, as are **nor** and **neither.** But note that **nor** is not always required after other negatives; thus, if an additional expression **merely** adds or amplifies, **or** is correctly used after it; but if an additional expression constitutes an important alternative, **nor** should be used. In, for instance, **He**

has no house or home, **home** is used as an equivalent of **house**
and is merely an added or amplified term; but in **He has no
money nor property, property** is used as an alternative. or
additional asset, as in estimating what he is worth, and **no** is
equivalent to **neither**. In such expressions as the following, the
second term is an equivalent, an amplifier, a kind of appositive
of the first: **I have no mind or inclination to help, I have no
aid or assistance in the neighborhood, I have not a rod or a
staff to comfort me, I have no coal or wood in the house** (that
is, no fuel). But in these, the second term—the one following
nor—is used as a significant alternative: **I have no heart nor
mind to help them, I have no friend nor acquaintance to turn
to, I have not a precept nor an example for guidance.**

The foregoing rule may be stated—perhaps more simply
—as follows: When **or** follows **no** or **not** as correlative connective, the relationship should be especially close; when **nor**
follows **no** or **not**, the second term is not closely related to the
first, may be an afterthought merely and therefore unimportant. In **Not a book or a magazine was lost, book** and **magazine** are so closely related as to constitute a unity, such as
printed matter or library or volumes. In **Not a book nor a
magazine was lost, magazine** appears as only an afterthought,
and the emphasis in the whole expression implies that almost
magical care was exercised in saving things—not a book nor
even a magazine was lost, so thorough were the rescuers.

As, in addition to being a pronoun (page 71), an adverb
(page 167), a conjunctive adverb of cause, degree, manner,
time (page 201), and a preposition (page 195), is sometimes
used as an introductory word to appositives and clauses and
other constructions. It introduces the appositive **leader** in
Grant as leader made a notable record. It introduces the
objective complement **captain** in **They liked John as captain.**
It may be introductory to the phrase **to what you mean** in **I
am in doubt as to what you mean,** though in this construction
as to may be regarded as a phrasal preposition. Note that in
comparative expressions in which **as—as** and **so—as** are used,
the latter member of the correlative is usually followed by a
nominative, as **He is as good as I** and **He is not so good as I.**
The final nominative is subject of **am** understood. Do not say
He is as good or **so good as me,** unless, as is explained on
page 195, **as** is regarded as a preposition. It is preferably a
conjunction in comparative statements, such as these, for the

reason that compared terms are better kept on the same level of syntax. If in **There is no such word as fail,** you take **fail** to be object of the preposition **as,** you make your comparison upon the unequal terms of nominative **word** and object-of-a-preposition **fail. There is no such word as fail (is)** represents the preferred syntax.

Note, however, that in comparative expressions in which the phrasal conjunction **as well as** (page 60) occurs, ambiguity may easily result. If you say **He plays as well as John,** you may mean that his playing is as good as **John's** or that he plays also. Again, in **I like Mary as well as Jane,** the meaning may be that I like Mary and Jane equally well or that I like Mary and Jane likes her also. For the sake of clarity, then, we must say **He and John play equally well** or **Both he and John play,** and **I like both Mary and Jane** or **Both Jane and I like Mary.** Such ambiguity is not so likely to occur when a personal pronoun follows the comparative conjunction, for the case inflection clarifies; thus, **I like Mary as well as her** must mean **I like Mary as well as I like her** or **I like both Mary and her;** and **I like Mary as well as she** must mean **I like Mary as well as she likes Mary** or **Both she and I like Mary.** But note that **You can read that as well as me** won't do, for **me** seems to be object of **can read** understood, whereas the meaning is **You can read that as well as I can read it.**

The rule regarding phrasal prepositions (page 191) pertains also to phrasal conjunctions. The error of proximity occurs with conjunctions also; thus, **Mary as well as the rest of the girls** *is* **going** and **All the girls as well as the matron** *are* **going.** The number of the noun or pronoun following a phrasal conjunction does not influence the predicate of the subject preceding the phrasal conjunction.

In the expression **as follows** or **as follow,** the singular or the plural form of the verb should logically be selected in accordance with the context. In **The items are as follow, as** is a relative pronoun referring to plural **items** and **follow** is thus plural, or the sentence expanded may read **The items are such as those that follow** in which **that** is plural to agree with its antecedent **those.** In **The record stands as follows,** the reference context is singular, that is, **The record stands as it** (the record) **follows.** Many authorities rule, however, that **as follows** is idiomatic and that it should always be used in the sense of **it follows,** and general usage at present accepts this ruling. The expressions **as regard** and **as regards** follow suit; that is, **your plans as (they) regard me** and **your plan as (it) regards me.** And the same authorities rule that **as regards,** like **as follows,** is idiomatic and static for **as it regards (as it follows).** The participial preposition in each of these commonly used expressions saves the day (though it may be a cowardly way out); thus, **the item** or **items following** and **your plan** or **plans regarding me.**

The correlatives **as—as** are used in affirmative statements and in questions to which affirmative answers are expected. The correlatives **so—as** are used in negative statements and in questions to which negative answers are expected. **This book is as thick as that one, isn't it** and **This book is not so large as that one, is it** illustrate these usages.

It has been seen on page 71 that **as** is a relative pronoun in such expressions as **This is the same as that is** and **There were such exhibits as I had never seen before.** And **as** in such expressions as **He is not so cruel as to do that** has been seen (page 206) to be an adverbial conjunction. But **as** should be used sparingly in both of these constructions, especially in the first. Say **Any one who** (or **that**) **can't see this must be blind,** not **Any one as can't see that must be blind.** Similarly, say **not that I know of** rather than **not as I know of.** Again, **as** must not be used for **whether. She did not say as she would go** is wrong; it should be **She did not say whether** (or **that**) **she would go. As** is more casual and general than **because,** and is preferably not used for it, therefore; thus, **I hid because I was afraid** is more immediate and explicit than **I hid, as I was afraid.** In the latter a comma is usually required before **as.**

Because implies **reason** and **why** (page 166). It is therefore superfluous, because repetitious, to say **The reason is because I was ill** and **That is because why I went. Reason** may be followed by **why** or **for** or **with; because** may be followed by **of.** It has been seen that, as phrasal prepositions, **on account of** and **because of** may be used interchangeably, but that **on account of** may never be used for **because. He went to Palm Springs because of illness** or **on account of illness** or **because he is ill** is correct, but **He went to Palm Springs on account of he was ill** is a solecism (page 198).

But has already been seen as adverb (page 167), conjunction (page 200), preposition (page 196), pronoun (page 71). The following examples of each particular use are set down here by way of review and of emphasizing the differences among these uses: As adverb, it means only, as in **I have but one;** as conjunction, it is contrastive or adversative or "subtractive," as in **He is going but I am not;** as preposition, it means except, as **Everybody is going but me;** as pronoun, it has the force of **who does not,** as **There is no one but believes him guilty.**

If is used chiefly—and preferably—to introduce condition or supposition, to mean granting or allowing or in case that. It should not be used for **whether** to introduce indirect questions. **He asked whether I could go** is preferable to **He asked if I could go.** Say also **I don't know whether I can** in preference to **I don't know if I can; See whether he is here** in preference to **See if he is here. If he is really ill he should go home** illustrates correct usage.

Lest means **that not;** it should not be used, therefore, with another negative in the same construction. If you say **Be careful lest you be not tempted,** the actual meaning is **Be careful to get yourself tempted,** that is, **Be careful that you get yourself not untempted.** The correct form is **Be careful lest you be tempted.**

Like has been explained to some extent on page 163. Some authorities rule that it should not be used as a conjunction. Others say (and the dictionaries follow) that it may be so used when it indicates resemblance and connects at the same time. In **He talks like a lawyer, like** is a preposition. But the sentence is ambiguous—you cannot tell whether he really is a lawyer or merely a layman who talks like a lawyer. In **He talks as a lawyer (talks),** you are equally in the dark. In **Dress as you said you would** there is ambiguity also: the sentence may mean wear what you said you would wear, or dress at the time or for the occasion at which or for which you said you would dress. **Like,** therefore, has its specific use as a conjunction of resemblance. **Dress like you said you would** means dress in the fashion or style in which you said you would dress; and **He talks like a lawyer talks** implies that he is a layman who resembles a lawyer in his talk. But this conjunctive use of **like** requires the greatest caution and cannot be unqualifiedly recommended. Many authorities rule that **as** is the preferred conjunction even in case of definite resemblance, and give to **as** the meaning of **like**.

Like is often wrongly used for **as if**, as in **He talked like he was angry** for **He talked as if he were angry** or **He talked as if angry,** and **They fought like they meant to win** for **They fought as if they meant to win.** In these examples there is no definite resemblance expressed, and the modification is clearly adverbial—he talked and they fought in a certain manner, **angrily** in the one instance, and **determinedly** in the other.

Only is an adverb of degree (page 170). It may be used as a conjunction meaning **namely, except that, but, were it not for;** but it should be sparingly so used. Say **I expected to go but I was ill** or **I expected to go; however, I was ill.** Do not say **I expected to go, only I was ill.**

Or is sometimes used like introductory **as** (page 206) to denote equivalence or apposition as in **The fawn, or young deer, is the most lovable of animals.**

Since may be used as an adverb (page 178) and a preposition (page 185) as well as a conjunction (page 201). It is a conjunction in **Since it is raining we are not going;** an adverb in **He left not long since;** a preposition in **We have been here since May.**

So is overused as an adverbial conjunction, where **accordingly, consequently, hence,** or **therefore** would also, as a rule, be correct. It is preferably used as an adverb of degree or as a demonstrative adverb, not as a conjunction of result. As correlative with **as, so** is merely an emphasizing antecedent in negative expressions (page 208), as in **He is not so well as he was.** It is used also to express consequence, especially before an infinitive, as **We should drive carefully so as to avoid accident;** to emphasize such affirmations as **I shall never go there again so long as she is there;** and in comparative questions that imply negative answers, **so** is correctly used as antecedent to **as,** as in **Do you mean to say that you are not so active as he.** If, however, an affirmative reply is expected to a question like this, it has been seen above that **as** correlates with **as.** In such expressions as **They did good work; hence, they shall have a**

holiday, **hence** or **accordingly** or **consequently** or **therefore** is preferable to **so**. In its original use **so** almost invariably expressed comparison, usually correlative with **as**, and this usage is still general and correct, as is its usage as an adverb modifying another adverb. It may be used as an adverb of degree in the sense of **very** but it tends to be overused in this way. Say **The child is very sick** rather than **The child is so sick**, not because the latter is wrong but because it illustrates a too common usage. Unlike **very, so** may correctly modify a verb directly, as **He was so disturbed that he called the police—** disturbed to a degree at which. But such modification may be easily used to excess.

Than in relation to **differ** has been explained on page 197 and in relation to incomplete comparisons on page 204. The expression **than whom** is (thanks to **than**) an awkward and pretentious one at best. By some authorities **than** is regarded as a preposition with **whom** as object. It is preferably regarded, however, as a conjunction. In such expression as **She is an actress than whom I like none better,** strained but correct, the latter part of the construction is really **I like none better than I like whom** (actress), **than I like whom** being an adverbial clause of degree modifying **better.** The objective case—**whom** —is required here. But note that **than who** may sometimes be required, as in **He is a leader than who no one is considered more highly,** which, read structurally, becomes **He is a leader no one is considered more highly than who (he) is.** Avoid as much as possible the **than whom** construction as well as the less necessary **than who** construction. If you feel that you must use either, be sure to get the case of **who** right.

Remember that **than** is always associated with comparisons, and thus with comparatives. Use, then, **He had no sooner arrived than** (not **when**) **he was called back.** Conversely, remember that **barely, hardly, only, scarcely** are not comparatives, and that they are therefore not followed by **than.** Use, then, **He had scarcely arrived when** (not **than**) **he was called back.**

That, as an introductory conjunctive relative before a noun clause, is as frequently understood as not, as **I deny I said it** for **I deny that I said it.** There can be no objection to its omission when such omission is consistent. Do not, however, omit it before one noun clause and use it before another, as

I deny I said it or that I meant to say it for **I deny that I said it or that I meant to say it** or **I deny I said it or meant to say it.**

The conjunction **that** follows **so** and **such** when result or purpose is expressed, as **They tried so hard that they were certain to pass** and **The driver made such mistakes in the route that we couldn't help being late.** (See pages 72, 73, 201 for other uses of **that.**)

Though and **although** are used interchangeably, euphony being the deciding factor. These are adverbial conjunctions of concession, meaning **notwithstanding, in case, granting, even if, conceding, however,** and usually introducing facts upon which consequences are based or results stated. **As though** (**as although** is never used) is preferably not to be substituted for **as if.** Say **It sounds as if a storm were brewing,** not **as though a storm were brewing;** that is, there is a sound that justifies the condition of a storm or that justifies the supposition that there will be a storm. The expression has nothing to do with concession, with yielding anything. **Though (Although) you are wrong, you evidently mean well** illustrates correct usage.

Unless is a conjunction used to show relationship between an independent clause and a dependent clause of condition, as **I shall come unless it rains** and **I shall not go unless you do.** Do not use the prepositions **without** and **except** for the conjunction **unless** in such constructions as the latter (see pages 196 and 199).

Whether is no longer used as a relative pronoun for **who** or **which,** as **Whether of the two is here.** It is used to introduce noun clauses, as **He asks whether he may go,** in which **if** in place of **whether** is wrong (page 209). **Whether** is also used correlatively with **or,** sometimes followed by **no** or **not** for the sake of emphasis. It has been pointed out (page 168) that the use of **no** or of **not** depends upon the word understood to follow. If the illustration above were extended to logical completion, **not** would be added to modify understood **go,** as **He asks whether he may go or not (go).** But in **He asks whether I have any marbles or no, marbles** is understood after **no;** to say **whether I have or no have** would be absurd. But after **whether** in such uses the negative extension of the clause is unnecessary, **whether** itself implying the alternative.

Chapter Eight

INTERJECTION

DEFINITION AND CLASSIFICATION

An interjection is a word or a term that denotes some strong or sudden feeling. It is used, as a rule, without any relation to other elements in a sentence, and is thus treated as an independent word or expression. An interjection is, thus, not an adjunct, and is not, in fact, a part of speech at all. Sometimes an interjection is a mere grunt or other emotional vocal sound; sometimes it is nothing more than a shrug of the shoulders or other gesture. Some authorities on the evolution of language hold that the interjection is the oldest form of expression, but this is and must remain conjectural.

Such words or forms as **ah, ahoy, alas, avast, aw, aye, boo, bosh, bravo, eh, goodby, ha, hail, halloa, hark, he-he, heigh, hem, hey, hollo, hoy, humph, hush, indeed, mum, nay, O, oh, ooh, oomph, ouch, pshaw, shoo, s'long, tch, te-hee, tut, well, what, whew, whoa, yea,** are representative simple interjections. Nearly all of them, it will be noted, have sound quality that suggests emotion, and they have no meaning at all beyond this. It is largely manner of utterance, remember, rather than word meaning itself, that makes a word an interjection. Many of the above words may be other parts of speech and, as such, may be used functionally and therefore unemotionally. Many slang expressions and practically all curse words are interjections, and every department of human activity has specialized interjections of its own, as **ahoy** in seamanship, **halt** in the military, **stop** in motor traffic, **whoa** in riding a horse, **fore** in golf, **ready** and **serve** in tennis, **aboard** in railway service, and so on.

Any word, any part of speech, any group of words may be used interjectionally, everything depending upon the degree of emotion brought to bear upon utterance. A few of the longer phrasal and clausal interjections are **do tell, farewell, forever and ever, heart of my heart, never again, not on your life, well done, well I never, woe is me, you don't say;** and any exclamatory expression followed by the exclamation mark, as **John! O new-born denizen of life's great city! Oh, that my head were waters, and mine eyes a fountain of tears!**

The exclamation mark follows an interjectional expression as a rule. If the interjection is a part of an expression that is itself not completely emotional, the exclamation mark should be placed at the point where the strong feeling ends. The ear and the context must decide where this point actually is. In **Oh dear! It is raining and I cannot go,** the first two words probably indicate strong feeling, and the rest constitute a declarative statement. But the whole expression may be exclaimed—**Oh dear, it is raining and I cannot go!** The sound of the voice and the quickness of utterance enable the ear to decide. Note that when an entire expression is exclaimed, the introductory interjection is set off by a comma. The exclamation mark should rarely if ever be used at two places in an expression, as, for instance, after an introductory interjection and at the end.

Many attempts have been made by grammarians to classify interjections elaborately, but such classification has proved unsatisfactory in the main. One person may differ from another in the words he uses to express emotion; almost everything depends upon temperament. The following classification is set down here for what it may be worth to one reader or another:

Attention	hey, ho, look, say, see
Aversion	foh, nonsense, ugh
Calling	ahoy, hallo, halloo, hello, hey, hollo
Contempt	fooey, humph, nonsense, poh, tut
Detection	aha, O-O, oho, and so, well I never
Departure	bye, farewell, goodby, s'long
Dread	ha, hah, no-no, oh, ugh
Expulsion	away, off, out
Exultation	ah, aha, hey, hurrah, hurray, whee
Interrogation	eh, ha, hey, huh, really, what
Joy	eigh, great, io, right, thank God
Laughter	ha-ha, he-he, te-hee, yi-yi
Pain	ah, eh, oh, ouch, ow, ugh
Praise	bravo, fine, good, O, well done
Salutation	greetings, hail, hello, hi, howdy, welcome
Silencing	easy, hist, hush, quiet, shh

Sorrow	ah, oh me, oh no, woe
Stoppage	avast, halt, stop, wait, whoa
Surprise	gee, gosh, hello, man, whew, what
Weariness	ho-hum, O me, whew
Wonder	indeed, O, strange, well-well, whew

You may find it interesting to insert among these various items slang and other exclamatory words that you yourself may have heard or used. The word lists are capable of extension; perhaps the classification headings are also.

Interjections are sometimes clipped forms or corruptions of words and phrases; thus, **lo** is short for **look,** once but no longer written **lo';** **adieu** is French through the Latin **ad deum,** meaning to God, that is, to God I recommend you; **goodby** is a clipped form of God be with you.

SPECIAL USES

Probably the two most commonly used interjections are **O** and **oh.** They are now used interchangeably by many writers, but there is a distinction between them that may be observed if the writer wishes. **O** denotes wishing, and it is used in direct address, that is vocatively (page 39). It is not followed by a comma or an exclamation mark or by any other mark of punctuation; it is supposedly so closely tied in feeling with what follows it that interruption of punctuation would violate the expression. Note **O pride of Greece! O Lord, we pray thee!** It frequently precedes nouns and pronouns that are independent by direct address, and no matter where it occurs it is always capitalized. **Oh** indicates sorrow, hope, longing, pain, surprise, and it may be followed by a comma, an exclamation mark, or by no mark at all. It is usually followed by a comma, however, and it is not capitalized unless it begins a sentence or a line of poetry. Note **Oh, I shall never get done!** and **But she is gone, and oh, the difference to me!** The exclamation mark usually follows an expression beginning with **O;** it frequently but by no means always follows an expression beginning with **oh.**

Interjectional words and phrases may occasionally be brought into grammatical relationships, but this is the exception rather than the rule. Sometimes an interjection is directly modified, as **Fie on your pride!** and **Oh for a place to go!** Here, **Fie** is modified by the phrase **on your pride** and **Oh** by the phrase **for a place,** both phrases being adverbial. Sometimes, especially when the interjection is followed by the objective case, grammatical construction may be arrived at by supplying understood words; thus, **Ah me!** must mean **Ah, pity me!** or **Ah, have mercy upon me!** and the syntax is easily seen. In the same way **Alas for John!** may be construed as **Alas, I am sorry for John!** and **Oh, for the wings of a dove!** must mean **Oh, how I wish I had the wings of a dove!** And again, interjectional words and phrases, like others, may perform the offices of nouns and pronouns, as **"Alas! Alas!"** cried he (object), **"Alas for her!"** is all he would say (subject), and **I am not moved by your pitiful "Alas!"** (object of preposition), and so on.

Interjections influence expression, giving it life and force and color. Many an exclamation, used without an appropriate interjection, may appear weak and unimportant. Butler's famous line "Ah me, what perils do environ the man that meddles with cold iron!" expressed in declarative rather than interjectional exclamatory form, loses significance almost entirely, as **The man that meddles with cold iron is environed with perils.**

But overused, interjections give the impression of "all emotion and no equilibrium" on the part of a speaker or writer. Whatever your "interjectional tendencies" may be, do not make an interjection of **listen** or **say** to introduce your every remark, or of **see** to conclude your every remark. These interjections have now become very tiresome and hackneyed. What's more—and worse—they are for the most part quite deceptive, for instead of being used to introduce and conclude respectively remarks that are momentous or, at least, sincerely arresting, they have come to denote the trivial and the superficial.

PART TWO

THE PARTS OF SENTENCES

The sentence is the unit of speech, that is, of expression. The isolated word or part of speech is, in the main, a detached tool only, to be kept handy and ready for use in association or relation with other words or parts of speech. True, a single word may "start a spirit" or "turn a revolution," but it is the exceptional word exceptionally used—and used always with such implied or understood ideas as to make it constitute a sentence in mind or emotion, or both. Nods, and Becks, and Wreathèd smiles may really be sentences.

The word—the part of speech—in and of itself is indeed nothing but a cold combination of letters. It usually needs the society of other words—other parts of speech—to give it vital spark. It is important chiefly just in proportion to its use in the formation of related and intelligible groups to express complete thoughts or sentences. A language—any language— is mastered only as its expressional unit of expression—the sentence—is mastered. This implies on the part of the student the ability to understand thoroughly through analysis the elements of which the sentence is composed.

The first part of this book treats of the parts of speech as mechanical tools and as associated units in the workmanship of expression. The second part—the content that follows— treats of the analysis of sentences into their component parts, the establishment of relationships that these bear one to another, and the nature and variety of these relationships. In the former, the parts of speech are presented as individual actors for the most part, portraying minor roles only for the purpose of "bringing out" their individuality. In the latter, they are presented ensemble—in action together before an audience. In studying them here in their natural roles you will necessarily find some repetition. They must appear as individual language units and as associated language units. The repetition is thus justifiable, for their "behavior" or "portrayal" as individuals is very often the same as it is as members of the company—the individual reflects the troupe, the troupe the individual. Moreover, the repetition will prove helpful in emphasizing and fixing correct practice in the use of English.

It is only by means of a thoroughgoing study of the sentence that students may be brought to understand grammar as something more than merely a code of hard-and-fast rules. Through the sentence, and through the sentence only, is he enabled to see that grammar is, more perhaps than anything else, a recording of language habit and custom. In language, as elsewhere, habit and custom connote continuous growth or change. They are ever-flowing, never dammed up, always a-stream. The grammatical rules that seem to be static, and seem to make expression static, are to a great extent records to be consulted, guides to be observed in spirit but by no means always in practice, frozen forms to be thawed by the warmth of live and breathing speech. These rules by no means always reflect current usage or tendency. Speech really dictates what language is and what it temporarily must be; print does not necessarily do so. The grammatical rule of one hundred years ago reflects the speech of one hundred years ago. Perhaps present-day speech still justifies the rule. More likely it does not; more likely change in speech habit and custom has to a degree if not entirely invalidated the rule.

The parts of speech as units are *ipso facto* the parts of sentences. But the parts of speech, as marshaled into working order in a sentence, associate themselves in various combinations. Nouns and verbs, for instance, often form working teams called subjects and predicates (page 224). Prepositions and participles followed by nouns or pronouns frequently associate to form modifying units. The articles are usually geared with nouns, preceding them alone or with modifying adjectives. And so on. While these combinations or groupings are classified under comparatively few headings in the following pages, it will be seen that they are more or less fixed or conventional but at the same time capable of wide variety of arrangement and placement. Certain sentence parts are prescribed, namely, subject and predicate. Certain other parts are optional or elective, namely, clauses and phrases and modifying words. But the latter are more or less prescribed also, since precision and richness of expression require more extended phrasing than merely subject-and-predicate sentences. All sentence parts must be logically arranged if sentences are to be understood, and this means that the good sentence must make its analysis (page 263) evident as it is unfolded to eye or ear. It means also that the individual elements of which the sentence is made up must bear testing for agreement or interrelationship by way of grammatical explanation or parsing (page 267).

The mere mechanics of sentence structure, though always important, must not be permitted, however, to obscure the fundamental office and purpose of the sentence itself, namely, the expression of thought or emotion. All else regarding it must be kept subordinate to this major function. The Latin origin of **sentence** is **sententia** or **sentientia** which in turn is formed from the Latin verb **sentire** meaning to think or to feel. The thought or feeling must therefore be given first consideration. Its manifestation by way of parts of speech and their arrangement is second—but close second.

Chapter Nine

SENTENCE CLAUSE PHRASE

SENTENCE

The simple sentence has been defined in many ways: It is a collection of words by means of which a meaningful idea is expressed about a being, place, or thing. It is a thought expressed in words so arranged and constructed as to have a subject—that about which something is said—and a predicate—that which expresses action or state or condition about the subject. It is a group of words so related as to express a complete thought by way of assertion or exclamation or interrogation or command. It is a set of words complete in itself, containing subject and predicate, expressing declaration, exclamation, question, or command. It is a related group of words consisting of subject and predicate with modifications, and expressing a complete thought.

It will be observed that these varied definitions all say the same thing: A sentence is a group of words *conveying* a complete thought by means of subject and predicate either or both of which may be understood, and—this is implied in all of them—either or both of which may be compound. The first part of this summary definition—*conveying* a complete thought—is theoretical and general; the second part—containing a subject and a predicate—is technical or grammatical and particular. Note the italicized word: In much writing and more speaking—especially of the modern school—subjects and predicates are likely to be implied, and groups of words that do not grammatically constitute sentences are permitted to stand alone as sentences. But the complete form is or should be always clearly conveyed or implied; thus, **Well, I never** really implies the complete expression **I am astonished** with correct grammatical subject and predicate. **On the contrary** may masquerade as a complete grammatical sentence meaning actually **The opposite is true. Not a word** implies **Don't tell** or **I'll say nothing,** and so on. In other words, any expression that clearly conveys or implies a complete thought may be regarded as a sentence both theoretically and technically.

But a serious danger may lurk just here for the young writer and speaker: Such a group of words, for instance, as **taking**

me by the hand or that I wanted should not be permitted to
stand alone as a complete sentence, for completeness is not
conveyed or implied or heard or felt in either group of words.
Each expression calls for related word groups consisting of
subject and predicate, expressed or easily implied, that will
yield a satisfied understanding or feeling; thus, **Taking me by
the hand he pulled me through the door** and **He took the
one that I wanted.** It is a serious mistake in English expression
to treat such dependent construction as either of these as independent, beginning it with a capital letter and following it
with a period. Such writing reflects loose thinking and lack of
respect for traditional English form. On the other hand, to
hold rigidly to the use of expressed subjects and predicates
when they may be easily implied, may very likely make speech
and writing seem stilted and mechanical.

The best speakers and writers do not think of disciplining
themselves to such rigid conventional practice. Rather, they
attain an engaging naturalness in their expression by such
variations in sentence forms as are illustrated in this:

Perhaps you think John was afraid? Not at all. He was,
if anything, inclined to be too daring under the circumstances. What a man! One night in the pitch darkness
of the jungle, he felt an ominous, upward-working coil
around his ankle. Not a sound out of him! But presently
—a sharp clip of the shears and a kind of sickening sizzle.
He had as quick as a flash cut the head off a rattler that
had already wriggled its way up to his waist line.

As indicated above, a sentence that states or asserts or
affirms is called **declarative,** as **Lincoln freed the slaves.** A
sentence that questions is called **interrogative,** as **Do you believe in democracy?** A sentence that commands or forbids is
called **imperative,** as **Do not enter.** A sentence that exclaims
or expresses emotion is called **exclamatory,** as **What fools
these mortals be!** An exclamatory sentence may or may not
contain an interjection (page 213), as **Oh, what a tragedy has
been enacted** and **What a tragedy has been enacted.** Prayers,
entreaties, positive requests and orders may be expressed as
either imperative or exclamatory; thus, **Please hand this to
him** and **Spare my child** and **Have mercy upon us, O Lord**
may be imperative or exclamatory sentences, though the last

two would normally be exclamatory and the first imperative or even declarative.

Any sentence under these four classifications may be expressed negatively by means of such words as **none, nothing, no, not, neither, nor, never,** or by such negative prefixes as **non, in, un, im, il;** thus, **He did not attend the party** is negative declarative; **Will he not attend the party** is negative interrogative; **Do not attend the party** is negative imperative; **What, not attend my party** is negative exclamatory. It is a mistake to devise all negative expression through the agency of **not**. **Nothing, none, never** are, as a rule, more emphatic than mere **not**. **I ask nothing, I will give him none, He is nonpartisan, This is unforgettable,** for instance, are stronger than **I do not ask for anything, I will not give him anything, He is not controlled by party, This is not to be forgotten.**

The **subject** of a sentence is that about which something is stated, asked, ordered, or exclaimed by the use of a finite verb. The **predicate** of a sentence is that action, state, or condition which is stated, asked, ordered, or exclaimed by the use of a finite verb. The word **finite** is most important in these definitions (page 138) for it means limited or restricted or bound by person and number and manner and time. Infinitives and participles are not thus bound; hence, they cannot be used as predicates. Only such verbs as have number, person, tense, and mode may be predicates. **The boy receiving good marks** cannot, therefore, be a sentence. It has a probable subject **boy.** But nothing is stated or asked or ordered or exclaimed about **boy.** Action or state is merely named, not asserted or affirmed. In **The boy received good marks** the verb is finite, and the expression therefore has subject and predicate, and is a sentence. The subject may be omitted—usually is—before verbs expressing command or wish, as **Go** and **Would he were here** for **You go** and **I would he were here.** And the subject is sometimes understood when it is the antecedent of a relative pronoun, as **Who dances must pay the piper** for **He who dances must pay the piper.**

The subject of a simple sentence is usually a noun or a pronoun, as **The rains came** and **He is the prize winner.** But it may be an adjective used as a noun, as **The good die young;** an infinitive used as a noun, as **To study is to progress;** a participle used as a noun, as **Walking is good exercise;** a prepositional phrase, as **In the beginning is the opening phrase of the Bible;** a clause (page 227), as **That you have wronged me doth appear in this.** The subject may, moreover, be any part of speech used merely as a name or used, out of natural function, as a noun, as (adverb) *Merely* **has an interesting history** and (conjunction) *But* **turns many a surprise** and (conjunctive adverb) *If* **is a mighty word** and (interjection) *Oh* **is too carelessly used,** and so on. In such wrenched uses as these latter, the word masquerading as a noun is usually italicized, that is, underlined in copy.

Most sentences, of course, consist of more than one word, as **Go** above, and of more than two words, as **Sam dances.** Both the subject and the predicate of a sentence are usually modified, as **The beautiful new car runs with ease.** Here the word **car** is itself subject noun (also called subject nominative, simple subject, essential subject, grammatical subject) and the word **car** with the three adjectives modifying it is called the complete or logical subject. Similarly, **runs** is the predicate verb (also called simple predicate, essential predicate, grammatical predicate) and the word **runs** with its modifying phrase **with ease** is called the complete or logical predicate. These names themselves are perhaps not important unless they may be made to mean something in grammatical relationships.

Note, for instance, that in **No one among all the pupils is more popular and at the same time more studious** the essential subject and the essential predicate—**one** and **is**—are by no means the most important words in the sentence. They are, however, important keys to construction. Until you discover what the essential subject is in the long complete subject, you cannot tell what person and number the essential predicate must be. And this discovery works in both directions: the essential predicate must be teamed with the essential subject. But **among all the pupils** is more important than **one,** and **more popular and studious** is more important than **is,** as far as the principal idea of the sentence is concerned. Nevertheless, **one** and **is** hold the secret of the grammatical construction; without them there would be no sentence.

Be sure, therefore, that the essential subject and the essential predicate of a sentence are correctly adjusted one to the other. If both of them stand, as in the above sentence, in long complete constructions, the error of proximity (page 191) may

easily occur. The word nearest the predicate, that is, may influence its number just as result of sound alone. In this sentence that word is **pupils**, after which the ear naturally pro-
vides **are**. But the essential subject is singular, and **One of the
pupils** *is* is the correct form even though more than one pupil
is really being thought of.

In normal order and placement the subject of a sentence
precedes the predicate and stands as closely to it as possible.
But it is frequently desirable to depart from this normal order
for the sake of avoiding monotony in expression. Successive
sentences should not all begin with subject followed closely
by predicate. Order and wording should be varied. In aiming at
such variety of construction, however, unusual placement of
a subject must not be permitted to violate rules of agreement.
In **There are a file and a typewriter in the office**, for instance,
file and typewriter is the subject, but its position after the
predicate may easily cause confusion regarding the number of
the predicate (page 159).

It has been said that a simple sentence contains but one
subject and one predicate, either or both of which may be
compound, as **Joe runs** and **Joe and Tom run** and **Joe and
Tom run and play**. The single members in such compounds,
as well as the compound group as a unit, may be modified by
elements to make extended complete subjects and predicates,
as **The boys of Groton and those of Exeter are in the best of
training and will meet tomorrow**. Here **boys** and **those** are the
essential subject, the former modified by **of Groton** and the
latter by **of Exeter; are** and **will meet** are the essential predicate, the former modified by **in the best of training** and the
latter by **tomorrow**.

Remember that essential subjects may be modified—extended or limited—by pronouns, adjectives, phrases (called
adjective phrases), appositives, and predicate nouns and adjectives; that predicates may be modified by adverbs and by
phrases (called adverb or adverbial phrases), and may be
"rounded out" by indirect objects and by complements—attribute, object, objective. In other words, complete subjects
consist of the former all pertaining to essential subjects, and
complete predicates consist of the latter all pertaining to
essential predicates (page 263).

CLAUSE

A clause is a group of words having a subject and a predicate. As a word group formed around subject and predicate,
a clause may be regarded as equivalent to a simple sentence,
but it constitutes, as a rule, a part or member of a compound
sentence or a complex sentence. A clause that carries or conveys the main predication in a sentence is called the principal
or the independent clause. A clause that enters into sentence
construction in the capacity or force of a noun or an adjective
or an adverb is called the subordinate or the dependent clause.

A compound sentence consists of two or more clauses that
are grammatically independent one of the other and that are
connected by expressed or understood co-ordinate conjunctions, as **The moon rides high and the night is old** and **He
came; he saw; he conquered.**

A complex sentence consists of one principal or independent clause and one or more subordinate or dependent
clauses, as **We are willing to help them because they are deserving** and **Though the weather is damp I do not think that
he will catch cold.**

A complex-compound sentence consists of two or more
independent clauses and one or more dependent clauses, as
**I do not know how you regard this action but I do know
what I think of it** and **He doesn't know whether he is to be
appointed but he freely admits that he deserves the honor.**

A complex-complex sentence is a complex sentence in
which a dependent clause is subordinate to another dependent clause, as **I was happy when I learned that he had been
appointed** and **No one doubts that the Monroe Doctrine represented sound policy when it was written by President Monroe
in 1823.**

These definitions are technical grammar definitions only.
The definitions of the simple sentence on page 222 apply to
each of these four also. But the thought in a compound or a
complex or a compound-complex or a complex-complex sentence is too large or extended to be confined within the structural limits of the simple sentence. A simple-sentence thought

can be expressed by means of a single subject and predicate either or both of which may be compound. A compound or a complex sentence-thought is too richly embroidered with attendant ideas to permit of their adequate expression through the agency of one subject and one predicate; two or more subjects and predicates are necessary. But the unity of the thought expression must stand unimpaired, as in the simple sentence.

A noun clause is one that is used in any way in which a noun is used. An adjective clause is one that is used in any way in which an adjective is used, that is, to modify a noun or a pronoun. An adverb clause is one that is used in any way in which an adverb is used, that is, to modify a verb, an adjective, or an adverb, and to express cause, comparison (degree), concession, condition, manner, place, purpose, time (page 201). Since we speak of a **noun clause** and an **adjective clause**, we may also correctly speak of an **adverb clause**. The last is commonly referred to as **adverbial clause**, and this too is correct usage, but the terms **nounal clause** and **adjectival clause** are rarely used.

The noun clauses are italicized below:

Subject	*That we are well prepared for war* is evident.
Object	He says *that the carrier is out of date.*
Appositive	It is reported *that the old man was murdered.*
Attribute	The story is *that the old man was murdered.*
Objective complement	His war experience made him *what you see him to be.*
Object of preposition	He had no idea of *what I was talking about.*
Object of infinitive	He is always ready to do *whatever he can.*
Object of participle	Saying emphatically *what he thought,* he turned and left the room.
Object of gerund	Saying *what you think* does not always pay.

The adjective clauses are italicized below:

He *who would have* must give.
The nation *that arms strongest* is the most secure.
The car *which was shipped from Detroit* has just arrived.

The adverb clauses are italicized below:

Cause	He went home *because he was tired.*
Comparison	This report is more complete *than that one* (*is*).
Concession	*Though it is raining* I shall not take my umbrella.
Condition	*If we are going to the circus,* please bring my coat.
Manner	He performed the ceremony *as the natives had told him to perform it.*
Place	They told him to go *wherever he wished.*
Purpose	They educated her in order *that she might enter a profession.*
Time	They told him to go *whenever he was ready.*

Who, which, and **that** usually introduce adjective clauses. These relatives are always construed in the dependent or adjective clause and always refer to an antecedent in the independent clause. But adjective clauses are sometimes introduced by other words which in such special constructions may be construed as relative pronouns; thus, in **The reason why he failed has never been explained** the adjective clause is introduced by **why,** equivalent to **for which;** in **Such as they gave we very gladly accepted** the adjective clause is introduced by **as;** in **There is not a car but will be reduced** the adjective clause is introduced by **but** (page 71); in **That is the town where he was born** the adjective clause is introduced by **where,** equivalent to **in which;** in **This is the week when we clean house** the adjective clause is introduced by **when,** equivalent to **in** or **during which** (page 180).

That and whether are frequently used purely as introductory words in noun clauses, as **He asked that I remain** and **They inquired whether we had seen him. That** in the first of these, and **whether** in the second, serve merely to introduce what follows and have no constructional relationship at all. They are, indeed, independent. But noun clauses are introduced by other words, and these are usually built into construction. In **I cannot tell what you mean** the noun clause is introduced by **what;** in **I asked why he did it** the noun clause is introduced by **why;** in **Tell me when he is coming** the introductory word is **when;** in **He inquired where I had been** it is **where;** in **He**

asked if he might come along it is **if** (though as explained on page 209 this is a colloquial usage, **if** being the equivalent of preferable **whether**).

In **He explained what he meant,** the noun clause **what he meant** is object of **explained,** and **what,** the introductory word, is object of **meant.** Noun clauses introduced by **how, what, when, where, why** usually follow such verbs as **ask, explain, inquire, know, wonder.** Note that the noun clause following **certain** and **sure** is properly construed as object of the preposition of understood, as **I am not sure why he came,** that is, **I am not sure of why he came.** Note also in this connection that the infinitive with its subject in the objective case is by some authorities called an infinitive noun clause. In **We expected him to stand highest in the test, him** is subject of the infinitive and **him to stand highest in the test** is the entire "infinitive clause" used as object of **expected.**

Every independent clause has a **sound** of completeness; every dependent one, a **sound** of incompleteness. Train your ear to listen for these notes of completeness and incompleteness. Independent clauses "make sense" on their own; dependent clauses do not. If you write **He gave me a pencil. Which was not sharp** you betray bad ear. The clause **Which was not sharp** sounds incomplete and is incomplete. It is a dependent fragment of a complex sentence which should read **He gave me a pencil which was not sharp.** This kind of fragmentary expression in regard to clauses parallels that mentioned on page 234 in regard to phrases. A dependent clause, like a phrase, is a hanging or subordinate part, and must be contained in the expression to which it is related, not separated as an independent element.

The clauses of a compound sentence are usually connected by co-ordinate conjunctions, such as **and, but, for, nor, or, while, yet.** A comma is placed before such conjunction in case there is danger that one clause may read into another and thus cause confusion of meaning; otherwise, no comma is required. If there is no connecting conjunction, the clauses, if simple, are customarily separated by commas; if long and involved, by semicolons. Observe the following: **The sun was setting and the golden glow was marvelous and I went down**

with Mary and Bill, and Clara met us at the station and **The old gentleman lived in Columbus for many years; toward the end of his life he moved to Omaha.**

The compound sentence may easily lend itself to loose usage. It is well to use it sparingly. Do not use it when simple sentences will serve your thought expression quite as well or better. In **The moon rides high and the night is old** (page 227), each part may quite properly be an independent simple sentence. But the two parts put together into a compound sentence make for fuller expression and convey a more unified spirit of meaning. This is not true in **John goes to school and Bill goes to college and Mary is at work.** Here the compounding is carried too far; it gives the expression a labored quality; it leaves a nervous and choppy and disunified impression. And, but, so are the offending connecting words, as a rule, in such stringy constructions. In **He came to the conference late and we had begun the discussion, but his tardiness disturbed us so we had to begin again,** for instance, the "stretched-out" co-ordinate clauses make loose and detached reading, and here, as in most similar instances, they are not equally important by any means (page 251). Note further that **The river has risen high, broken over its banks, and defied all control since the heavy rains** is preferable to **The river has risen high and it has broken over its banks and it has defied all control since the heavy rains.** Nothing whatever is lost by the shorter, more compact form; something is, indeed, gained by way of economy and directness. Some authorities rule that such compounding of a predicate is allowable only provided the verbs are in the same tense, as here. Otherwise the compound form is desirable.

The compound sentence may, however, very often make for emphasis, as **I was not only thrilled by the story but I was enchanted by the style.** Repetition of subject and of auxiliary was "hammers" or stresses the thought. Say **I was not only thrilled by the story but enchanted by the style** and your sentence is grammatically correct but by no means so emphatic as its compound equivalent above. From the point of view of mere grammar, all such sentences may be regarded as either simple or compound provided subjects are the same and predicates agree in voice, mood, and tense (page 153). While a compound subject or a compound predicate, or both, in a simple sentence may be economical and emphatic to a degree, it too frequently happens that such construction bungles expression and makes it heavy. In **John and Mary enjoyed the performance and applauded it wildly,** for instance, the simple sentence form hardly does justice to the thought expressed. The latter idea seems to be an independent consequence of the former, too fully charged with meaning to be teamed with it. The compound form **John and Mary enjoyed the performance and they applauded it wildly** distributes meaning more emphatically than mere compounding in the simple sentence can do, and in addition builds a little toward climax.

But both the appositive and the infinitive may economize for the clause, as they may for the complex phrase. In **There goes Jameson who was elected president,** the idea is a simple one but the construction is complex. Say preferably **There goes Jameson, president-elect** or **the newly elected president.** Again, in **That is the truck that will do your work,** the idea is really simple rather than complex, and the complex construction may be avoided by the use of the infinitive, as **That is the truck to do your work.** As in the use of the compound sentence, some authorities regard the extended or complex form as somewhat more emphatic than the simple form, and it may be in some uses. In the main, however, any construction that makes for economy makes, by that very token, for emphasis.

PHRASE

A phrase, as far as grammatical considerations are concerned, is a group of two or more related words not containing a subject or a predicate. In general usage the word **phrase** is both noun and verb meaning expression and to express in words, as in **His phrases are eloquent** and **He phrases his ideas eloquently.** And the term **phraseology** is used collectively in general reference to style and diction, and abstractly in reference to manner and quality of expression. Grammatically the word **phrase** is used principally to refer to a prepositional phrase, an infinitive phrase, or a participial phrase, as, respectively, **in the winter, to try hard, seeing the end.** But as well as and **beautiful snow** and **according to** and **for the sake of her** are likewise phrases, as is any other dependent word group without subject and predicate. The phrase is used in sentences chiefly to modify; but it is used also to connect. In whatever use, it must stand so closely to the word or other

element that it modifies or connects as to permit of no misunderstanding (page 186).

Phrases are classified on page 188, which should be consulted. The following illustrations in italics are set down here
by way of review in different kinds of combinations:

Noun and adjective and adverbial prepositional phrases respectively:

Of all things is a commonly used expression (subject of **is**)
The girl *in red* is the one I mean (modifies the noun **girl**)
They arrived *at noon* (modifies the verb **arrived**)

Noun and adjective and adverbial infinitive phrases respectively:

To be good is *to be happy* (subject of **is** and attribute after
is)
He assigned us work *to do* (modifies the noun **work**)
He struggled *to overcome defeat* (modifies the verb **struggled**)

A participial adjective phrase:

Studying all night long he was worthless the next day (modifies the pronoun **he**)

A gerund noun phrase:

Studying all night made him ill (subject of **made**)

Participles do not, as a rule, modify verbs, adjectives, or
adverbs; participial adverb phrases are thus unusual.

Note that the adjective prepositional phrase may be used to
limit, as **parents of five children;** to describe or picture, as **A
sunset of red and gold greeted us at the top of the hill;** to complete attributively (attribute or predicate complement), as
The refugees seemed in great anxiety; to explain (explanatory
modifier or appositive), as **The town of King's Row had more
than its share of scandal.**

Note also that the absolute phrase (page 39) is, as a rule,
adverbial by nature though it is by no means always so construed; thus, in **Mary having at last arrived, we were able to**

proceed it denotes time, and in **The storm becoming fiercer and fiercer, we were detained at home** it denotes cause.

Phrases are sometimes economical, sometimes extravagant. A single word or two may very often be found adequate substitute for a phrase. On the other hand, emphasis and significance of expression may require the more important part of speech—noun—preceded by a preposition, to the less important part of speech—adjective or adverb. In **The car runs with ease** the adverbial phrase **with ease** may be reduced to **easily**. In **She is a girl of great charm** the adjective phrase **of great charm** may be reduced to **very charming**. And **The car runs easily** and **She is a very charming girl** are quite as good as, respectively, **The car runs with ease** and **She is a girl of great charm** (pages 79 and 162).

When, however, the noun modified by a phrase is more or less colorless and when the object of the preposition is subject of thought (though not necessarily of verb) the phrase is preferable to its adjective or adverb equivalent; thus, **a gleam of glory** is stronger than **a glorious gleam**, **a heart of gold** than **a gold (or golden) heart**. And in **She hopes to win the prize,** the infinitive phrase both economizes and emphasizes the complex noun-clause form **She hopes that she may win the prize.** The appositive form does the same for the adjective clause in **Thompson, who is my best man, arrived last night,** as **Thompson, my best man, arrived last night** (page 232).

An isolated phrase or dependent clause is usually unintelligible. It must not be used, therefore, as a complete sentence unless implied matter is clear and definite (page 222). **Seeing some one in the distance** conveys an idea only, not a complete thought. Built into relationship with subject and predicate, this participial phrase may of course constitute an important part of a complete statement, as **Seeing some one in the distance, John decided to turn back.**

Equally as objectionable as the fragmentary phrase (or clause) masquerading as a complete sentence is the sentence in which phrases are permitted to roam loosely and "nervously" and repetitiously. In **She looked quite pale and very faint** and **He was keen and eager and anxious to get off to a good start,** overphrasing is permitted to make expression wordy and wasteful. In **John's father, a large man and stylishly** dressed, looking anxious about his son, and quite out of breath, loomed on the scene to every one's relief, extraneous phrasal details are permitted to make expression heavy and confused.

Chapter Ten

COHERENCE AND UNITY

(Review)[1]

Most of the errors in expression treated in the foregoing pages are errors in coherence and unity, that is, errors resulting from the violation of these two principles of sentence construction. Coherence and unity apply also to forms of expression that are longer than the sentence—to paragraph and to theme—but once achieved in the sentence they are the more easily achieved in combinations of sentences that make a paragraph, and in combinations of paragraphs that make a whole theme. And they apply, further, to "composition" beyond the realm of mere English expression—to music, to painting, to sculpture, to architecture—to every sort of expression in which author or artist or other worker is concerned with giving ideas concrete manifestation.

Coherence means the proper adjustment and arrangement and relationship of the parts of a sentence (or longer form); it means "sticking these parts together" in close and natural and logical order. The verb **cohere** comes from two Latin words meaning to hold or stick fast together, as parts of the same mass. Without coherence, expression cannot be completely clear. Unless all parts of a sentence are clearly and logically connected and related, vagueness or ambiguity is certain to result. But if similar or related parts are placed as closely together as they possibly can be—are made to **cohere** —understanding will be made easy and immediate.

Unity means oneness of thought in a sentence (or longer form); it means that a single complete thought—neither less nor more than this—should be expressed in a sentence. It does

[1] In the exposition immediately following there are many page references to the sections in the first part of this book. If the student will consult each of these conscientiously he will avail himself of a thorough-going review of the principles of correct English.

not mean that all sentences have to be short. But a long sentence has unity only provided a single thought is kept prominently to the fore, subordinate ideas being kept subordinate in construction but definitely "tied" to that single thought. If this can be done easily and naturally in a single expression, then unity is achieved. If it cannot be done, then by this token the signal is given that there is too much matter for a single sentence, and more than one sentence is required. And so, here as elsewhere in expression—in all kinds of expression—the unity of thinking processes is the be-all and the end-all of concrete composition. If a thought in and of itself does not constitute a unified whole, it cannot be expressed by means of a clear and unified sentence.

The principles of coherence and unity cannot be kept rigidly apart and distinct in their operation. A sentence that lacks coherence very likely lacks unity also; a sentence that lacks unity is probably lacking in coherence as well. If you say **Either Mary or Jane are going** your sentence lacks unity because **are** conveys the idea of plural, and **either-or**, connecting singular subjects, the idea of singular—one is going, not both. But your sentence lacks coherence too, because the idea of one expressed in the subject does not consistently cohere with or "stick to" the idea of more than one implied in **are** (page 156).

The principle of coherence is violated chiefly by failure to observe the rules of agreement or relationship. The principle of coherence is respected by the arrangement of phraseology so that modification and reference are unmistakably exact and clear. A predicate, for instance, must agree with its subject in person and number; thus, **One of the boys is going** is coherent and **One of the boys are going** is incoherent (page 160); **I don't believe that I shall ever again visit this place** is coherent and **I don't ever believe that I shall visit this place again** is (probably) incoherent (page 179).

In **John told Bill he was wanted elsewhere** the ambiguity of pronominal relationship or reference prevents coherence —he doesn't know whether to "stick to" John or to Bill. You may say **John told Bill that Bill was wanted elsewhere** or **John told Bill that John was wanted elsewhere**. But neither is good. Direct discourse is usually required for the correction of this kind of incoherence, as **John said to Bill, "You are wanted** elsewhere" or **John said to Bill, "I am wanted elsewhere"** (page 50).

In **The automobile is now a necessity; everybody uses them** and **Nobody has done their work,** incoherence of reference makes for slovenliness and lack of precision, rather than for ambiguity. In the first, plural **them** is made to refer to singular **automobile;** in the second, plural **their** is made to refer to singular **Nobody.** The first requires **it** for **them;** the second, **his** for **their.**

Perfect coherence requires that a pronoun refer to a noun that is important in construction rather than to one that is used subordinately or, worse yet, to one that is understood. If you say **In O'Neill's *Strange Interlude* he is at his best,** you make nominative **he** refer to possessive **O'Neill's;** if you say **He is an excellent pianist, which is the instrument I like best,** you make the relative **which** refer to a word **(piano)** not in the sentence. The latter—"blind reference"—is the more serious of the two; but both should be avoided in the cause of clearness. Say **O'Neill is at his best in *Strange Interlude*** or **When O'Neill wrote *Strange Interlude* he was at his best** and **He is excellent at the piano which is my favorite instrument** or **The piano is the instrument which I like best, and he is an excellent pianist** (page 50).

The pronouns **it, they, you, one,** in their impersonal uses, may frequently cause incoherence in sentence structure. In such usage they have been seen (page 63) as general or indefinite in reference, rather than specific or definite. **It,** for instance, in such expressions as **It rains** and **It seems to me** and **It is warm** is merely introductory or, at least, merely generalizing in regard to condition or probability or time. Sometimes its reference resides in an appositive, as in **It is necessary to work** and **It so happens that he won,** in the first of which the infinitive **to work** is in apposition with **It,** and in the second the noun clause **that he won** is in apposition with **It.** Both are convenient idiomatic forms of expression but both are wordy and roundabout for, respectively, **Work is necessary** and **He happened to win.** Another idiomatic use of **it** that may frequently become incoherent occurs in such expressions as **It was John** and **It is they** and **It has been years** and **It is the Scriptures** in which the attribute complements differ in number or gender, or both, from the subject **It.** There is no logical explanation to be made of these constructions, for they are idioms—the set ways of a language.

It is used most incoherently—and superfluously—in **In the paper it says rain** and **In the book it tells how to make the cake** and **In the prospectus it explains the route,** and in other similar constructions; for its antecedent, if not the word immediately preceding it, is some vaguely understood word or idea. **The paper predicts rain** and **The recipe in the book tells how to make the cake** and **The route is explained in the prospectus** or **In the prospectus there is an explanation of the route** are more definite, less wordy and awkward.

They is used without personal or specific reference in such expressions as **They are building a house there** and **They usually display the flag on holidays; you** in such as **You turn to the left to reach the grounds** and **You must never race the engine; one** in such as **One never knows** and **One must always be prepared.** All are, again, idiomatic, and unobjectionable unless carried to excess. But **That restaurant serves good food** is better than **They serve good food at that restaurant, Coffee is served at that counter** than **You get your coffee at that counter, A man should always be ready to serve his country** than **One should always be ready to serve one's country** (page 59).

In general, the more definite pronominal reference is, the clearer and more coherent the expression in which it occurs will be. The use of **which** and **it** and **this** and **that,** for instance, to refer to whole statements (page 73) is dangerous at best, though literature abounds with just such indefinite references. They are probably more objectionable so used in negative statements than in affirmative ones. In **He says I am ill, which is not true, which** apparently refers to his statement. In **He says I am ill which I am not, which** apparently refers to the adjective **ill.** In **He says I am ill but this (or it) is not true, this** or **it** may refer to the statement or to the idea of illness. In all of these—and in still other possible variations—the pronominal reference is cloudy or vague because of its indefiniteness. **He says I am ill but I am not** and **I am not ill though he says I am** and **It is not true that I am ill** are simpler and clearer ways of conveying the idea.

Pronouns, like verbs, must be kept in rational and consistent sequence, otherwise incoherence in regard to person, number, and gender (in regard to time where verbs are concerned) may result. You say **When one enters one** (or **he**) **sees a portrait,** not **When one enters you** (or **they** or **we**) **see a portrait,** for **one** is third person, singular number, common gender (**he** is correct in the same impersonal use), and it is incoherent because non-sequential to refer to it with a pronoun that is not also third, singular, common (page 64). In **I had arrived late but Tim comes even later,** the verbs are not in coherent or consistent sequence—the present **comes** is not sequential to the pluperfect **had arrived.** Say either **I had arrived late but Tim came** (or **had come**) **even later** or **I arrived late but Tim came even later.** Similarly, say **I have been happy to see you** or **I am happy to have seen you,** not **I have been happy to have seen you,** for, as a rule, the present infinitive follows the perfect indicative or the perfect infinitive follows the present indicative (page 152).

Incoherence may result from wrongly associated correlatives. **Either,** for instance, is not coherent with **nor; neither** is not coherent with **or.** Say **Not only Dick but also Harry will be there,** not **Not only Dick as well as Harry will be there,** for **not only** and **as well as** do not cohere or "stick together" as correlatives (page 201).

In the same way, it has been seen (page 174) that two negatives—the double negative—used closely together in the same construction make for redundancy. Do not use an expression like **I haven't never seen it** in place of **I haven't ever seen it** or **I haven't seen it** or **I have never seen it.** But it is correct to use two or even more negatives in the same sentence provided they modify different words (verbs as a rule); thus, **I cannot say that I shall never see him** and **Not only is he not going himself but he will not allow me to go** are correct, for the negative words are distributed in modification. The correlative conjunctions **not only—but** in the latter example simply emphasize the negative adverb in each clause.

Superfluous words muddle or confuse construction, as a rule, and thus make for incoherence. In **At wherever he is, I must go to him,** for instance, **at** repeats **wherever** and to a degree delays understanding (page 195). In **To whom did you**

give it to, either initial or final **to** is superfluous and grasp of meaning is again delayed.

It is unnecessary to use both **because** and **reason** in the same construction (page 166). Though they are different parts of speech, they nevertheless have or imply similar meanings, and, used together, are therefore repetitious. **I like it because it is so beautifully drawn,** not **The reason I like it is because it is so beautifully drawn.** Many sentences beginning with **reason** contain attribute clauses that should begin with **that,** not with **because;** thus, **The reason is that he is ill,** not **The reason is because he is ill.** But the conjunctive adverb **because** is correctly used to answer the question **why** in simple statements of fact, as **I ate it because I was hungry** and **He left because he was ill.**

Incoherence is frequently caused by the misuse of the conjunctive adverbs **because, so, when, where, while. Because** should be used only as an adverbial conjunction, not as introductory word to a noun clause. **Because you were elected does not justify your being superior in attitude** is wrong, as is also **The condemning fact about the man is because he is rich.** In both sentences **because** introduces a causal idea, and therefore requires a causal clause, but the clause in each is given the construction of a noun—subject in the first and attribute in the second. The one should read **Your being elected** (or **The fact of your election) does not justify your being superior in attitude,** and the other **The condemning fact about the man is that he is rich.**

When and **where,** it has been pointed out (pages 176 and 178), deceive when they are used to introduce attribute clauses, for they indicate time and place respectively, whereas the subject that they elaborate requires, as a rule, straightaway definition instead. Use **Work is agreeable occupation; drudgery is disagreeable occupation,** not **Work is when one is agreeably occupied; drudgery is where one is disagreeably occupied.**

While is sometimes incoherently used for **when,** and vice versa. The former means **during the time that;** it has in it the idea of continuance or duration. **When** means **at the time at which** or **at a time that;** it denotes fixed time by contrast. **He**

came while you were out is correct; that is, **He came during the time that you were out.** He jumped when he heard the bell ring is correct; that is, **He jumped at the time at which he heard the bell ring** (page 241).

While is frequently incoherently used for other more appropriate co-ordinate and subordinate conjunctions. It is better to say **John danced and (or but) Mary sang at the school entertainment** than **John danced while Mary sang,** for the latter may convey the idea of simultaneous performance. Again, **While he seems happy, he feels his loss deeply** may be misunderstood; the evident meaning is expressed by though— **Though he seems happy, he feels his loss deeply.** **The summers are short and hot, and (or but) the winters are long and cold** is similarly preferable to **The summers are short and hot while the winters are long and cold.** And both while and when are incoherently used as conjunctive adverbs meaning if. Use **Do your best if you wish to get ahead,** not **Do your best when (or while) you wish to get ahead.**

So is sometimes incoherently used for **provided.** Use **He will pass provided he does his work,** not **He will pass so he does his work.** So should not be used for though. Use **Though you torture me, I will not tell,** not **So you torture me, I will not tell.** Such incoherent uses of so constitute illiteracy. So should be used sparingly to introduce result clauses, as in **I was hungry, so I cut the cake.** **Being hungry I cut the cake** and **Because I was hungry, I cut the cake** and **I was hungry; therefore, I cut the cake** are preferable. So is, again, a cause of incoherence when it is used excessively to connect co-ordinate clauses, as in **I went and so I saw her and so I was convinced of my error.** This sort of loosely run-on sentence reflects detached and incoherent thinking (page 210).

Perhaps incoherence is caused more frequently by so-called dangling constructions than by anything else (page 144). The dangling element may be—usually is—a participial phrase, as **Leaving the house a large maple is seen on the right** for **Leaving the house one sees a large maple on the right.** But it may be a gerund phrase, as **On returning from the city, guests were found at the house** for **On our return from the city we found guests at the house** or **When we returned from the city we found guests at the house.** It may be an infinitive phrase, as **To thread the needle the light was turned on** for **To thread the**

needle she turned the light on. It may be on a prepositional phrase, as **After a hearty lunch the sofa looked unusually attractive to him** for **After a hearty lunch he thought the sofa looked unusually attractive.** It may be an elliptical clause, as **You must not eat those apples until ripe** for **You must not eat those apples until they are ripe.**

But such expressions as **by and large, in the long run, taken on the whole, whatever the case may be, be that as it may** do not fall under this rule. These phrases and clauses are used independently or elliptically, as a rule, and they dangle by "idiomatic permission," as it were, just as single words sometimes do; thus, **Be that as it may, I nevertheless feel that John is right** and **Generally speaking, autumn is the best season here** and **As for that, well, I never expected anything else** are not to be regarded as incoherent expressions because they contain parts that are not closely woven into grammatical construction (pages 145 and 184).

It is especially important that the agent of an action denoted by a participle or an infinitive be easily discernible to a reader or a listener. But any word, phrase, or clause that is left in a sentence with no connection or relationship, or with a false connection or relationship, may be said to be dangling or suspended. It is usually incoherent, and is thus wasteful of time because it delays understanding. Adjectives, for instance, modify nouns and pronouns (page 79); adverbs modify verbs, adjectives, and adverbs (page 162). If you say **His speech was well** for **His speech was good,** or **She spoke sincere** for **She spoke sincerely,** you really dangle or suspend relationship, and delay quick and intelligent grasp of your meaning. While the misuse of adjectives and adverbs, as here illustrated, is not usually included under the subject of dangling modifiers, **well** and **sincere** are nevertheless without correct attachment in these respective sentences, and they therefore dangle in their constructions.

All rules pertaining to coherence are important, probably equally important. But most authorities insist that the rule of placement should be labeled most important. This rule says that words and phrases and clauses must be placed as closely as possible to the expressions they modify (page 186). In **I have only one,** only is coherently placed in modification of **one.** In **I only have one,** only is incoherently placed; it does not modify **have.** In **The rain fell in torrents just as we reached the garage,** the phrase **in torrents** is coherently placed in modification of **fell.** In **The rain fell just as we reached the garage in torrents,** the phrase **in torrents** is incoherently placed; it does not modify **reached.** In **An old general in the World War told us his army experience which was most interesting,** the clause **which was most interesting** is coherently placed in modification of **experience.** In **An old general told us his experience in the World War which was most interesting,** the clause **which was most interesting** is incoherently placed, and thus seems to modify **World War.**

In all such sentences as this, it is imperative that the relative pronoun agree with its antecedent in gender, number, and person, its case depending upon its construction in the clause of which it is a part. Needless to say the antecedent must be clearly discerned; otherwise confusion of number and person may result. In **She is the one who is always ready,** for instance, it is easy to see that **who** refers to **one** which in turn refers to **she.** But in **She is the only one of them who is always ready,** the antecedent of **who** may not be clear at first glance; the meaning probably is, however, that she is the only ready one in a group, and **who** is therefore feminine, singular, third, since **she (one)** is antecedent. In **She is one of those who are always ready** and **She is one of the few who are always ready,** however, **who** refers to **those** in the one instance and to **few** in the other, and is therefore common gender, third person, plural number.

Serious incoherence may be caused by the so-called split constructions. Material is sometimes inserted, for instance, between the members of a verb phrase, as **He has to my great surprise and certain knowledge run away from home.** It is preferable here to keep the verb phrase intact, as **To my great surprise and certain knowledge he has run away from home.** But this rule does not apply, of course, to the idiomatic placement of adverbs between auxiliary and principal verbs, as **He has secretly returned home** and **I had never before seen a car burn** (page 170).

Such split construction as **Tompkins during the time that he was away played a great deal of tennis,** is unnecessarily incoherent, for the phrase and the clause that separate the subject and the predicate of the independent clause could just as

well follow **tennis, as Tompkins played a great deal of tennis
during the time that he was away.** Sometimes such split or
separation is justified for the purpose of making a sentence
periodic, that is, for postponing the principal idea to or
toward the end (page 256). But it is usually better, in working for periodic structure, to place all subordinate constructions before the subject, as **During the time that he was away
Tompkins played a great deal of tennis.** Sometimes this sort
of incoherence results in squinting construction (page 171),
such as **The boy who tries in nine cases out of ten wins** in
which the phrases **in nine cases out of ten** may modify backward—**tries**—or forward—**wins;** and **The agent assured me
when the papers came he would do it** in which the "squinter"
clause **when the papers came** may modify the preceding **assured** or the following **would do.** In the first of these, the
ambiguous phrase should open the sentence for it colors the
entire thought; thus, **In nine cases out of ten the boy who
tries wins.** In the second, the ambiguous clause must be placed
according to meaning, either **When the papers came the agent
assured me he would do it** or **The agent assured me he would
do it when the papers came.**

True, the comma may very often be depended upon to
clarify grammatical relationships. But it should not be resorted to as a "lazy way out," or as a device to "doctor" inex-
cusably loose and incoherent modifications. The aim should
always be to make construction so tight and close-up as to require the minimum of clarifying punctuation. Say **With one
angry look he dashed our hopes,** not **He, with one angry look,
dashed our hopes** or **He dashed, with one angry look, our
hopes. Being suddenly called to duty, the captain was obliged
to leave his sick boy** is preferable to **The captain, being suddenly called to duty, was obliged to leave his sick boy.**

The comma is sometimes depended upon to clarify what
might otherwise result in a run-on construction, or, at least,
in a confused arrangement, especially after prepositions and
conjunctions. But while, so used, it may remedy, it rarely
"cures." Rearrangement of phraseology is, as a rule, desirable,
not to say imperative, in such expressions as **The cleaner came
in with plain yellow soap and mop** and **The Queen's only
recreations are occasional walks and drives in Hyde Park and
knitting** and **The Queen gets recreation by knitting and driving in Hyde Park.**

Place a comma before **and mop** in the first, before **and knitting** in the second, before **and driving** in the third, and you do something to obviate the run-on confusion—something that "isn't too much trouble" once the sentences are on paper. But tighter and more coherent arrangement should be made. The first will cause no trouble if the article *a* is inserted before **mop**, but **The cleaner came in with a mop and plain yellow soap** is a better arrangement inasmuch as the phrases build rhythmically from short to long (page 101). And **The Queen's only recreations are knitting and occasional walks and drives in Hyde Park** and **The Queen gets recreation by knitting and by driving in Hyde Park** indicate more painstaking expression.

For the sake of both coherence and unity, distinction must be made between a prepositional phrase having a compound object and parallel prepositional phrases connected by a co-ordinate conjunction. In **The Queen gets recreation by knitting and sewing** the preposition **by** has a compound object—**knitting and sewing.** But in **The Queen gets recreation by knitting and driving in Hyde Park** the preposition *by* does not have a compound object—**knitting and driving**—unless, indeed, the sentence means to say that the Queen knits in the park. In order to prevent an absurd run-on reading, therefore, another *by* is preferable to govern **driving in Hyde Park;** a comma is a lame preventive. **By knitting** and **by driving** are parallel prepositional phrases modifying **gets** independently of each other and connected by **and.**

The split infinitive may violate the principle of coherence seriously when it is used to such extreme as it is in **I want you to not ever again think of doing such a thing** and **I am happy to with the sincerest and most honest intentions in the world say this to you** (page 140). And it is always preferably avoided when it does not make for emphasis or convenience or rhythm of expression—when, in other words, it does not "come naturally." Remember that in **to run,** for instance, the *to* is almost as much a part of **run** as *ing* is of **running,** and that **to rapidly run** is only a less violently broken English form than **run-rapidly-ning** would be. But many writers and speakers find a unity and conciseness and rhythm in such expressions as **to thoroughly understand** and **to emphatically denounce** and **to so purify,** and there can be no objection to such "compact splits" as these. They are, moreover, very much and very persistently with us.[1]

A degree of incoherence may be caused when logical time order is violated in an expression. In **We left after we had said goodby** and **I entered the hall after I bought the tickets,** for instance, the time sequence is reversed. The reader is, in a way, required to "think backwards." In **After we said goodby we left** and **After I bought the tickets I entered the hall,** and in **If you work faithfully you will succeed** and **When the bell rang everybody jumped,** normal order of events is observed, and the expressions have the additional merit of periodicity.

While it may not always be difficult for a reader or a listener to follow compound or complex construction having different subjects in its clauses, it is preferable for the sake of coherence to keep subjects similar or, at least, related. Unnecessary change of subjects, especially in compound sentences, may divert and dissipate attention; thus, **I met Frank at the parkway and the car was waiting there** may just as easily and more coherently be put **I met Frank at the parkway and I found the car waiting there,** *or* (simple sentence) **I met Frank at the parkway and found the car waiting there,** or (complex sentence, and best of the three) **I met Frank at the parkway where I found the car waiting.** Similarly, **After much deliberation John has made up his mind, and he is not in favor of the movement** is more coherent than **After much deliberation John has made up his mind and his decision is unfavorable.** But it is by no means always possible to retain this unity of subject, especially in compound and complex sentences that are long and involved.

The members of a compound predicate should as a rule be kept in the same number and person. They are preferably kept in the same tense and voice also. In the event that change of tense or voice (or both) is necessary, it is regarded as preferable to repeat the subject and thus write a compound sentence. But this rule applies chiefly to the long simple sentence. **He ran fast but was overtaken** and **He came yesterday and is going to remain a week** are both good sentences. But if they are made longer they are probably better expressed as

[1] See *Get It Right* by the same author, published by Funk and Wagnalls Company.

compound sentences, as **He ran fast to the very end of the course but just at the turn he was overtaken by the former champion Anderson** and **At long last he came to us yesterday with all of his precious specimens and he is going to remain with us indefinitely.** Of course, such violent and illogical change of tense as **He tried hard and fails** and **He ran slowly and then dashes ahead** (page 151) is incorrect; both verbs should be kept in the same tense, past or present. This **sort** of error is sometimes made by a speaker or writer with the mistaken idea that he is employing the historical present (page 149).

The misplacement of correlative conjunctions is another common cause of incoherence. If you say **Gene neither cares for peaches nor nectarines,** you place the correlatives **neither-nor** in such manner as to make them connect the verb **cares** with the noun **nectarines.** The connection is, therefore, ungrammatical or illogical. Obviously, the two conjunctions are intended to connect the two nouns **peaches** and **nectarines,** and they must stand as closely as possible to them, as **Gene likes neither peaches nor nectarines** (page 202).

It is violation of the principle of coherence to use a co-ordinate conjunction—especially **and**—to connect terms that pertain to widely different and unrelated ideas of functions. If you say **This is the man who climbed Mount Everest and who has just eaten the raspberry jam,** you correlate two actions that are entirely unrelated and disproportionate. Even a more logical subordination, such as **This man who has just eaten the raspberry jam climbed Mount Everest,** does not make the sentence acceptable. Two independent sentences are required to express two such completely unrelated thoughts, unless, of course, humor is the object. Comic effects are not infrequently produced by means of just such irrational relationship of ideas as is here illustrated.

Note that the **and who** construction in the above sentence is grammatically correct for the reason that **and** connects the **who** clause that follows it with the preceding **who** clause. Care must be taken not to connect a relative clause with a principal clause by a co-ordinate conjunction. In other words, **and who, and which, and that, but who, but which,** and so on, presuppose relative pronoun constructions preceding them for the sake of logical co-ordinate connection (page 75).

The co-ordinate conjunctions connect elements of equal value and importance—two clauses of equal rank, two phrases, two adjectives, two adverbs, two nouns, two verbs, and the like. They are not used to connect a noun with an adjective, for instance, or an infinitive phrase with a participial phrase, or an adjective clause with an adverb clause. **She began to cry and murmuring her grief to me** is incoherent because and does not connect co-ordinate or similar elements. Say, rather, **She began crying and murmuring** or **She began to cry and (to) murmur.**

Do not make a phrase co-ordinate with an independent clause, as in **We went to the circus and to see (or seeing) the elephants perform.** This should read **We went to the circus and saw the elephants perform** or **We went to the circus to see the elephants perform.** Note, however, that though **The truck upset with all our baggage in it** is likewise better than **The truck upset and with all our baggage in it,** the latter form is sometimes justified because of its exclamatory nature. By this interpretation it is better written **The truck upset—with all our baggage in it!** The expanded form would be **The truck upset, and it was just our bad luck that all our baggage was in it** or **The truck upset, and—worse luck—all our baggage was in it!**

The principle of unity is violated whenever anything essential is omitted from an expression, whenever there is any incompleteness that makes for misinterpretation or double interpretation or other doubtfulness in regard to intended meaning. This does not apply, of course, to those English constructions that are habitually or idiomatically incomplete, such as the elliptical infinitive—**let me (to) go**—and the imperative—**(You) Go away please.** But it does apply to such incomplete expressions as **This is as good if not better than that** and **I like this better than any in the world,** in which, respectively, as is required after **good** and **other** after **any** to make the sentences correct (pages 100 and 204).

In **I have rarely seen a finer woman than my mother; never than my father,** the omission of a **finer man** after **never** leaves **father** of dubious gender. Although there can be little question about the meaning, economy in expression has gone too far here—the omission has made possible a ridiculous interpretation.

Omissions may, indeed, cause such serious disunity as to throw entire expressions out of gear—to make absurd meaning or to convey a meaning different from the one intended. The restaurant that advertises itself as **a first-class place to eat** invites to elephantine indigestion. The omission of **at which** after **place** makes the slogan grammatically absurd. And in such expressions as **When but five years old my parents brought me to America** and **As far as his being guilty, I don't believe a word of it**, omission of parts plays havoc with full and correct expression of thought. In both of these the dependent parts are really dangling clauses (page 242), and they are made so by omissions. **When I was but five years old I was brought to America by my parents** and **As far as his being guilty is concerned you may say that I believe him innocent** or **I don't believe he is guilty** are complete readings.

Such serious violations as the foregoing are more likely to occur in complex sentences than in simple or compound ones for the reason that complex constructions, as the name implies, are more involved and, thus, more easily get out of hand. But it has been seen (page 158) that the omission of the second **the** in the sentence **I want to see the president and the secretary** makes great difference in meaning; and that (page 193) incomplete comparisons may be both ridiculous and ambiguous, as **He has a temper equal to a lion** and **I like John as well as Bill.**

Not only does the so-called stenographic or telegraphic sentence lack unity, but by the very token of its disunity it lacks courtesy. To write anywhere but in a telegram **Yours received** and **Contents noted** and **Room reserved** and **Goods sent,** and other abbreviated expressions, is to be disrespectful to your reader. These expressional short cuts are not used in conversation. They would be as ridiculous in conversation as such fully written forms as **Your letter has been received** and **We are reserving a room for you** would be in telegrams.

Probably the most serious violation of unity by way of incompleteness is that of making a fragmentary expression stand for a complete construction, as **I saw the house. Where he lived** for **I saw the house where he lived,** and **Having nothing to do that afternoon** for **Having nothing to do that afternoon I went to the circus** (page 222). The ear alone interprets **Where he lived** and **Having nothing to do that afternoon**

as incomplete. To write either of these fragments as if it were
a complete sentence—beginning with a capital letter and ending with a period—indicates a kind of illiteracy.

Putting too much in a sentence is likewise a violation of
the principle of unity. **The president of our club is a man
about thirty years old and he is very much liked but sometimes he has to take very strict measures with us members**
illustrates this sort of disunified construction (page 231). Too
many details are given; the sentence is stringy and wordy;
conjunctions are used to link a chain of unorganized ideas.
More compactly and unifiedly stated the sentence should
read **Our thirty-year-old president is very much liked in spite
of the fact that he has to take very strict measures with us
members.** And the sentence in which ideas are totally unrelated represents a violation of unity as well as of coherence,
as **It rained yesterday and John returned the book** and **He ate
the jam and climbed Mount Everest** (page 248).

Akin to the foregoing is the error of using too many conjunctions—making excessive co-ordination. A series of additions—**ands**—or subtractions—**buts**—makes for a kind of disunity that is characteristic of childish chatter. **They came for
dinner and they stayed all night and they left after breakfast**
and **She felt ill but she decided to remain at school but she
was obliged to go home after all** and **He came early and
stayed late but nobody paid any attention to him but Mary
but he didn't seem to mind** illustrate this type of disunity.

Excessive subordination may be equally damaging to the
principle of unity, as **This is the book that he brought from
the library that is situated on the green that was once the
camp site of Washington's army.** This "tandem" or "house-
that-Jack built" kind of sentence is usually the result of loose
and disordered thinking. It has been called the afterthought
habit. The offending connectives in such violations of unity
are usually **that, which, who, when, as, since, though, for.**
Note these further illustrations: **I gave the book to the boy
who went to college with my brother who left when the war
broke out** and **This is the sort of outing that they like for the
young people of the community in which I have lived ever
since I was a child** and **He was dressed in sport clothes for he
was to act as referee at the games for which unusual prepara-**

tions had been made. All such piling-up of phrases and clauses violates coherence as well as unity.

For the correction of such sentences as those above, complete reorganization is, as a rule, necessary. These are more coherent and unified and emphatic readings: **They came to dinner, stayed all night, and left after breakfast. Though she felt ill, she decided to remain at school; however, she was obliged to go home after all. This is the book that he brought from the library—the library situated on the green where Washington's army once encamped. Though he came early and stayed late nobody but Mary paid any attention to him; however, he didn't seem to mind. I gave the book to my brother's college friend who left at the outbreak of the war (or I gave the book to the college friend of my brother who left at the outbreak of the war). They like this sort of outing in the community where I have lived since childhood. Unusual preparations had been made for the game; even the referee was dressed in sport clothes.**

. Incorrect clause subordination may often be another cause of disunity in expression. There can be no singleness or oneness of desired impression if minor ideas are emphasized by placement in principal clauses and important positions, if major ideas are subordinated to dependent clauses and unimportant positions. If you say **He floated idly on the surface of the water while** or **as the alligator moved closer and closer upon him,** you make his floating on the water a major idea and the approach of the alligator a minor one, and this, to say the least, is probably not justified in the circumstances. **While** or **As he floated idly on the surface of the water the alligator moved closer and closer upon him** represents more logical subordination (page 255).

Again, it is inconsistent with the principle of unity to say **My ankle hurts and I shall therefore run the race,** because it is inconsistent with expectancy for one to run, and especially to run a race, when his ankle hurts. Any statement that does violence to natural and logical sequence of ideas is disunified. The additive conjunctions **and** and **therefore** are used to add one like element to another, to build logical sequence. The sentence should read **My ankle hurts but I shall run the race just the same.** The adversative conjunction **but** is correct for the two ideas expressed are opposite or contrary to normal practice (page 209).

Any expression that is inconsistent, that evokes irregular or fantastic mental pictures, that is partly figurative and partly literal, is lacking in both coherence and unity. If you say **Our road is rough but our sailing is clear ahead,** you mix earth and sea, land travel with sea travel, vehicular traffic with navigation, in your effort to enforce and beautify your expression with figure. If you say **Let's get down to brass tacks and attack the problem at its very root,** you mix hardware with horticulture. Such mixed pictures as these make too great demands upon the mind and the imagination of a reader or a hearer. He cannot very well concentrate upon the intended underlying idea because he is obliged to stretch his fancy from one image to another unrelated one.

Equally bad is an expression that is half literal and half figurative, such as **He became very successful after being weighed in the scales of failure.** It is better to keep the statement literal throughout—**He became very successful after experiencing many failures**—than to make it disunified and incoherent by fringing cold fact with figure. If you say **Fifty per cent of the time he is trying to scale Parnassus,** you mix the language of commerce with the language of poetry. If you say **Madame Curie triumphed in the laboratory as Wellington triumphed at Waterloo,** you make an ill-matched, disproportionate comparison. Perhaps the classic example of incoherence and disunity caused by the mixing of figures of speech, is that of the witness who emphatically declared from the witness stand that the handwriting on the wall was as clear as a bell. To this incompatible marriage of calligraphy and carillon the sarcastic examining attorney replied: "In other words, I understand you to say that you smell a rat and think it should be nipped in the bud, and that you have discovered a tempest in a teapot that you think should be taken with a grain of salt!"

Of course, all such expressions as these may be couched in correct English—may, indeed, represent a worthy desire to make thought not only clear but beautiful and impressive as well—but they are by no means to be recommended in the cause of coherence and unity. Unless you are quite sure that you can carry your figurative language through logically and consistently, you will do well to hold strictly to literal expression. Meaning may be gathered from mixed figures, but never quickly or easily, and usually with attendant dangers of vagueness, ambiguity, and absurdity.

The foregoing exposition of the working principles of coherence and unity represents the usages and misusages that are most common in daily expressional intercourse. Others, having to do particularly with the different parts of speech, are explained in Part One of this book, to which page references above are made.

Chapter Eleven

EMPHASIS AND VARIETY

Studious and affected correctness in expression does not necessarily make for force and engagingness. Correctness is, of course, important to these ends, and it should always be aimed at first. After it is achieved the next step should be to make writing and speaking stronger and more engaging, if possible, by means of certain devices of selection and arrangement of materials.

It has been seen on page 252 that, for one thing, proper subordination of minor ideas is important for emphasizing major ideas in independent clauses. The mind decides what is subordinate and what is not, especially when it is concerned with making impressions and winning convictions. If you say **Though he had not been a promising runner, he won the race,** you have, first of all, the emphasis of contrast in your thought—no promise contrasted against winning. You establish emphatic relationship between the two ideas by putting the winning of the race in the principal clause, and the attendant circumstance of his having been unpromising in a subordinate clause. And, again, you construct for climax by placing the important idea last, after the suspense of his not being promising and the consequent probability that he might very likely lose. Say **He had not been a promising runner though he won the race,** and you falsify relationships to a degree. Worse, you subordinate the winning to the lack of promise, and you "tack on" ideas rather than build for challenge and stimulus.

If you say **While his leg was being amputated, he calmly smoked a cigarette,** you emphasize the fact that he had the nerve and the self-control to smoke nonchalantly while the surgeons took off one of his legs. If you say **While he calmly smoked a cigarette, his leg was being amputated,** you emphasize the fact of the amputation and give secondary importance to his smoking during the operation. The principle of subordination, as pointed out above, must be decided in the mind of the speaker or writer. You make a mountain of a mole-hill if you say **That girl who was married yesterday used to spurn all the fellows** instead of **That girl who used to spurn all the fellows was married yesterday.**

Important words and ideas should be placed first or last in a sentence, for these are the emphatic positions. Last position is more emphatic than first. To build toward emphasis as you proceed to the end of your sentence is to create suspense step by step upward until a culminating point or a climax is reached. This sort of expectant or surprise sequence may be applied, of course, to longer units of expression. But a striking or arresting beginning is likewise important, for it clinches attention. Parenthetical or thrown-in words and phrases and clauses belong midway in a sentence, not at the beginning, not at the end. Use **Shots rang out close by, and, almost before I knew what had happened, my pal lay dead** rather than **Close by, shots rang out and my pal lay dead almost before I knew what had happened.**

Periodic structure is structure that postpones to the end or almost to the end of an expression the important word or idea in it. If you say **A long time ago while I was in active service in the navy, I saw a huge battleship turn turtle,** you do not "unlock" your expression until the term **turn turtle** is reached. That is the key to the suspense preceding. The periodic sentence is thus seen to be emphatic by both arrangement and position, and also by subordination inasmuch as the minor ideas are assigned to phrase and dependent clause. If you turn the sentence around, as **I saw a huge battleship | turn turtle | a long time ago | while I was in active service | in the navy,** you make the sentence loose, that is, you disregard arrangement and sequence in behalf of emphatic periodic structure, and utter the ideas as they occur more or less haphazardly to your mind. Note that in the loose form the sentence may be brought to a close at any one of the vertical lines. A period may be placed at any one of these points, and a complete grammatical sentence precedes it. This cannot be done so frequently, if at all, in a periodic sentence, for as explained above, the periodic order is, as a rule, the climactic order.

Excessive periodic order may defeat its own aim by over-emphasis, and it may thus tend to artificialize expression, to make it heavy and monotonous. Other devices for emphasis may thus well be mixed with periodicity. Sometimes balanced structure may be desirable. By this is meant the placement in similar constructions of two or more ideas that are similar or opposite in meaning, so that they pair or balance one another. It is much easier to understand—it ought to be much easier to say—**Man proposes and God disposes** than **Man considers ideas to be put into force but whether they are to be carried out lies with God.** The superiority of **Worth makes the man; the want of it the fellow** over **A man is made by the true worth that he possesses, whereas we call him a mere fellow if he hasn't true worth** is evident at once to both ear and eye. In the same way the balanced **Nothing venture, nothing gain** is better than the stodgy **You must be prepared to take risks if you wish ever to possess anything;** just as the balanced **One was radiant, one was glum, one was somewhere between** is better than the heavy and incoherent **One was radiant but glumness marked the features of the second, and the third was neither radiant nor glum but half and half.**

Antithesis is an opposition or contrast of ideas, emphasized by the position of the contrasting terms, as **false and fair, up and down, in and out.** It invites balanced structure, but, as indicated above, balanced structure pertains to both similar and antithetical expression; thus, **Man proposes and God disposes** is both antithetical and balanced; **an eye for an eye and a tooth for a tooth** is balanced but not antithetical.

Words, phrases, clauses, and entire sentences and paragraphs may be placed in balance. Balance in any unit of expression makes for economy as well as for rhythm and memorableness. Many epigrams get themselves remembered as result of their balanced structure. The *Psalms* and the *Proverbs* teem with both balance and antithesis, as do the most frequently quoted sayings of the great authors of the world. But balanced expression should not be used to excess. Like excessive periodicity, it may easily defeat its own ends by being overused. No other form so easily falls into the merest patter and trickery. Indeed, balanced structure may become downright dishonest in that people may be "carried away" by the smartness of expression and fail to get the meaning behind it (if any). Too often the popular slogan that depends upon balance for its catchiness, is quite meaningless.

It has been pointed out that the historical present tense (page 149) is sometimes used for emphasis by virtue of the fact that it enlivens or vivifies. The same is true of the active voice as opposed to the passive. It is more emphatic to say **I heard a shot** than **A shot was heard by me.** The passive voice may, indeed, be vague or ambiguous when the agent of action is impersonal and has to be implied. If you say **The heavy truck was seen dashing down the hill toward the help-less little coupé,** you leave in doubt the answer to the question, seen by whom. The expression is much more emphatic in the active form, as **The bystanders saw the heavy truck dashing down the hill toward the helpless little coupé.**

Repetition is an invaluable device for emphasis. Used in-expertly, it is also a dangerous one. In all of the best litera-ture, especially in the Bible and Shakespeare, repetition for the sake of emphasis is to be found in abundance. Such poems as Poe's *The Bells,* Southey's *The Cataract of Lodore,* Brown-ing's *Through the Metidja to Abd-El-Kadr* depend upon the skillful repetition of sounds for their effects. Euphony or agreeableness of sound depends upon nice choice of diction. Skillful repetition, used for the sake of emphasis, is always euphonious. Unskillful repetition, made as result of impover-ished diction and vocabulary, is invariably harsh and crude, and thus unemphatic. Such letters as **h, j, s, x, z,** and soft **c** and **g** do not, as a rule, yield pleasant sounds, though they may, of course, be used deliberately for unpleasant effects. In **Whom did you two go to to get those two gadgets,** the repeti-tion of sounds is not agreeable, and the whole sentence savors of laziness and indifference in regard to expression. But in **day after day, day after day** and **alone, alone, all, all alone** the effect of repetition is not disagreeable, for the long rhythmic vowel sounds tend to echo the meaning desired, namely, utter monotony in the one case and utter isolation in the other. Special care should be taken to avoid awkward and monotonous repetition after phrasal adverbs (page 192), such as **laughed at at the club, ask for four for the fourth.** On the other hand, for sheer impact of impression such repeti-tion as **over and over and over again, many and many and many a day, for ever and ever and ever** may be made to serve excellently in bringing emphasis to bear.

Sometimes abrupt change or renewal of construction may be used for the sake of emphasis—"shock emphasis," it is frequently called. **The man stood his ground and shook his fists, apparently meaning exactly what he said** is weak in comparison with **The man stood his ground and shook his fists. He meant exactly what he said.** The use of **and** or **but** or **then** or **so**, or of some other conclusive conjunction, as the opening of the emphatic summing-up in such expression, may add to its force. A change from indirect discourse to direct may likewise be made to do much by way of emphasis and impressiveness; thus, **He shouted to the crowd that he was ready to stand by his promises to the death** is weak in comparison with **He shouted to the crowd, "I am ready to stand by these promises to the death!"** Direct discourse is usually more emphatic than indirect, but its continuous use for emphasis —like the continuous use of any other device—may easily become monotonous and confusing.

While economy of expression makes for emphasis as well as for other merits of composition, there are times when the extension or elaboration of a term may be a most effective means toward emphasis. Many examples are to be found in literature in which enumeration of detail following a general term or statement emphasizes by proportion better than any other method could do. Observe these excerpts in which extension of terms is aided by repetition:

No matter which way you manipulate the knob, the result is the same. Turn it up, the lid comes open. Turn it down, the lid comes open. Turn it to the right, the lid comes open. Turn it to the left, the lid comes open. Push it in, pull it out; hit it suddenly; move it slowly and gradually—it's all the same. The lid automatically responds, and accident is therefore impossible. It is so simple and so sure that a new-born babe, sound asleep, could operate it!

* * * * * * * * * *

Cheese, butter, firewood, soap, pickles, matches, bacon, table-beer, peg-tops, sweetmeats, boys' kites, bird-seed, cold ham, birch brooms, hearthstones, salt, vinegar, blacking, red-herrings, stationery, lard, mushroom-ketchup, staylaces, loaves of bread, shuttlecocks, eggs, and slate-pencils: everything was fish that came to the net of this greedy little shop, and all these articles were in its net.

—CHARLES DICKENS' *The Chimes*

Thirty years ago Marseilles lay burning in the sun one day. A blazing sun upon a fierce August day was no greater rarity in southern France then than at any other time, before or since. Everything in Marseilles, and about Marseilles, had stared at the fervid sky, and been stared at in return, until a staring habit had become universal there. Strangers were stared out of countenance by staring white houses, staring white walls, staring white streets, staring tracts of arid road, staring hills from which verdure was burnt away. The only things to be seen not fixedly staring and glaring were the vines drooping under their load of grapes. These did occasionally wink a little, as the hot air barely moved their faint leaves.

•   •   •   •   •   •   •   •   •   •

The universal stare made the eyes ache. Towards the distant line of Italian coast, indeed, it was a little relieved by light clouds of mist, slowly rising from the evaporation of the sea, but it softened nowhere else. Far away the staring roads, deep in dust, stared from the hillside, stared from the hollow, stared from the interminable plain. Far away the dusty vines overhanging wayside cottages, and the monotonous wayside avenues of parched trees without shade, drooped beneath the stare of earth and sky. So did the horses with drowsy bells in long files of carts, creeping slowly towards the interior; so did their recumbent drivers, when they were awake, which rarely happened; so did the exhausted labourers in the fields. Everything that lived or grew was oppressed by the glare; except the lizard, passing swiftly over rough stone walls, and the cicada, chirping his dry hot chirp, like a rattle. The very dust was scorched brown, and something quivered in the atmosphere as if the air itself were panting.

—CHARLES DICKENS' *Little Dorrit*

This method of securing emphasis also has its dangers. It may become monotonous or deadly repetitious if it is not carefully managed. But if it can be placed against a figurative setting and be made to complete a unified and coherent picture, it may be made vastly more alive and satisfying than any mere generic phraseology can ever be.

It has been said on page 226 that the normal order of

sentence expression is subject, predicate, complement, as **The good man lives a useful life.** But there are many variations from this arrangement that may be successfully used for emphasis and variety. In questions and exclamations, for instance, subjects and predicates may be (usually are) transposed, as **Where has he gone** for **He has gone where** and **What happiness she has had** for **She has had what happiness.** In the imperative sentence the subject **you,** though understood before the predicate, is not as a rule expressed, as **(You) go,** but as in the foregoing cases the imperative auxiliary may precede the subject, as **Do (you) go.** Negative statements frequently violate normal order, usually for emphasis, as **Never was there a more beautiful day** and **Not only does he prefer it but he will have it in no other way.** Sentences beginning with adverbs, especially adverbs of place and manner, very often have the subject after the predicate, as **Here is an apple** and **There are the boys** and **Secretly entered from the right her most precious lord and master.** In comparative statements the subject of one member of the comparison is likely to follow the predicate, as **The harder he worked the more hopeless seemed his outlook.** In sentences in which the subjunctive is used, as **Had we seen you** and **Were you to go with me I should be happy,** the normal order is again violated.

All of these deviations from normal order make for variety of sentence expression, for elasticity or resilience in framing thought into expressional form. And by this token, they make likewise for emphasis. In addition, variety of expression may be achieved through the use of many different substitutes for noun subjects even when the normal order is strictly observed, as (pronoun) **They have decided,** (adjective) **The really beautiful is rare,** (adverb) **The whys and wherefores are important,** (infinitive phrase) **To see is by no means always to believe,** (gerund) **Seeing is by no means always believing,** (verbal noun) **His dancing, I thought, was very awkward,** (prepositional phrase) *By the way* **is a hackneyed phrase,** (noun clause) **That he had failed me was known by all.**

Similarly, predicates and complements may be varied in form as well as by substitutions, as may also the modifiers of subjects and predicates and complements. There is, indeed, almost infinite variety to be brought to bear upon every phase of sentence construction, provided the speaker or writer is learned in both diction and grammar. If his vocabulary is so limited as to be actually impoverished, and if his knowledge of grammar is so narrow and confined as to enable him to use only the simpler constructions and arrangements, his expression cannot help being weak and monotonous.

It is by this time evident that there is constant interplay between the devices for emphasis and those for variety. Whatever makes for emphasis makes also for variety, and vice versa. Indeed, even well-devised repetition yields a degree of variety. Given a good command of diction; ability to use the different kinds of sentences with facility—declarative, interrogative, imperative, exclamatory; simple, compound, complex, compound-complex, complex-complex; loose, periodic, balanced; familiarity with the many different constructions explained in the foregoing pages; freedom to introduce and conclude sentences with any part of speech and any grammatical combination of terms, it would seem to be impossible to be dull and dry-as-dust in the manner of saying what you have to say. It has been insisted by more than one authority on the subject of English composition that, with all of these mechanical devices of expression at command, any one who is tiresome or monotonous in what he has to say must be either very ignorant or very lazy, or both.

Chapter Twelve

SENTENCE ANALYSIS

By sentence analysis is meant the division or separation of a sentence into its component or constituent parts for the purpose of explaining their relationships and of defining them in accordance with these relationships.

The traditional type of sentence analysis involves these steps: Tell what kind of sentence according to the listing on page 262, read the independent clause or clauses, and the dependent clause or clauses; in regard to the dependent clauses, tell what kind of clause each one is, how it functions, and how the relationship to independent clause or clauses is established; name the essential subject and predicate of every clause in the sentence and also the complete subject and predicate, beginning with the independent clause or clauses; point out and explain all modifying words and phrases in all clauses.

Observe the analysis of this sentence:
The three adventurers advanced slowly toward the last outpost.

This is a simple declarative sentence. The essential subject is **adventurers**; the complete subject, **The three adventurers.** The essential predicate is **advanced**; the complete predicate, **advanced slowly toward the last outpost.** The essential subject **adventurers** is modified by the definite article **The** and by the numeral adjective **three.** The essential predicate **advanced** is modified by the adverb of manner **slowly** and by the adverbial prepositional phrase of direction **toward the last outpost,** in which **toward** is the preposition and **outpost** is its noun object modified by the definite article **the** and the limiting adjective **last.**

Note now the analysis of this sentence:
If the weather is clear we shall go in the new car which is Harry's pride and joy.

This is a complex declarative sentence consisting of one independent clause and two dependent clauses. The independent clause is **we shall go in the new car,** of which **we** is both essential and complete subject, **shall go** is the essential predicate, and **shall go in the new car** is the complete predicate. **In the new car** is an adverbial prepositional phrase of manner modifying **shall go,** in which **in** is the preposition and **car** is its noun object modified by the definite article **the** and the descriptive adjective **new.**

The first dependent clause is **If the weather is clear.** This is an adverbial clause of condition modifying the predicate—**shall go**—of the independent clause. **If** is a conjunctive adverb modifying **shall go** and **is,** and serving as the connection link between the conditional clause and the independent clause. **Weather** is the essential subject of the conditional clause, and **the weather** is the complete subject. **Weather** is modified by the definite article **the.** **Is** is the essential predicate of the conditional clause, and **is clear** is the complete predicate. **Clear** is an adjective used as predicate complement or attribute complement, completing the predicate **is** and describing the subject **weather.**

The second dependent clause is **which is Harry's pride and joy.** This is an adjective clause modifying **car** of the independent clause. **Which** is a relative pronoun used as subject of the verb **is;** its antecedent is **car,** and by this antecedence it becomes a conjunctive relative making the whole adjective clause a modifier of **car.** **Is** is the essential predicate of the adjective clause; **is Harry's pride and joy** is the complete predicate. The phrase **pride and joy** is the compound predicate noun or attribute complement of the adjective clause, modified by the possessive proper noun **Harry's** and connected by the co-ordinate conjunction **and.**

Another method of sentence analysis, originally advocated by those who felt that purely verbal analysis was unsatisfactory, is diagraming. Most contemporary grammarians are reluctant either to use or to advocate sentence diagraming because of their feeling that it tends to become an abstract exercise or an end in itself. If so, then it could have small value in achieving the goals for which sentence analysis is undertaken. Those who wish to learn the standard system of diagraming can find it explained in detail in almost any English handbook published before 1940.

Various new methods of sentence analysis have recently been evolved. An example of such a method is that of Charles C. Fries, explained in *The Structure of English,* which criticizes the traditional type of analysis explained above as unscientific because it starts with the total meaning of the sentence and then uses this meaning as the basis for analysis; in other words, it labels but does not analyze. A sentence, Fries believes, consists of words, but the total meaning of the sentence is much more than all the dictionary meanings of the individual words put together. What gives the sentence its meaning is a combination of these lexical meanings plus the structural meanings, that is, the relationships in which the words stand to each other. Sentence analysis in his view thus involves the study of "the patterns of form and arrangement that constitute the devices to signal structural meaning." [1] It must be kept in mind, then, that structural linguists regard a sentence as a structure and not as a group of words. The details of the system which Fries sets up to analyze sentences are far too complex to present here, but it may be summarized as consisting of the rejection of many of the traditional parts of speech and a division of all words into the classes of "form-words" and "function-words."

Among other recent developments has been IC (immediate constituents) analysis, which involves progressive breaking down of the sentence ending in its reduction to morphemes so that the "successive hierarchical structure" can be observed. This method is also too complicated to be treated in any detail here, but can be examined in Barbara Strang's *Modern English Structure* or R. S. Wells' article in *Language,* Volume 23.

A final method which should be mentioned is that proposed by the transformational grammarians. The concept of transformation comes from the field of mathematics, in which it deals with the process of changing the form but not the value of an expression. As used in linguistic analysis it has the double application of (1) replacing a class by a member of that class, or vice versa and (2) changing one element of such a complex structure as a sentence so that the other elements remain the same. Thus, for instance, **Chris was**

[1] P. 57.

Chapter Thirteen

PARSING AND SYNTAX

Parsing means telling what part of speech a word is, classifying it as a part of speech, and explaining its grammatical inflections and relationships.

Syntax or construction means explaining predicative, qualifying, and other word relationships according to the rules of grammar. It means, in other words, telling how and why a part of speech functions as it does in a given sentence. Syntax is, as a rule, included under parsing—as the last item in the listed items of the parsing. But strictly speaking syntax or construction pertains only to agreement or relationship, and is therefore really a separate or different kind of explanation from that of parsing. The two words—syntax and construction—are used interchangeably.

Take, by way of illustration, the short simple sentence **Boys attended:** There are five items to be stated about **Boys** in parsing it—**noun, common, masculine, plural, third;** that is, general classification, **noun;** special classification, **common noun;** gender, **masculine;** number, **plural;** person, **third.** The words gender, number, person, and so on, may be repeated after each designation, but it is a waste of time to do so inasmuch as **third** implies person, **masculine** implies gender, and so forth.

There are ten items to be stated about **attended** in parsing it—**verb, finite, weak, notional, intransitive, active, indicative, imperfect, plural, third.** As with the noun, the general classification comes first, namely, the part of speech—**verb.** After that there are for finite verbs nine different classifications, the last two—number and person—being relational or agreement items of parsing decided by the subject **Boys.** A finite verb or predicate agrees with its subject in number and person. A verbal—infinitive and participle—having no subject in the finite sense, is therefore not parsed for number and person and mode, the word **infinitive** or **participle** being used for mode in the parsing scale.

267

In giving the syntax of **Boys** you say: **Boys** is in the nominative case subject of the predicate **attended**. In giving the syntax of **attended** you say: **attended** is predicate of the sentence, agreeing with its subject **Boys** in plural number and third person, or, preferably, in third plural.

Pronouns follow the same parsing plan as nouns. Their syntax must include antecedence, if any. Take, for instance, the pronoun in **The man who works is independent: who** is **pronoun, relative, masculine, singular, third.** Its syntax is nominative case, subject of **works** in the dependent clause, in agreement with its antecedent **man** in masculine, singular, third.

In parsing adjectives and adverbs give classifications and degree of comparison. In explaining their construction tell what they modify. Similarly, in parsing conjunctions and prepositions and interjections, give classifications; then tell, of prepositions, the words between which relationship is shown and the kind of phrase in which used; of conjunctions, the words or phrases or clauses connected and the kind of connection established (co-ordinate or the various kinds of subordinate relationships); of interjections, word and phrasal relationships, if any.

Remember that, while the subject of a finite verb is always in the nominative case, the subject of an infinitive is always in the objective case (page 139); that nouns and pronouns used as attribute complements and appositives are always in the same case as the words to which they refer, are usually of the same part of speech and, thus, of the same gender, number, and person; that a pronoun agrees with its antecedent in gender, number, and person, but its case depends upon the construction of the clause in which it stands; that objects of verbs and of prepositions, objective complements, and indirect objects—whether words, phrases, or clauses—are always regarded as being in the objective case; that nouns and pronouns construed as independent or nominative by direct address or as absolute in construction, are always regarded as being in the nominative case.

In some systems of parsing and syntax the declension of pronouns is included, as are also the parts of verbs (especially irregular verbs), and the complete comparison of adjectives

NOUNS AND PRONOUNS

	General Classification	Special Classification	Gender	Number	Person	Case	Syntax
door	noun	common	neuter	singular	third	nominative	subject of made
noise	noun	common	neuter	singular	third	objective	object of made
hinges	noun	common	neuter	plural	third	objective	object of on
house	noun	common	neuter	singular	third	objective	object of in
I	pronoun	personal	common	singular	first	nominative	subject of came
its	pronoun	personal	neuter	singular	third	possessive	modifies hinges; antecedent is door
that	pronoun	relative	neuter	singular	third	nominative	subject of woke; antecedent is noise
everybody	pronoun	indefinite	common	singular	third	objective	object of woke

VERBS

	General Classification	Special Classification	Auxiliary or Principal	Transitive or Intransitive	Weak or Strong	Voice	Mood	Tense	Person	Number	Syntax
made	verb	finite	principal	transitive	strong	active	indicative	imperfect	third	singular	predicate of independent clause
came	verb	finite	principal	intransitive	strong	active	indicative	imperfect	first	singular	predicate of adverbial clause
woke	verb	finite	principal	transitive	strong	active	indicative	imperfect	third	singular	predicate of adjective clause
swinging	verb	participle	principal	intransitive	strong	active		present		singular	modifies door

ADJECTIVES AND ADVERBS

	General Classification	Special Classification	Degree	Syntax
the	article	definite		modifies door
a	article	indefinite		modifies noise
frightful	adjective	descriptive	positive	modifies noise
the	article	definite		modifies house
Just	adverb	degree		modifies adverbial conjunction as

PREPOSITIONS AND CONJUNCTIONS AND INTERJECTIONS

	General Classification	Special Classification	Kind of Relationship or Connection	Syntax
as	conjunction	adverbial	time	connecting adverbial clause of time with made, predicate of independent clause
on	preposition	simple	adverbial	shows relationship between swinging and hinges
in	preposition	simple	adjective	shows relationship between everybody and house
Alas	interjection	simple	independent	

and adverbs. These may be important adjuncts of the process in the case of those whose native tongue is not English or of those who require review in inflections.

Before the parts of speech in a sentence can be correctly parsed and construed, the sentence must itself be seen and understood as a whole; that is, sentence analysis must necessarily come first if the intimate relationships of the words in a sentence are to be perfectly defined and classified. For the sake of reviewing the foregoing exposition study the following sentence and the parsing of its parts of speech in the tables above:

Alas! Just as I came, the door, swinging on its hinges, made a frightful noise that woke everybody in the house.

Note that case is included under parsing in the first paradigm above, that declensions of pronouns and parts of verbs are not given, and that exposition of syntax is necessarily somewhat abridged. It goes without saying that the classical system of parsing explained above is valid only if the conventional classification of the parts of speech is used. An entirely different system has to be used for each of the various approaches mentioned at the end of Chapter Twelve (see pages 265-66).

INDEX

BOOKS OF DISTINCTION
FROM WARNER BOOKS

__EDWIN NEWMAN ON LANGUAGE
by Edwin Newman   (97-459, $6.95)

Both STRICTLY SPEAKING and A CIVIL TONGUE are now combined in one definitive book on our mother tongue. EDWIN NEWMAN ON LANGUAGE will laugh with you at the errors others make and increase your delight in the wonder of words.

__IN SEARCH OF HISTORY
by Theodore H. White   (30-299, $4.50)

This is a book about the people who, making history, have changed your life—and about a great correspondent who listened to their stories for forty years. Now he has woven all those stories into this splendid tale of his own. "IN SEARCH OF HISTORY is the most fascinating and most useful personal memoir of this generation."
                                        —*William Safire*

To order, use the coupon below. If you prefer to use your own stationery, please include complete title as well as book number and price. Allow 4 weeks for delivery.